SECOND EDITION

ADVANCED REPORTING

SECOND EDITION

ADVANCED REPORTING

DISCOVERING PATTERNS IN NEWS EVENTS

DONALD L. SHAW
University of North Carolina at Chapel Hill

MAXWELL MCCOMBS
University of Texas at Austin

GERRY KEIR

WAVELAND
PRESS, INC.

Prospect Heights, Illinois

For information about this book, write or call:
  Waveland Press, Inc.
  P.O. Box 400
  Prospect Heights, Illinois 60070
  847/634-0081

CONTENTS

Part II   Beats, Interviews, and Sources   53

Part III   Community Connections   105

Part V   Entering the Event   249

Part VI Professional Issues   301

PREFACE

We were happy when Waveland asked us to revise this text because there have been many new developments and technological advancements that have occurred since the first edition was published more than a decade ago. The second edition of the text has been extensively rewritten—approximately 80 percent of the material is new. This edition has a slightly different title, and the order of how the authors are listed has also changed.

Computers put the same power in the hands of reporters that once was available only in industry or university labs. Reporters who win prizes today often use the computer to help gather and organize facts. Yet, the same computer technology that puts so much power in the hands of journalists also puts the same power in the hands of consumers. For example, some people use e-mail to learn about events or the Internet to make reservations at a local restaurant. Thus today, the established mass media must survive in a highly competitive market of information, transmitted by many different media, and easily accessed by media audiences. Reporting and writing skills must be excellent for any medium—or journalist—to stand out.

The 1995–1996 arrest and trial of football star and celebrity O.J. Simpson—charged with the murder of his ex-wife and her friend—showed the power of audience interest to swamp the programming of even "serious" news programs such as ABC's distinguished *Nightline* (which devoted 55 programs to the extended ongoing events). Not far behind in the amount of media attention given to the trial were the *New York Times* and *Washington Post*. The mass media have never before faced such competition from each other. The traditional television networks compete with as many as 100 or more other channels on some cable systems.

In this text, we take the point of view that journalism has long been an important profession and will remain so in the future. We focus on the skills that reporters need to acquire and that can be applied to new as well as established media in the 21st century, not on any particular medium. Future journalists may use their skills to gather and present information, independent of any established medium, or they may work for a specific medium—such as newspapers, magazines, television, radio, cable, Internet, and so forth—as various media evolve into 21st century forms. It will always be important for students to learn how to select, gather, organize, and present information and to know how to evaluate how audiences learn about and use public information. Having good skills and ethical dedication is as important for journalists as it is for lawyers or physicians if the public is to be well served.

The second edition attempts to show how journalists can integrate the broad array of skills that are required by the new interest in public journalism, now being used by many news media to serve audiences more closely. Using contemporary communications theory, the text discusses not only ways that the press can set the issue agenda, but also its obligations to explore community issues over time—that is, to put them on the agenda as a matter of proactive journalism. In addition, because journalists of the future will need to use computers in a variety of ways, not just as word processors, we have presented many examples of how computers can assist journalists.

Acknowledgements

While most of this book was written by Gerry Keir, Max McCombs, and me, a group of journalists and scholars assisted us in putting together some special materials, helped organize student examples, and wrote portions of some chapters. We include below some background information on each of them.

Bill Cloud teaches journalism at the University of North Carolina. For many years he worked at the *Miami Herald* and at Long Island's *Newsday*. He has been a reporter and copy editor, among other assignments and, for this text, assembled 5 student articles (which appear in chapter 6) that demonstrate the use of research, polls, and interviews.

Jon Hill worked as a journalist for more than a decade for several North Carolina newspapers, the *Thomasville Times*, *Wilson Daily Times*, and the *Greensboro News & Record*. He assisted with chapter 9 on self-administered surveys, co-wrote chapter 16 on objectivity, and co-wrote chapter 18 on the future of the press.

Brad Hamm, like Jon Hill, now completing his doctorate in journalism at the University of North Carolina-Chapel Hill, worked as a journalist on the *Salisbury Post* in Salisbury, N.C. He wrote chapter 11, "Using Databases for Reporting," showing how students can make use of interviews and computers to provide context and data for stories.

Bob Nowell, who wrote a special chapter (12) on reporting teams and computer-assisted journalism, has been managing editor of the *Chapel Hill Newspaper* and, more recently, has worked as a copy editor for the innovative *Raleigh (N.C.) News & Observer*. He teaches at North Carolina Central University in Durham.

Ed Caudill worked for years as a reporter and as a copy editor for newspapers in Ohio. Now a journalism professor at the University of Tennessee at Knoxville, he helped write a special chapter (15) that shows how newspapers, magazines, television, and radio work to equalize the opportunities to acquire information during presidential campaigns.

Martha FitzSimon helped write chapter 16 on objectivity. Ms. FitzSimon holds an M.A. degree in journalism from the University of Texas and, for six years, has worked with The Freedom Forum Media Studies Center in New York as publications manager. Before that, as a freelance writer, she contributed to newspapers in New Jersey. She is the author or editor of many Center studies.

In addition to the assistance of those mentioned above, I used this text in manuscript form in the spring of 1996 for a reporting class and benefitted from student comments. We also owe a special thanks to Professor Stuart Showalter, Professor of Journalism at Goshen College, who was a visiting scholar at UNC-CH during 1995–1996 and a participant in the reporting class in which the new version of the text was tested. He provided a number of insights that we were able to incorporate into the book.

The second edition was planned in good part, and some of it was written, while I was senior fellow at The Freedom Forum Media Studies Center in New York in 1992–1993. This book must be considered one of the many books inspired by that program, offered to journalists and communication scholars, and for which I would like to express my gratitude. I extend my thanks especially to Ev Dennis, the superb founding director of the Center.

About the Authors

Journalism is a first love of all the authors. Gerry Keir for several years was managing editor and then became editor of the *Honolulu Advertiser*. Today he works in public relations in Honolulu. Max McCombs, who teaches at the University of Texas at Austin, worked as a journalist covering local government and economics on the *Times Picayune* in New Orleans. Dr. McCombs is widely known as a scholar of media effects, especially of the agenda-setting power of the press. Recently, I worked as a reporting intern at the *Minneapolis Star Tribune* as part of an American Society of Newspaper Editors program supported by the Knight Foundation, but I also have worked as a reporter for the *Asheville (N.C.) Citizen, Asheville Times*, and the *Burlington (N.C.) Times-News*. Presently I teach reporting at the School of Journalism and Mass Communication at the University of North Carolina at Chapel Hill.

Donald L. Shaw
Chapel Hill, N.C.

PART I

THE PROFESSION OF JOURNALISM

Chapter One

PATTERNS

> My approach to my work is really a kind of derivation or vulgar-
> ization of the Platonic idea, with the distinction between the real-
> ity and the appearances. My view is that events can best be
> interpreted—must be interpreted—in the light of some underly-
> ing pattern of forces, circumstances, and design.
>
> —Walter Lippmann
> *Oral History Collection of Columbia University*

Walter Lippmann, one of the preeminent journalists of the twentieth century, provided insightful perspectives in his columns about
national and world events. In a career that stretched across the first
half of the twentieth century, Lippmann influenced political leaders,
scholars, business leaders, and—not least—other journalists. In
1951, interviewed as part of Columbia University's oral history program, Lippmann said he always examined news events with a view to
finding the underlying patterns that explained the facts. For Lippmann, knowledge of history provided one important way to locate the
significance of events in the stream of passing time. In Lippmann's
view, the enduring patterns of forces "don't change nearly so much as
the reader of the newspaper would imagine they did."

Patterns exist in many forms. They exist across time but also among
events that occur simultaneously, interwoven like the threads of a colorful quilt or a bright Scottish plaid. Sociologists search for patterns
in contemporary groups. Psychologists seek patterns in the behavior

3

of individuals. Chemists find patterns in the basic elements—indeed, the regularity of elements enabled chemists to guess that some were not yet discovered because of breaks in the patterns.

Journalists, like chemists, are challenged to find the patterns in events or in perspectives and have a responsibility for spending part of their time searching for the reasons *why* things happen the way they do. Sometimes events can be explained by placing them within history, as Lippmann suggested. Other times journalists may want to search for patterns within a contemporary context, using surveys, databases, interviews, or any of several other key journalistic methods.

Events always have causes, and events are usually the visible part of an ongoing process, like earthquakes—the final, violent outcome of a series of deep underground shifts of earth, marked by faint rumblings that can be picked up by seismographs, if at all. Important human events are similar. For example, the 1991 riots experienced in Los Angeles were the culmination of racial misunderstandings, a depressed economy, and a sense among many of lost hope over a long period of time.

A series of stories that appeared in the *Detroit Free Press* in the 1960s won a Pulitzer Prize after reporters used the work of then-reporter Philip Meyer, who employed survey research to document a widespread sense of discontent and hopelessness. The riot in Detroit was the event that actually, and tragically, broke out after faint rumblings were ignored. The riot in which 43 people died was like an earthquake that was foretold by the faint rumblings below the earth's surface. One year later, reporter Meyer led a follow-up survey that showed the potential for another outbreak, despite efforts by Detroit officials to improve race relations and the economic climate of the city.

Seeing Events, Making Events

Reporters use their eyes to see events, and that is vital. However, the old adage that seeing is believing can be deceptive. Reporters use a variety of methods to identify patterns, of which seeing is only the first and most important. Reporters are aware of the historical evolution of events, as Lippmann suggested, but they also use survey research, database investigations, field experiments, and other techniques to supplement the standard interviews and to document sources.

Reporters can search for patterns in many ways. They can compare the reactions to events of women versus men, or older versus younger citizens. Reporters can compare reactions to events of people with higher versus lower incomes, or Democrats with Republicans. They can compare nonwhites with whites. Reporters can compare different people within the same period of time as well as compare people across time. Of course, there must be reasons to make these or any comparisons.

However they search for patterns, reporters should constantly ask themselves two important questions:

1. What are the key facts about this event?
2. What are several meaningful perspectives about this event?

If the president is quoted in a news story as attacking the opposition party, then the reporter should ask, What are key facts that the president is using or seems to be using, and what are other perspectives about these facts? Even during times of domestic and international crisis, the job of a reporter is to seek key facts from events and a variety of responsible perspectives on those facts. Reporters do not take sides, but they have a responsibility to introduce the pluralism of different perspectives into the public dialogue. In his 1922 *Public Opinion*, Lippmann wrote:

> But in the end knowledge must come not from the conscience but from the environment with which that conscience deals. When men act on the principle of intelligence they go out to find the facts and to make their wisdom. When they ignore it, they go inside themselves and find only what is there. They elaborate their prejudice, instead of increasing their knowledge.

Regardless of the medium, journalists are challenged as never before to use both old and new techniques to gather, organize, and disseminate information. The technologies that allow millions relatively easy access to large pools of information also provide opportunities for journalists to report about events in different ways, to search for the patterns of events.

Lippmann saw events as nested in history and sought historical patterns. Journalists also apply the perspectives of sociologists, using survey data to compare different types of groups, or apply the perspectives of scientists, artists, political scientists, or others to find the patterns in which events occur. One event is usually just a single square, however important, in a quilt in which all the squares are stitched together. Squares are added every day to the quilt of human existence.

If we move back a little, we may see that the squares often suggest interesting pictures—in fact, many pictures. These are the patterns of our collective lives.

Journalists in a Changing World

Professional journalists do not have to pass a bar examination as do lawyers, or a state examination as do physicians, but the challenges of covering trends and events in contemporary society require a high level of skill in gathering and processing information. Journalists write about people who are both in and out of power, and journalists highlight those areas of social life that press for attention. One can argue that journalists are professionals because what they write about is important. In addition, having the skills to use today's available technology to access, gather, process, and present information also qualifies journalists as professionals.

The End of Old Media Communities

Communication changes us in ways of which we are not even aware. Faxes, telephones, relatively easy travel, computer databases, electronic mail, and many other developments allow individuals to contact people and pursue interests far beyond the local community. Local communities, around which so much of our lives are organized with schools, local government, and so forth, no longer dominate our lives as they did in the years immediately after World War II.

Through the information sought and shared, individuals who live in different communities can communicate with others who may share certain interests, for example, Elvis Presley or *Star Trek*. Contemporary communication technologies allow individuals to bypass local communities to participate in a larger world, much as industry has done for the last half of this century. Many, if not most large industries (such as IBM and General Motors) and services (such as the press, wire services, and banking) are international in scope, extending far beyond local communities. The very concept of serving a local geographic community as a way of ensuring the success of a medium may be jeopardized. Many traditional media, such as newspapers, need to experiment with other ways of providing information to their communities.

The End of Old Journalistic Beliefs

Journalists have an important set of skills and an obligation to blend them with their more widely informed views. Journalists work in a world of new challenges in which some old assumptions are not valid. For example, it has been said: If you build a better mousetrap the world will beat a path to your door. However, that is not true in the field of mass media. Newspapers and national news magazines are excellent in their use of information and graphics—they have never been better—yet readers are not beating a path to their doors, as circulation steadily drops. Network television executives have had similar experiences. Readers, listeners, and viewers are not loyal and are as willing to turn to convenient alternative information sources as they are to bypass their local retail store for the lower prices of Wal-Mart.

The old journalistic rule—if an event happens, we will cover it—does not fit a world in which people find themselves living in a variety of communities (including the electronic community of the computer literate). Some readers belong to the environmental community, the feminist community, or the pro-life community and may find those communities more interesting and involving than the geographic area in which they happen to live. Therefore the old rule—concentrate on the local community—may be good only if you know what that community might be for your audience. The community may be a lot more than where your audience lives. Many people do not think much about where they live, and many do not even know the full names of their neighbors, especially in cities but increasingly in smaller towns as well. Therefore, serving the "community" means what? It means many things.

The End of "Vertical" Organizations

The old rules of concentrating on covering news about the leadership of communities and organizations—the important people at the top— do not fit the turmoil that most organizations are undergoing as communication empowers people at all levels of society, even at the very bottom. In the past, information filtered down from leaders through intermediaries to the people who, without access to events and information, had no reason to question it. After all, did not political presidents, church leaders, academic deans, teachers, coaches, and many others at the top of power triangles have our best interests at heart? Today, we know from our access to the massive array of available information sources that leaders sometimes have their own interests at heart. At least we are aware of alternatives.

Now we can communicate with others easily and, with faxes and computer networks, for example, organize our own resistance—listen only to those who think like we do. As a result societies are increasingly polarized, as mass media audiences seek out perspectives conforming to their own. An individual with a computer, a modem, and the time to use them may not need mass media. However, that individual is still a mass media target.

Communication accessibility may even imperil old hierarchical institutions such as political, religious, and educational organizations—for example, access to information helped end communism in the former Soviet Union. As another example, consider that Catholic official doctrine rejects artificial birth control, yet in the United States many married Catholics at the "bottom" of the church structure use artificial birth control at about the same rate as do other married couples. Politicians from president to mayors are finding that it is not enough to announce policy—they must sell it. Journalists who concentrate only on established news leaders at the top will miss the ferment of activity that is bubbling throughout organizations all the way down to the bottom. Their stories will not be relevant to anyone but leaders. Journalists, like leaders, can get out of touch. Many are.

The Need for Perspectives

Journalism is as much in transition as other professions. Times are changing but also are challenging and exciting for those willing to seize new opportunities for gathering and presenting community information needed for intelligent policy decisions.

Women do not always see events the same as men do. White people do not always see events the same as minorities do. The rich see events differently from the poor. One perspective is not always better than another; perspectives differ. The challenge of journalists is to identify "major" perspectives—such as that of a general or mayor or president—and then provide as many other perspectives as reasonably possible, given the constraints of time and money. If journalists provide the *official perspective* only, they are mostly writers. If journalists *diversify perspectives, look for patterns, deepen the search*, journalists are reporters. Many journalists are writers, not reporters, and think little about how others, rather than officials, might view events. That practice needs to change.

Journalists are educated in a richly humanistic tradition, incorporating the sciences and the arts. Whether or not they have the opportunity for extensive schooling, they should always be reading, watching, attending, learning. Journalists should be widely read and actively seek to learn new things every day from many sources. As overseers of society, journalists should be open to all kinds of information. Journalists should form a picture in their minds of interesting trends in the society; they should notice changes and how those changes affect society. Consider the situations below and how they currently challenge society.

U.S. cities are in trouble, with white citizens deserting the central cities for the suburbs, leaving a declining tax base and diminishing commitment to those left behind—often members of minorities who lack the economic freedom to adjust to changing times. Families are in trouble, with high divorce rates, abandoned or abused children or spouses, and a declining ability of churches or other institutions to help.

Recently there has been much discussion of the privatization of work in our society. Companies, government, and even universities hire people on a part-time basis to meet the demands of times when workloads are heavy and budgets decreasing, leaving millions of people without permanent employment or a chance to obtain inexpensive health insurance. There are many instances where thousands of middle managers and thousands more blue-collar workers are laid off as industries downsize and the United States becomes fully integrated into a free-market, global economy. Universities and colleges are in trouble, as escalating tuition and other costs cause parents and students to ask cost-benefit questions such as: "Am I getting my money's worth?" While humanists cringe at such questions, all institutions are being forced into new levels of accountability. However, this process provides many new economic opportunities for those with energy, innovation, and the ability to seize new opportunities. They need information.

Changing Media Use

News media follow history and resist significant change in organizing news beats and allowing journalists to be proactive. That is true despite the fact that newspapers have been in decline in terms of market penetration since the 1930s, mass radio since the 1950s, mass magazines since the 1970s, and network television since the 1980s. The old formula—react to the news as it happens, and not a minute before—is seriously out of date. Journalists need to participate more in society if the media which employ them are to thrive, or even survive. Journalists need to be *active*—not *reactive*—professionals.

Many of our ideas about how communities and mass media interrelate are outdated. The control over what people see, read, and listen to is gradually passing into the hands of audience members. While news media provide forces to pull social systems together through a common focus on events selected as important by journalists, new communication technologies tend to dissipate the impact of messages by putting key choices about when and where to receive the message in the hands of audience members. Audiences also choose their own messages.

In the eighteenth century, when newspapers were few and illiteracy widespread, newspaper reading was a social activity in alehouses and teahouses. Newspapers brought people together. A century later the inexpensive penny press allowed readers to buy their own newspapers so reading became an individual behavior. Early in the 1920s radio sets were relatively limited in number, and radio listening was often a family activity with families engaging in democratic discussion to select program choices. The same is true of television in the early 1950s. Radio and television, like newspapers, were first used widely in bars, the modern equivalent of alehouses, but soon moved to homes. Radio and television also pulled people together at first.

But transistors and other modern developments now allow individuals to own their own sets, so that radio listening and television viewing are today individual rather than collective social behaviors. Tape and video players and recorders, combined with a wide range of cable television choices and video and audio programs and formats, enable audiences to control the time and place of programs. Even the news can be purchased on audio tape.

The pattern seems to be that technology first favored mass media and collective social use of a medium; then technology shifted to individual use of the collective message; and now technology encourages individual assembly of the collective message. The result of this development is that news media are in competition as never before. The same satellite technologies that encourage publication of a national medium like *USA Today* also undercut the significance of collective national messages and shared experiences when individuals talk directly to each other via the same satellite and bypass the mass media altogether. Journalists must therefore be aware that audiences use the mass media as a system. In other words, few members of an audience depend entirely on newspapers or television or magazines or radio.

Most people listen to the radio while commuting, read the newspaper in the morning, and in the evening catch a television news or entertainment program, read a magazine, or attend a film. Public information is part of a social system. Therefore it makes less sense for any medium, such as newspapers or television, to act as if the competition is between media when audience members are most likely to use media that are easy and convenient at any particular time. Therefore, each medium today is free to turn to exciting experiments with reporting rather than simply providing information according to old formulas. Experimentation, in fact, is needed for economic survival.

That is the promise of the First Amendment, a right preserved for the people to have access to key facts and to different perspectives on those facts. The First Amendment does not promise a conservative government or a liberal one. It does not promise a democratic government or a dictatorial one. It does promise a pluralistic set of perspectives rather than a single official view.

Seizing the Agenda

Journalists are not professionals in the same way as are lawyers and doctors. Journalists are not required to pass a certifying examination—indeed it would probably be a violation of the First Amendment to place such a restriction on the field. Some journalists cannot spell. Some are not especially responsible in gathering facts. Yet most journalists are interested in informing their communities in a responsible way so that citizens can make informed decisions and live better lives. Journalists usually love to report or to write, or both. Some like to report more than write, and some prefer writing over reporting. If journalists do their work in a consistent and responsible way, communities benefit from exposure to responsible views.

Communication scholars have documented that the news media have some power to set an agenda of public issues. That is very great power. The news media do not know, any more than do other institutions, the "solutions" to the many challenging problems of our complex and dynamic social system. But the news media have the ability to shift the spotlight of attention from one topic to another.

Members of the public focus only on a few issues at any one time. This is also true for a community as a whole. Communication scholars have documented that individuals closely follow about two to three public issues at any one time, with lesser attention to several minor

Box 1-1

Fear of Crime Far Outweighs the Reality

Polls are a key news source for finding out what is on the mind of the public. In the case of fear of crime, the public's state of mind may be vastly different from the reality of crime portrayed in state and federal statistics. Once again we are reminded that good reporting uses a variety of techniques to *triangulate* on reality.

In his book, *Public Opinion*, Walter Lippmann contrasted the world outside with the pictures in our heads. What this comparison reveals in the case of crime is that public feelings reflect the media's selective portrait of the world more than the actual reality of the world.

In the mid-1990s public opinion polls asking people to name the most important problem facing the country found more than one out of four Americans concerned about crime. This high level of concern persisted over many months despite the fact that crime statistics showed little or no increase in the incidence of actual crime.

What was driving this public concern over crime? According to a research project at the University of Texas, a major influence on the public's response to pollsters was a heavy barrage of news coverage and infotainment TV programming on crime. There were cover stories on crime in the news magazines, a heavy dose of crime stories on TV news magazines, and a proliferation of reality shows on TV featuring crimes.

Summing up the situation in *The Public Perspective*, Jeffrey Alderman, Director of Polling for ABC News, noted that polling data shows the news industry can reshuffle the American agenda by deciding to focus on a topic such as crime.

issues. For example, a man who has just lost his job is interested in the performance of the economy. A family facing a problem with drugs may be interested in law enforcement or public health issues. However, there is always some overlap of interests and, collectively, the end result is an array of slowly shifting public concerns.

When a "new" issue arises, it overshadows an "old" one. In the 1990s, for example, some people expressed concern that the heavy emphasis given to the global and tragic AIDS disease might push attention (and funding) away from such "old" illnesses as breast cancer and tuberculosis, both on the rise around the world. Such concerns are valid given the findings of communication research.

One can argue that seizing part of the public agenda is a journalistic moral obligation, if done responsibly, similar to the obligation of dentists who, in the 1950s, pushed for the introduction of fluoride in community water systems after studies showed that fluoride reduced dental cavities. One could argue that it is as much a journalistic obligation to focus on social problems as it is the obligation of a doctor, who happens upon an injured accident victim, to provide needed medical attention. It is as much an obligation as that of a lawyer who sees the need to provide pro bono time for destitute defendants helplessly caught in a tangled legal system, regardless of whether they are eventually judged guilty or innocent.

The view that journalism must passively concentrate only on events that were initiated by someone else (press conference) or that have already happened (meetings, car accidents) does not fit a world that needs to move ahead with improved information to meet upcoming changes. In other words, the honored notion that we will print all the news that happens and is fit to print is nineteenth-century in origin and very outmoded for an age in which many citizens have access to the communication technology to gather the information they want, when they want it, and in the form they want it. Today many audiences are using emerging technologies to gain information, making the mass media that provide a dull, reactive, and formula-driven menu each day seem out of date. But the mass media can, and must, adapt.

If the press has the power to put items on the agenda, does it also have a responsibility? Many would say no, that the press has the responsibility only to cover events that happen, such as accidents, speeches, or news conferences. If so, then the press is likely to be responsive only to news leaders. Indeed, some studies show that those in power are far more likely to be quoted than those out of power. News media beats focus on police, courts, mayors, and businesses rather than on workers, minorities, civil liberties, or human health. In other words, news beats reinforce the political and economic organization of society more than they explore the social issues that envelop people where they live, work, hope, and fear.

Pulling People Together

There is yet another view. There is evidence that the press agenda of social issues is shared among readers and viewers, although agreement on solutions to social problems may not be. One could argue that communities are much more important than geographic locations, and that a community is made up of people who share issues rather than geographic space. Agenda-setting research suggests that journalists, along with political leaders and leaders within other institutions, play an important part in building a sense of community. The sheer explosion of informational opportunities represented by cable, many small magazines, direct mail, and other sources also has resulted in a decline in the ability of a few large mass media to suggest a common agenda for all of us. This may be one reason that so many people grasp single issues, nourished by small media, and resist all attempts by the larger community to compromise. The need for journalists to create meaningful community agendas is very great. The need for journalists to use all their professional skills has never been greater.

References

Auletta, Ken. *Three Blind Mice: How the TV Networks Lost Their Way*. New York: Random House, 1991.

Faludi, Susan. *Backlash: The Undeclared War Against American Women*. New York: Doubleday, 1991.

Lippmann, Walter. *Oral History Collection of Columbia University*, New York: Columbia University, 1950.

____. *Public Opinion*. New York: Harcourt, Brace & Co., 1922, p. 149.

Meyer, Philip. *Precision Journalism: A Reporter's Introduction to Social Science Methods*. Bloomington: Indiana University Press, 1973.

____. *The People Beyond 12th Street: A Survey of Attitudes of Detroit Negroes After the Riot of 1967*. Detroit, MI: Detroit Urban League, 1967.

Phillips, Kevin. *Boiling Point: Democrats, Republicans, and the Decline of Middle-Class Prosperity*. New York: Random House, 1993.

Rheingold, Howard. *The Virtual Community: Homesteading on the Electronic Frontier*. Reading, MA: Addison-Wesley, 1993.

Rogers, Everett M. and James W. Dearing. "Agenda-Setting Research: Where Has It Been, Where Is It Going?" In *Communication Yearbook*, James A. Anderson, ed., pp. 555–94. Newbury Park: Sage, 1988.

Shaw, Donald L. "The Rise and Fall of American Mass Media: Roles of Technology and Leadership." Roy W. Howard Lecture presented April 4, 1991, at Indiana University, Bloomington.

Shaw, Donald L. and Shannon E. Martin. "The Function of Mass Media Agenda Setting," *Journalism Quarterly* 69, no. 4 (Winter, 1992): 902–20.

Leon V. Sigal. *Reporters and Officials: The Organization and Politics of Newsmaking*. Lexington, MA: D.C. Heath, 1973.

Stone, Gerald. *Examining Newspapers: What Research Reveals About America's Newspapers*. Newbury Park, CA: Sage, 1987.

Chapter Two

THE SKILLS OF THE PROFESSIONAL JOURNALIST

"It's not the gold. . . . It's finding the gold."

—Lynn Gunn
"Ten-year California gold miner"

In the 1920s, journalists mostly relied on interviews and documents to reconstruct the key facts about events. Even if journalists see events, the perspectives provided by eyewitnesses and documents are valuable. As a reporter, you could cover a college football game merely by watching the game and the scoreboard. But the game story would be enriched if you examined a simple document—the printed program—allowing you to match the players' numbers with their names and actions on the field. It would be enriched still more if you looked at the game statistics to compare the teams, and still more if you interviewed coaches and key players. Journalists did all this in the 1920s and earlier, and they still do today.

Three legs steady the platform of a reporter's fact-gathering methods:

1. observing events,
2. studying documents about events, and
3. interviewing eyewitnesses or other interested parties.

Lawyers, doctors, and other professionals have exactly the same requirements. In the last few years reporters, like physicians, have expanded the types of methods they can use. Reporters still use documents, of course, and often trace the records of individual people and institutions.

Yet with help from computers, reporters can also use documents in a more creative way. Many documents exist on paper temporarily before the information recorded on them is transferred to a computer file, where it can be accessed by someone who knows how to interact with computers. Officials have such access, but many reporters are just now learning how to match their skills to the information sources that are available today. The *Raleigh (N.C.) News & Observer* developed a computer program that could read salary records of public employees in the health field—public information. These records showed that some state employees were earning more in overtime pay than they earned from their annual base salaries. This information enabled the *News & Observer* to determine that the state, cutting back state jobs during lean budget years without cutting back on services, was doing what many industries are doing—working people harder (with their consent) rather than hiring anyone new. For nurses at a state psychiatric hospital, extra hours were part of their weekly routine, as reported in the *News & Observer*:

> "There are not enough nurses," says Kathryn Forehand, a veteran nurse who earned $34,365 in overtime pay last year. "So you work when you're needed. Because that's what you have to do."

> "Sometimes it's voluntary, sometimes it's mandatory because you cannot walk off and leave the unit uncovered," says Beatrice Cox, a nurse supervisor who often works double shifts with chronically ill patients.

The Education and Skills of a Journalist

Journalists need to be able to perform several important tasks. Below is a sketch of the journalistic process.

Community Issues. Journalists often should stop, look, and listen, just as railway warning signs advise. Journalists also should read constantly and remain tuned to television, radio, magazines, and other sources of community information and issues. Films shown in theaters or on television often focus on social issues of local importance. Journalists should be aware of many community issues.

Gathering Information. Journalists are challenged as never before to adjust to the advanced technologies of the computer age. Formerly, journalists could rely on what they learned from seeing an event, supplemented with some information from interviews and documents at the scene (or from police departments or courts). Today, however, journalists need to be able to examine records assembled in databases and, if necessary, to conduct a content analysis of those documents to gather unique information. Likewise journalists should understand the simple mechanics of a survey, including the processes of sampling, question construction, and data analysis. These are the professional skills of journalists. For example, journalists at the *Pittsburgh Post-Gazette* compared the economic recovery of the region's once-prosperous steel towns along the rivers with that of the region as a whole by gathering information from publicly available databases. While the view collectively was somewhat dismal, there was room for optimism here and there.

Organizing and Blending Information. Journalists need to be able to blend the information they have gathered with that gathered in other ways and for other purposes. Journalists need to learn to use their computers as libraries to access other stories and perspectives on the same topics. Contemporary journalists need to blend as well as organize information.

Writing Information. Journalists can take advantage of many evolving ways to present information, especially graphics. Visual information is not only easier for readers to absorb, it saves space. Visual information is more efficient than verbal information in sketching complex processes or events, such as details of a train wreck or the path of a hurricane.

Writing styles change. We write shorter sentences than most journalists did a hundred years ago. Earlier readers may have understood long sentences better than their contemporary counterparts, although we cannot be sure of this. The writing style of Charles Dickens is easy to understand, as is Ernest Hemingway's. One wrote long sentences, and one short, but both reflected the literary style of their times. We reflect ours, and journalists who read a lot can see evolving styles in the pages of the *New Yorker* and other magazines, or in the *Washington Post* or *New York Times*. Mass media are not equal when it comes to influencing writing (and reporting) styles—which is all the more reason journalists should read, watch, and listen all the time.

Storing Information. Journalists also are aware that news media are using newer technologies to store information. The same newspaper that, after it was read, was then used to wrap fish, is now ending up in electronic "storage bins" that can be reached by personal computers and marketed as a by-product of the news media in the future. Readers can construct their own histories of local stories, or of the years of their birth or marriage. Some media are already marketing old information in new ways. Journalists are beginning to think about *information* rather than just about current stories and news. This shift is subtle but profoundly important for journalism as a business.

Contextualizing Information. Journalists realize they work within established journalistic traditions. Like other professionals, journalists have standards, and all stories need to be weighed against the ethical standards of the field. Journalists sometimes fail, but they always should present perspectives on events in a manner as fair as possible to all involved. Truth is hard to determine, but journalists should attempt to present information that can be backed up with reasonable facts. That is as close to the truth as journalists can get. There also are historical and cultural traditions in journalism (even television is more than half a century old). Journalists should be aware of patterns and traditions, even as they also seek new ways to carry out the tasks of journalism.

Presenting Information. Information must be displayed in an interesting, readable, and inviting format so people will choose to read it. Today, computer graphics are increasingly used to present the main points or provide more specific information associated with a news article. Journalists need to be able to imagine ways to tell stories without words.

Evaluating Audiences. Journalists should understand how audiences use news and entertainment media, what role these media play in their lives, and—most especially—how audience members learn. In the past, editors have relied on surveys, letters, and telephone calls as the main measure of how well a medium is doing. Of course circulation is an important indicator. Despite frequent feedback from audiences, mass media managers have not been able to stop the decline in daily newspaper circulation, the drop in network audiences, and the decline in general magazine circulation. Journalists need to learn how to do their job from the audience's point of view.

Editors and publishers sometimes produce high-quality stories the same way year after year, insisting this is what readers and viewers still want or at least *should* read and watch. It is as if car manufacturers decided to build high-quality cars the same way they did in the 1960s and fill up acres with unsold, high-quality cars for which there were no interested buyers. This is what is happening in the world of mass media also, except we call it declining circulation. Audiences are still buying "cars," although perhaps not the ones we had hoped.

The failure of some mass media managers to adapt to the shifting audience—the failure to seize the opportunities afforded by the changing technology—is as irresponsible as the car manufacturers whose decisions have resulted in massive layoffs. The fault is not in automobile buyers; the fault is not in the much-blamed audiences. Journalists must learn to lead audiences by following them. All other professional groups do. That is the exciting challenge of learning about your audience.

How Journalists Enrich Perspectives

In the mid-nineteenth century, reporters began to use interviews to fill the pages of newspapers. There are limits to what an interview can tell you. Interviews are limited to the perspectives and quotes of one or a few individuals, and major events always generate a variety of perspectives about key facts. Therefore journalists can enrich stories about events and trends by enlarging the number of people interviewed. The survey is one way to do that. Using a representative sample, a journalist and his or her associates can interview people of different age, race, class, gender, geographic region, political affiliation, and other comparative factors. In a sense, a survey is a single interview that is expanded—in a careful and controlled way—to cover many people.

Yet there is a difference between an interview and a survey. With a single interview, you can adjust the questions to fit the responses and moods of the single individual to whom you are talking. With a survey, the questions are written out in advance and asked in exactly the same way to everyone interviewed. A survey is like a play in which one part, that of the interviewer, is spoken verbatim as written, while the parts of those interviewed are written by each respondent as he or she answers.

Because most people—but, significantly, not all people—have telephones in the United States, most mass media survey interviewing is done by telephone. News media often determine a topic quickly and compile a questionnaire for telephone implementation. Major polling companies such as Lou Harris and Gallup still conduct some surveys door to door, and sometimes news media also do door-to-door polling.

As telephones spread, more people use them for polls, even in countries once under control of the former Soviet Union in Eastern Europe.

Seeing and Checking Events

Some of the most significant events do not happen in front of your eyes. For example, daily acts of discrimination on the basis of race or gender may be hidden, and those that engage in them may not even be aware they are acting with prejudice. The United States has long prided itself on efforts to root out discrimination and provide equal opportunity for all citizens regardless of race, gender, age, or ethnic background. The First Amendment stands as a protection for different views. Yet prejudice and discrimination linger in the United States.

Sometimes a news medium can test actions and beliefs that elude other fact-gathering techniques. For example, reporters will not often find anyone saying: "Yes, I am prejudiced against (blacks, gays, women, old people, young people, liberals, conservatives, and so forth)." Nearly everyone says, and believes, they are without prejudice. The ABC News program *PrimeTime Live* attempted to determine whether blacks and whites were treated differently. The program sent two men about the same age (in their 30s), of similar socioeconomic background (middle class) and appearance (casual wear) to shop for housing. Their reception was secretly filmed with small, unobtrusive cameras. The black shopper was served more slowly, sometimes ignored, and shown different homes than was the white shopper. The film vividly demonstrated differences in reception. The story suggests that what society says and what society does are not yet the same.

In the nineteenth century, *New York World* reporter Elizabeth Ann Cochrane, known as Nellie Bly, feigned mental illness so that she could report about the typical treatment in asylums of the day. In the early 1990s, a journalist from Israel pretended to be a neo-Nazi to win the confidence of key leaders in what he claimed to be a large and growing new Nazi movement in Germany. Creating events is not a new way of checking on the performance of social agencies or even private businesses that provide goods and services for the public.

A Collection of Methods and Perspectives

Reporters seldom use a single method. More often interview information is combined with information from documents or from attending and witnessing events. Sometimes, reporters can add information generated from databases or content analysis, or from surveys. Occasionally, as with the ABC News example, reporters actually enter events to test things out. One can visualize stories as layers of different perspectives on information and can visualize how a story might change as different perspectives are added, as illustrated on the following pages by the hypothetical coverage of a football game between the University of Texas and the University of Arkansas, long-term rivals.

SEEING THE EVENT. Imagine that your editor asks you to watch a football game between the Texas Longhorns and the Arkansas Razorbacks, a game of keen interest in the region. The editor asks you to write a story using the information from the scoreboard and from what you learn as a member of the crowd. You know only what you see and hear. Your story is likely to read something like this:

Version 1: Seeing the Event

"Longhorns Defeat Razorbacks"

The Texas Longhorns delighted a roaring home crowd today when Texas edged Arkansas 17–14 after Texas kicked a 38-yard field goal in the final nine seconds of the game.

Crowds ran onto the field to tear down the goal posts despite efforts of police to prevent them, and the players seemed in danger of being mauled by some enthusiastic supporters.

The Longhorns scored one touchdown and the extra point in the first and third quarters, while the Razorbacks scored touchdowns with extra points in the second and fourth quarters.

ADDING DOCUMENTS. Reporters could report some events simply by keeping their eyes open. A simple document, however, can change nearly all stories. With a football program you can match numbers of players with their names. Another document, the collected game statistics, adds another perspective to what you see with your own eyes. As a result your story will reflect the addition of these perspectives.

Version 2: Seeing the Event PLUS Reading Documents

"Longhorns Defeat Razorbacks"

The Texas Longhorns delighted a roaring home crowd *estimated at more than 62,000* today when Texas edged Arkansas 17–14 after *place-kicker Tim Simmons* kicked a 38-yard field goal, the

36th—and most important—successful field goal of his career, in the final nine seconds of the game.

Crowds ran onto the field to tear down the goal posts despite efforts of *approximately 100* police officers to prevent them, and the players seemed in danger of being mauled by some enthusiastic supporters.

The Longhorns *dominated the game in total yardage, gaining 452 yards on the ground and 127 in the air versus 173 yards on the ground and 73 in the air by Arkansas, but Arkansas was able to take advantage of Texas fumbles—a record nine—*to score touchdowns in the second and fourth quarters.

ADDING INTERVIEWS. With documents the story is enriched, but there are no people, just facts and figures, so you undoubtedly will want to interview key players and perhaps coaches. You may also want to interview others. Every individual has a different perspective on a game. Coaches see it differently from quarterbacks, who see it differently from defensive linebackers, who see it differently from the fans in the upper decks, who see it differently from fans lower down at the 50-yard line. There is seldom one perspective on a game or event. It is almost as important that journalists provide a variety of perspectives on facts as to provide the facts themselves. Quotes from interviews would add enriching perspectives to our story.

Version 3: Seeing, Document PLUS Talking

"Longhorns Defeat Razorbacks"

The Texas Longhorns delighted a roaring home crowd estimated at more than 62,000 today when Texas edged Arkansas 17–14 after place kicker Tim Simmons kicked a 38-yard field goal, the 36th—and most important—successful field goal of his career, during the final nine seconds of the game.

Crowds ran onto the field to tear down the goal posts despite the efforts of approximately 100 police to prevent them, and players seemed in danger of being mauled by some enthusiastic supporters.

Simmons, interviewed after the game, said, "I closed my eyes and prayed. I didn't open them until I heard the cheering."

The Longhorns dominated the game in total yardage, gaining 452 yards on the ground and 127 in the air versus 173 yards on the ground and 73 in the air by Arkansas, but Arkansas was able to take advantage of Texas fumbles—a record nine—to score touchdowns in the second and fourth quarters.

Coach Bill Jones said that Texas was lucky to win, given the mistakes made in the game. "We just squeezed by," he told reporters in a postgame press conference.

ADDING SURVEY DATA. Interviews add a human perspective on events and enrich the findings of other methods. Each method and each source provide another perspective on events, and reporters should always ask themselves: What are the key facts, and what are other perspectives on these facts? It is conceivable that survey data might be available regarding some aspect of the game, providing data that would not be readily available from regular interviews or documents. See how some survey data might change this story.

Version 4: Seeing, Documents, Interviews PLUS Survey Data

"Longhorns Defeat Razorbacks"

The Texas Longhorns delighted a roaring home crowd estimated at more than 62,000 today when Texas edged Arkansas 17–14 after place kicker Tim Simmons kicked a 38-yard field goal, the 36th—and most important—successful field goal of his career, during the final nine seconds of the game.

Crowds ran onto the field to tear down the goal posts despite the efforts of approximately 100 police to prevent them, and players seemed in danger of being mauled by some enthusiastic supporters.

Simmons, interviewed after the game, said, "I closed my eyes and prayed. I didn't open them until I heard the cheering."

Although no one was hurt in the postgame rampage on the field, a survey carried out in Austin last year by a major polling firm found that many in the city feel that the intensity of feeling between fans of these long-time football rivals is too intense and perhaps even dangerous. The survey shows that a number of fans said they may start watching future games on television.

The Longhorns dominated the game in total yardage, gaining 452 yards on the ground and 127 in the air versus 173 yards on the ground and 73 in the air by Arkansas, but Arkansas was able to take advantage of Texas fumbles—a record nine—to score touchdowns in the second and fourth quarters.

Coach Bill Jones said that Texas was lucky to win, given the mistakes made in the game. "We just squeezed by," he told reporters in a postgame press conference.

FIELD EXPERIMENT. The findings from each method add a dimension to the story of the game. The newspaper could have looked ahead and conducted a field experiment to test the survey findings about feelings getting too intense. For example, the newspaper might have sent two reporters, both the same age and gender and dressed alike, to the fan section of each side, with directions to root for the opposite side (with courtesy and common sense). Then the story might have another dimension.

Version 5: Seeing, Documents, Interviews, Survey Data PLUS Field Experiment

"Longhorns Defeat Razorbacks"

The Texas Longhorns delighted a roaring home crowd estimated at more than 62,000 today when Texas edged Arkansas 17–14 after place kicker Tim Simmons kicked a 38-yard field goal, the 36th—and most important—successful field goal of his career, during the final nine seconds of the game.

Crowds ran onto the field to tear down the goal posts despite the efforts of approximately 100 police to prevent them, and players seemed in danger of being mauled by some enthusiastic supporters.

Simmons, interviewed after the game, said, "I closed my eyes and prayed. I didn't open them until I heard the cheering."

Although no one was hurt in the postgame rampage on the field, a survey carried out in Austin last year by a major polling firm found that many in the city feel that the intensity of feeling between fans of these long-time football rivals is too intense and perhaps even dangerous. The survey shows that a number of fans said they may start watching future games on television.

The Longhorns dominated the game in total yardage, gaining 452 yards on the ground and 127 in the air versus 173 yards on the ground and 73 in the air by Arkansas, but Arkansas was able to take advantage of Texas fumbles—a record nine—to score touchdowns in the second and fourth quarters.

Coach Bill Jones said that Texas was lucky to win, given the mistakes made in the game. "We just squeezed by," he told reporters in a postgame press conference.

The Austin Newspaper sent two reporters, both men in their late 20s, to sit in the fans' section, one for each team, with instructions to root politely—cheers only, no words—for the other team.

Both reporters received hard glances and, in one case, abusive language from other fans—"Go back where you came from," or "What are you, some kind of a—hole?" One Texas fan threatened to throw an empty beer bottle—alcohol is not allowed in the stadium—and an Arkansas fan threatened to strike one reporter with an umbrella. Each reporter left his assigned section at the end of the first quarter.

DATABASE INFORMATION*.* You can see that the story continues to evolve as layers of information are laid over the top of what you can see with your own eyes. You can even go further and tap a database such as Vu/Text, DataTimes, Nexis, or Dialog, available in many newspaper offices. For example, you could conduct a search of stories in key newspapers for the past five years in which the word "football," "fans," and "riot" or "violence" (for starters) occur within 50 words of each other. If so, you might find that fan intensity has surfaced as a factor in other college football games in recent years. That might change the story still further.

Version 6: Seeing, Documents, Interviews, Survey Data, Field Experiment, PLUS Database Information

"Longhorns Defeat Razorbacks"

The Texas Longhorns delighted a roaring home crowd estimated at more than 62,000 today when Texas edged Arkansas 17–14 after place kicker Tim Simmons kicked a 38-yard field goal, the 36th—and most important—successful field goal of his career, during the final nine seconds of the game.

Crowds ran onto the field to tear down the goal posts despite the efforts of approximately 100 police to prevent them, and players seemed in danger of being mauled by some enthusiastic supporters.

Simmons, interviewed after the game, said, "I closed my eyes and prayed. I didn't open them until I heard the cheering."

Although no one was hurt in the postgame rampage on the field, a survey carried out in Austin last year by a major polling firm found that many in the city feel that the intensity of feeling between fans of these long-time football rivals is too intense and perhaps even dangerous. The survey shows that a number of fans said they may start watching future games on television.

The Longhorns dominated the game in total yardage, gaining 452 yards on the ground and 127 in the air versus 173 yards on the ground and 73 in the air by Arkansas, but Arkansas was able to take advantage of Texas fumbles—a record nine—to score touchdowns in the second and fourth quarters.

Coach Bill Jones said that Texas was lucky to win, given the mistakes made in the game. "We just squeezed by," he told reporters in a postgame press conference.

The Austin Newspaper sent two reporters, both men in their late 20s, to sit in the fans' section, one for each team, with instructions to root politely—cheers only, no words—for the other team.

Both reporters received hard glances and, in one case, abusive language from other fans—"Go back where you came from," or "What are you, some kind of a—-hole?" One Texas fan threatened to throw an empty beer bottle—alcohol is not allowed in the stadium—and an Arkansas fan threatened to strike one reporter with an umbrella. Each reporter left his assigned section at the end of the first quarter.

A computer search of the sports stories about college football games—a search for words indicating fan violence during or at the end of the games—shows that several college games have deteriorated into fist fights and violence at the end, especially if the home team is victorious over a powerful archrival. There were more outbreaks during the past two years than in previous years.

A journalist is part historian, creative writer, social scientist, humanist, and also part of many other professions and skills. Yet journalists have a different role from other professionals. Where doctors seek to provide information for a specific individual, journalists need to provide the key facts, along with an array of perspectives on those facts, for a more general audience. If a journalist provided only a single point of view on each event, it would be as if a doctor refused to consider the opinions of other doctors. Doctors sometimes disagree. News sources nearly always do.

When journalists use a variety of reporting methods, they necessarily enlarge the perspectives on the key facts of a story. The final story in our mythical football game between Texas and Arkansas is much richer than the story based on simple observation, or even simple observation supplemented with some statistics and interviews. Journalists have the duty to gather, organize, and present key facts, but they also have the duty to present a variety of perspectives on the key facts.

It takes time, courage, and methodological skill to present a variety of perspectives, to find patterns in events. Those who object to coverage from a "liberal" or "conservative" press are really objecting to a pluralism of views. "Liberals" don't want so much "conservative" news—"conservatives" don't want so much "liberal" news. Both sides suspect a conspiracy. Those of us who deeply treasure the orderliness of society want to listen to and obey the directions from leaders—such as presidents, coaches, deans, business executives—who sit at the top of clearly defined organizational triangles. For such leaders, a pluralism of views different from their own threatens their position as well as the very nature of how society functions. Of course most leaders in business, politics, culture, arts, and social life do not want to be challenged. Therefore in the minds of many, pluralism threatens the neat order of society.

The Active Audience

There is another view. If the power triangles are not challenged by information reflecting many views, they become too rigid, like Egyptian pyramids with massive stones pressing down on the layer below. That process characterized much of human history. It led to economic and social progress but also sometimes to human misery.

Communication technology has put communication means within the hands of average people, from telephones to faxes, from cable television to direct satellite transmission, from home computers to laptops. With these means, average people can communicate with each other and talk back to leaders at the top of triangles. Communication technology once favored the leaders over followers, as in Germany in the 1930s when the Nazis made skillful use of propaganda. Today communication favors people talking with other people, and so the once-rigid pyramids of human organization are becoming more like Christmas trees with small lights blinking at every level. The star at the top remains brightest but still is only another star.

The Challenge for Journalists

In such an information-rich environment, what can journalists add? Journalists will not compete well for audience attention when consumers can gather much information themselves. Soon no one will need newspapers for determining what films are playing or the current price of stocks. (Many already can retrieve such information directly via the Internet.) Yet journalists remain focused on the public life of communities, and journalists remain in the best position to dig up key facts and to provide a diversity of perspectives on those facts. The survival of the news media may depend on the ability of journalists to do a better job of enriching the ways in which simple events can be viewed and considered. In other words, *finding patterns in the news representing a diversity of viewpoints has become one of the most important aspects of journalism.*

This is an important step beyond publishing everything that is fit to print (or broadcast). It means journalists need to use all their skills to locate the patterns of our collective lives so that we know where we are going.

References

Emery, Edwin and Michael Emery. *The Press and America: An Interpretive History of the Mass Media,* 5th ed., p. 260. Englewood Cliffs, NJ: Prentice Hall, 1984.

Gunn, Lynn. "Ten-year California gold miner." *New York Times*, Aug. 30, 1993.

Krueger, Bill and Pat Stith."On the Ward, Overtime Pays." *The Raleigh News & Observer*, May 30, 1993, p. A1.

Michelmore, David L. and Bob Donaldson. "Can Mill Towns Revive?" *The Pittsburgh Post-Gazette*, November 29, 1993, p. A1.

"True colors." *PrimeTime Live*, September 26, 1991.

World Association for Public Opinion Research (WAPOR). *International Journal for Public Opinion* (various issues).

Chapter Three

VANTAGE POINTS

... All policies, whether in the area of health, education, social welfare, or industrial development, are dependent upon the success of interested parties in generating beliefs about an uncertain world.

—Oscar Gandy Jr.
Beyond Agenda Setting: Information
Subsidies and Public Policy

Writing skills are essential for both print and broadcast journalists if they are to communicate effectively the critical patterns in each day's news. Equally essential is another set of skills—observational skills. If they are poor observers, even the best writers have little to say, no matter how clever their sentences. Creativity in journalism lies in the ability to make acute observations of what is happening in the world. This ability to discover patterns, even in the most ordinary and obscure corners, is what makes Mike Royko, Studs Terkel, Jimmy Breslin, and Molly Ivins outstanding journalists. They are superb writers, but they also are superb observers of minute details in everyday life—Chicago transit riders, conversations about sports, activities in Manhattan taverns, and dozens of other settings familiar to ordinary people. These journalists' ability to highlight familiar experiences is what makes them effective communicators.

A journalist who is a good writer but a poor observer is like a painter with keen technical skills who has little to put on canvas. The results in both cases are pictures of poor quality. Good journalism demands two distinct sets of talents and skills—observation and writing, and skillful observation must precede the writing.

Although newsroom positions typically have titles such as *reporter* or *staff writer* that seem to emphasize writing and presenting news reports, there has to be something to report. Editors and news directors assume that when you sit down to write, some time already has been invested in observing what is happening in some segment of the community. After all, journalism is an empirical activity. You have to gather facts before you can report them. Good journalism, of course, is more than a set of facts. It is a coherent set of information about some key pattern. Recognizing such patterns requires considerably more than casual observation of what is happening in your community.

Some of the common, rudimentary techniques of observation are learned early by journalists and journalism students. Short telephone interviews, the rewriting of press releases, and using such background documents as minutes of meetings and reports are staples of simple journalistic observation. Using these techniques alone and the routine facts that they provide to prepare news reports makes a journalist little more than a newsroom bureaucrat, much like the bureaucrats at the county courthouse and at dozens of corporate offices who plod through file after file every workday.

While most journalists have an image of their own work that is considerably different from their image of the work of bureaucrats, newsrooms and their staffs share many of the characteristics of government and corporate office environments. It is precisely because of the bureaucratic routinization of so much of the daily work in the newsroom that it is possible to produce a daily newspaper or evening newscast day after day on a very tight schedule.

If you regard journalism as a trade, as nothing more than a set of routine job skills and tasks, then there is no reason to go beyond this comparison. However, the distinguishing mark of a profession, and of professional education, is to move beyond rote procedures and traditional practice. The purpose of education is to stimulate analytic thinking, not just to teach technical job skills. An educated professional is someone who is reflective about his or her work and has some sensitivity about what it all means, why things are done the way they are, and how they could be done differently and more effectively.

Routine Shortcuts

As soon as you strive to go beyond the traditional practice of professional journalism and begin to think about how most journalists go about observing their communities, you realize that journalists' daily observations of the world do rely to a considerable degree upon a great many routine shortcuts.

Press conferences, handouts, routine reports, and brief conversations with key officials head the hierarchy of sources upon which journalists rely for the facts that fill their stories. Even on major newspapers, such as the *New York Times* and *Washington Post*, with their large reporting staffs and emphasis on journalistic enterprise, routine shortcuts are extensively employed. Leon Sigal's examination of the *Times* and *Post* found that enterprise reporting—direct observation, in-depth interviews, or extensive examination of records and library materials—accounted for less than a third of these newspapers' staff-produced stories. Most of the news originates with materials prepared by others—what Oscar Gandy calls *information subsidies* furnished to news organizations by interested parties from business, government, and interest groups.

The disadvantage of this kind of reactive, bureaucratic reporting is obvious. News organizations can become passive conduits for the views and objectives of others. In those situations, the patterns reported are those framed by persons who have a vested interest in the outcome. They are not patterns developed by more dispassionate observers. Under such circumstances, all the traditional rhetoric about serving the public and playing a special role in a democratic society becomes very hollow. To echo David Barsamian, the media become "stenographers to power."

Even when the most expert and well-intentioned news sources are used, there is another problem with these routine shortcuts—an over-reliance on a few techniques of collecting information. Social scientists for decades have been concerned with the inherent structural biases in information based on a single observation technique. Every means of observing people and their communities has some limitations. Information based on several distinctly different techniques of observation, a kind of *triangulation* on reality, provides a better picture of the world than information gathered through any single technique. Preoccupation with one or two routine techniques of reporting is the hallmark of a trade, not of a profession. Use of a variety of observation techniques in depth is the hallmark of a creative professional.

To evaluate how good our techniques are for observing patterns in the local community, consider these two standards:

factual adequacy—accuracy, precision and completeness of the facts; and

efficiency—the cost of collecting the initial basic facts about an event or topic, plus the cost of gathering additional facts to increase the scope and depth of the picture.

Under the pressure of deadlines, which seldom are more than a few days and more frequently are just a few hours or even minutes away, newsrooms emphasize the second criterion, *efficiency*. The routine sources of observations—those press conferences, handouts, and brief interviews—are efficient methods of gleaning the highlights and most salient features of daily events. Furthermore, because these techniques are restricted largely to observations of official sources to whom the facts can be attributed, there is at least a passing grade on the criterion of *factual adequacy*.

However, as this text will show repeatedly, the factual adequacy of the news that is collected through these routine shortcuts—or through any restricted set of observation techniques, for that matter—is very limited. A true professional understands and employs a broad *strategy* of journalistic observations, not just the rote application of a few, commonly employed *tactics*.

Strategic Observations

Relatively little news is observed directly by reporters. There are not that many reporters to record the myriad happenings of each day, and the occurrence of major portions of the daily news is not neatly scheduled. For much of the grist of the daily news—fires, deaths, crimes and accidents—you rely upon a source, either someone who was present to observe the event or, more commonly, someone whose official duties involve collecting facts about what has now become the focus of your news story. Sometimes you obtain these facts in a brief interview with the source; other times you read their report. In any event, traditional journalistic practice has two major characteristics:

• Journalistic observations are *indirect*, based upon the reports of sources who, as witnesses or officials, are in a position to possess some of the facts about what happened.

• Journalistic observations are *episodic*, usually limited to the reporting of a single event that occurred in the past few hours.

But journalists' observations are not necessarily limited to single events within the ken of one or two sources. Increasingly, it is important to report situations broader than those comprising the news events of the past twenty-four hours. Although the majority of political reporting, for example, is narrowly focused on the political events and hoopla of the day, it is necessary to push beyond these ritualistic and sometimes superficial events to get at the real meaning of a political campaign and how it affects voters.

This is what the *Wichita Eagle* and the *Charlotte Observer* attempted to do during the 1992 presidential election. Through elaborate combinations of polling to discover what issues concerned voters, in-depth follow-up coverage in the newspaper, and a variety of community forums, these newspapers made an effort to connect the presidential campaign with their readers in a meaningful way.

More and more in recent national elections journalists have turned to polls and survey research as instruments for observing and understanding the political news of the day. In the abstract, there is little difference between the traditional interviewing of politicians and campaign managers and interviewing a sample of voters in a poll. In both instances, you rely upon others to tell you what is happening and why. However, sources such as campaign managers have a vested interest in both the outcome of the election and the content of your news story.

Individual voters also may feel some vested interest in the outcome of the election, although for many it is a matter of rather peripheral concern. In any event, the vested interests of hundreds of voters interviewed in a general-population survey will balance out in the end far more evenly than the strong interests of a few political sources. The key point here is that rather than relying upon a few sources who are conveniently at hand and are clamoring to speak, the use of polls and surveys yields *systematic* observations about general voter sentiment. This approach also opens the door to numerous other news stories about community patterns that are difficult, if not impossible, to report from an episodic, news-event perspective.

In 1992 Los Angeles was racked by days of rioting, following a state jury verdict that acquitted the policemen accused of beating black citizen Rodney King. News coverage of the rampant arson and disorder was thorough and revealed many previously unreported community patterns.

This news coverage was a good example of Walter Lippmann's definition of news as a part of life that has obtruded into the public arena. Only when events and problems reach the attention of major social institutions, such as the police and fire departments or the mayor's office, do they commonly become news and receive broad public attention. It is at these institutional locations, the sites where most problems eventually surface, that news organizations establish their beats.

This emphasis on episodic reporting—what has sometimes been called the event orientation of the press—means that many social problems and situations do not capture the attention of reporters until they have reached a crisis level. Los Angeles is one case in point. Child abuse, hunger, discrimination in housing and lending, and numerous other social concerns appearing in the news in recent years existed long before the news media put them on the national agenda.

When many of these community situations become part of the daily agenda of our government and social institutions, the pervasive event orientation of the press still may result in a failure to recognize them as something that transcends a story about one or two individuals, one or two events circumscribed by time and place. Police reports, for example, are episodic reports of crime and have been a staple of journalism for centuries. Most news organizations, especially local newspapers and television stations, monitor these police reports and report at least some of them. But until recently few news organizations had any kind of ongoing monitoring of crime as a social problem.

The *Austin American-Statesman* has taken advantage of new technologies to add another dimension to its reporting of crime in the capital city of Texas. Touchtone telephones can be used to access the newspaper's computer, which stores a variety of community information—everything from stock quotations and movie reviews to crime statistics. Crime news—individual stories about specific criminal acts—still appears in the newspaper. However, readers of the *American-Statesman* also find a "Neighborhood Crime Reports" map (figure 3.1) in the newspaper dividing the city into six areas. Note the instructions above the map. With the advent of computer databases that can be accessed directly by the news audience, we have the beginnings of a system in which episodic reports about individuals are elements in social trends, not just isolated incidents.

Although most of our social institutions, such as the police or courts, continue to deal primarily with individuals and their activities rather than tackle broad social situations, a broader perspective is emerging. In the last decade or so, journalists have recognized a need

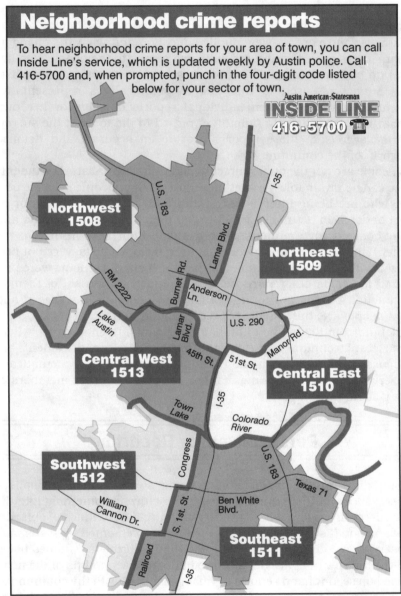

Neighborhood crime reports

To hear neighborhood crime reports for your area of town, you can call Inside Line's service, which is updated weekly by Austin police. Call 416-5700 and, when prompted, punch in the four-digit code listed below for your sector of town.

Austin American-Statesman
INSIDE LINE
416-5700 ☎

U.S. 183

I-35

Northwest
1508

RM 2222

Burnet Rd.

Lamar Blvd.

Anderson Ln.

Northeast
1509

Lake Austin

Lamar Blvd.

U.S. 290

Manor Rd.

45th St.

51st St.

Central West
1513

Central East
1510

Town Lake

I-35

Colorado River

Southwest
1512

Congress

U.S. 183

Texas 71

William Cannon Dr.

S. 1st St.

Ben White Blvd.

Railroad

I-35

Southeast
1511

Source: Austin Police Department

Staff graphics

Figure 3.1

A map showing codes so readers can obtain neighborhood crime reports
Reprinted by permission of *Austin American-Statesman*.

to observe social trends in their community systematically. For example, journalists have examined such topics as how teachers, students, and parents view public education and what the changing character of central cities and suburbia means to the people who live and do business there. To report these kinds of stories, journalists use survey research to interview systematically a representative community sample. Each individual reports only his or her own behavior, perception, or opinion in regard to the topic of the survey. In the aggregate, these reports provide an accurate and detailed portrait of the community.

People are not the only sources available to journalists. Documents also can be invaluable—sometimes more so than people because people who are being interviewed, either as traditional sources or as respondents in a survey, are aware of their role as informants and may consciously or unconsciously shade their responses. On the other hand, most of the documents used by journalists were not prepared with a journalist in mind. Typically, these documents were prepared for some other purpose, and a reporter's perusal of them is incidental. This is not to argue that documents are not biased and that people are, but usually the biases found in documents are quite different from the biases of human informants. In chapter 10, where a variety of techniques for extracting information from documents are discussed, the point is made that documents can be systematically observed in much the same manner as voters or other members of the general public.

Perspectives for Reporting

If we diagram the major points made so far about journalists' observations of their communities, the picture is something like the top row of figure 3.2, where traditional routine techniques of episodic observation (listed on the left) have been supplemented by systematic observation techniques (listed on the right). All the techniques listed on the top row of figure 3.2 also are indirect observations of the news based on secondhand reports of what is happening in the community. In news stories based on any of these techniques, attribution of the information to a source is a key element in the writing.

On some occasions journalists are eyewitnesses to news events. Many of the events reported by the news media are scheduled in advance and go into the planning books of city editors and TV assignment editors. Take a look at this morning's newspaper and count how many of the local stories could have been scheduled in advance. A journalist can plan to attend and to directly observe the city council meeting, a court trial, a planning board hearing, or a political speech. Of course, because there is only a limited number of reporters, many of these events end up being reported on the basis of indirect observation.

There is one category of news where direct observation is the norm—sports. The press box is the working arena for the sports reporter, who observes the performance of a professional baseball club, high school football team, or local college basketball team through his or her own eyes. Use of direct observation to report sports—as compared to the various techniques of indirect observation

	Episodic	**Systematic**
Indirect	**I** Interviews Reports and Documents	**II** Polls and Surveys Content Analysis Social Indicators
Direct	**III** Public Meetings Sports Events Eyewitness Accounts	**IV** Participant Observation Field Experiments

Figure 3.2

Types of observations made by journalists

used to report most public affairs news—results in some major differences in the styles of writing and reporting found in these two kinds of stories. Occasionally, the style of reporting typical of sports is applied to other types of news in the form of "I was there" features or color stories. Frequently, these are sidebars to the principal report of the news event, but they can expand public understanding of complex events.

Political scientist David Paletz and his colleagues contrast the highly abstract and stylized news reports of the Durham, North Carolina, city council with the actualities, the kinds of events that an emphasis on direct observation might highlight. For example, at one meeting a group of people came to protest a proposed public housing project. Since at this point the project was under the control of the public housing authority, there was considerable doubt that the council had any jurisdiction at all. After a long discussion on this point, one of the members suggested that it was not proper for the council to take any action at all. The audience booed and yelled. As a result the council debated at length a motion to establish an investigative committee and then debated at greater length whether the committee should report to the council or to the housing authority. After further outcries from the audience, it was decided to have the committee report to the council. This lengthy, vacillating, and raucous portion of the council meeting was tersely summed up in the next morning's newspaper.

> After much discussion of proper procedure, the offering of a motion, substitute motion and a substitute for that, the council voted over- whelmingly to look into the matter further.

Public affairs stories typically have low readership and frequently don't appear in local TV newscasts at all. What kind of audience would there be for sports stories written in this same dry style?

Direct observation of an event or situation, whether it is a city council meeting, local sports event, or the consequences of a hurricane, falls into category III of figure 3.2. The adjacent box on that row, category IV, lists a systematic form of direct observation, a technique called *participant observation* (see chapter 13). This type of reporting has been used in journalism and social science for more than a century.

A *Chicago Tribune* reporter took a job as an ambulance driver to gain information for his Pulitzer Prize-winning series on abuses in private ambulance service. A *New York Times* reporter moved into an upper West Side neighborhood for several months to gather information about the patterns of daily life in Manhattan. Journalist Hunter S. Thompson spent more than a year riding at various times with the Hell's Angels motorcycle gang. Sometimes it is necessary to be inside a situation in order to fully understand and report it. This is where the technique of participant observation is powerful and revealing.

Also listed in category IV are field experiments. In contrast to participant observation, where the reporter attempts to be an unobtrusive observer of behavior in its natural setting, the *field experiment* is a deliberately obtrusive technique in which the journalist or social scientist wants to see how people respond to a specific situation. For example, the Texas Department of Health wanted to know how often retailers violated state laws when confronted with underage teenagers attempting to buy cigarettes. The department set up an experiment to find out. In this experiment, teenagers employed for the research project attempted to buy cigarettes at 165 different stores and were successful more than 60 percent of the time. (This and other field experiments are discussed in detail in chapter 14.)

How else could this situation have been observed? Sometimes, a participant observer can wait around for things to happen. In other situations, it is better to be more obtrusive and to conduct an experiment. Both techniques are examples of systematic, direct observation.

Descriptions and Explanations

Any discussion of all the techniques outlined in figure 3.2 must include thoughtful consideration of the purpose for the reporting. Why bother with a particular story at all?

Simple answers to the questions of "Why?" and "For what purpose?" are provided by the traditional event orientation of journalism and the routine use of news values to identify the most important features of those events. From these perspectives the purpose of journalism is to *describe* the salient features of the major events of the day. However, increasingly journalists define their task as including some *explanation* for the day's news. For this reason, journalists are turning to survey research, content analysis, participant observation, and a variety of other observation techniques. Developed over decades of social science research and practical journalistic experience, these techniques can provide both the basic data for describing what is happening in our communities and the procedures for analyzing this data in ways that help us to explain what is happening.

Although the participant observer, for example, has a convenient vantage point for compiling detailed descriptions of daily life in ghetto neighborhoods, mental wards, or high schools, the real strength of participant observation is the opportunity to penetrate beneath these daily routines and to understand the reasons behind the observed patterns of behavior. In short, through participant observation and the other observational techniques discussed in this book, reporters can pursue detailed *hypotheses* that explain the "why" of surface behaviors.

Hypotheses might seem out of place in a discussion of news report-ing, but they are not limited to science and its observations of the world. Journalists use hypotheses every day. In journalism our hypotheses usually are called *story lines* or *themes*. Sometimes you just call them *hunches*. In any event, they guide your thinking and your gathering of information. Neither in science nor in journalism is it really possible to observe the world around you in a thoroughly neu-tral and comprehensive way. As philosopher of science Carl Hempel once remarked, "Those who aren't looking for anything in particular seldom find anything in particular." Neither scientists nor journalists can afford the luxury of very many empty searches.

Hypotheses guide our observations and the collection of facts for inclusion in a news story. They also help us structure these facts. After all, the purpose of journalism is not simply to report *facts per se*. World almanacs and other statistical reference works in the library do that. The purpose of journalism is to provide *information*. Although you may not have thought about it very much, reporters must always organize their facts into stories built around some theme or hypothesis. One way of thinking about the lead of a news story is to regard it as the statement of a hypothesis that is to be supported with a variety of facts organized into coherent information about an event or situation.

Strategic Planning

There are dozens of potential hypotheses to be explored in every community. How should the limited resources of your newsroom be allocated to this continuing process of exploration? Even with a superbly organized beat system and close attention to each day's breaking events, there is no guarantee that your audience will receive a comprehensive, in-depth understanding of the most important situations in the community. Comprehensive coverage is more likely to result if there is a strategic game plan.

To this point our discussion of vantage points for reporting has emphasized *how* to focus our attention. Every profession, from foot-ball to journalism to medicine, involves tactical skills. A large portion of the training for any profession involves the acquisition of skills. In some colleges and universities the training for journalists is totally tactical and rote. However, the journalist or editor who wants to achieve more than a few bylines and a few annual awards needs a strategic game plan. In addition to professional skill in *how* to focus attention, you must know on *what* to focus attention.

There is no single strategic game plan that will work for every community or newsroom. Creating a game plan for covering a local community, region, or larger area requires thought and imagination. Every journalist will not feel comfortable with the same plan. You must devise your own.

Unfortunately, the kind of game plan required for productive journalism is much more complex than the game plan required to win a football game or even to produce a winning football season. Obviously, the geography to be covered is considerably larger than one hundred yards, and the duration of the enterprise considerably longer than 60 minutes. However, there is one striking similarity—winning strategies in both journalism and football are composed of dozens of tactical moves. A single play or drive does not, by itself, win a football game. A single story, or even series of stories, does not constitute comprehensive coverage of a community.

There is at least one other similarity as well. Success requires a variety of plays. That is why so much of this chapter was spent on developing an overview of the various types of observation, and why the goal of this book is to teach the tactical details of numerous reporting techniques. Our picture of the local community is a mosaic constructed from many tiny pieces. When the pieces are fashioned with a strategic plan in mind, the resulting picture depicts a clear and understandable pattern.

Constructing the Game Plan

The best game plans will result from a journalist's creative imagination, but the game plan does not have to start from absolute scratch. Numerous sources, both journalistic and scholarly, are available to stimulate and guide your thinking. Not only can these sources provide ideas about what to focus attention on, they also suggest numerous comparisons that help put your local situation in context. Your community can be compared with nearby communities, with similar communities elsewhere, or with state and national averages.

A recent examination of the comparative well-being of 162 countries suggests a variety of ways in which the health, happiness, and prosperity of any community can be assessed. The economic well-being of a community is an obvious starting point because the daily news regularly reports numerous economic and business indicators. Typically, each of these indicators—the unemployment rate, current interest rates for home mortgages, or average prices of gasoline—is the subject of an isolated story. Too frequently even those isolated stories provide minimal information about the trend over time for that single indicator, but a mosaic that pulls together a number of these indicators into a comprehensive picture of the community's economic well-being can illustrate whether life is getting better or worse for most people in the community. Among the economic elements that can be incorporated in your mosaic are constantly changing figures, such as weekly bank deposits, and more slowly evolving figures, such as the total value of the community's housing or the total value of property tax assessments. Knowledge of the community's economic well-being also can be a central clue for covering many other stories that will help explain what the future holds in store for the community.

Economics is just one aspect of a community's well-being. Michael J. Sullivan III's *Measuring Global Values: The Ranking of 162 Countries* explored many others.

Education and knowledge are indicated by more than the obvious statistics from the local school district about the number of high school graduates, enrollment in the local junior college, and the dropout rate in the public schools. The national census conducted every 10 years collects detailed information on the level of education attained by each individual, which means that a comprehensive measure of your community can be compared directly with many other locales. Other not-so-obvious indicators of knowledge or access to means of knowledge include library circulation figures, telephone penetration, newspaper penetration in your market, and possibly available figures on how many people own computers and fax machines.

The *health status* of a community is well documented by public health departments operating at virtually every level of government. The available information ranges from the incidence of dozens of diseases that are reported by doctors and hospitals—everything from chronic ailments to the latest wave of the flu—to the amount of money paid for various treatments from public funds. All of this is an important local element in the ongoing national debate on health care.

Social justice is considerably more than reports from the police beat or the latest crime statistics. These are only two of the windows, albeit the most frequently reported, on social justice. There is a lot more information available at your local courthouse. How many persons are awaiting trial? For what offenses? What punishment is meted out as a result of trials and plea bargains? How fair are these outcomes? And don't forget that not all questions of justice involve the criminal statutes. Our courts are filled with lawsuits of every description. How litigious is your community? For what reasons do community residents—and their lawyers—go to court?

Ecological balance is one of the most interesting aspects of society. examined by Sullivan in *Measuring Global Values*. Contemporary concern with the environment, which covers a vast multitude of activities and situations, could itself be the basis of a major game plan. Almost certainly it will be a central aspect of any broader game plan for community coverage. Sullivan's approach to ecological balance is broad. There are the obvious aspects, such as pollution measures,

---

Box 3-1
Index of Social Health

The Index of Social Health measures our nation's progress in responding to sixteen major social problems ranging from infant mortality to poverty among the elderly. Researchers at Fordham University's Institute for Innovation in Social Policy prepare this annual report from a wide variety of data gathered by the federal government. The basic idea of the index is to describe the social well-being of the United States with a single number on the familiar 100-point scale.

The most recent index released by the Fordham researchers gave the country a score of 40.6 points for 1992, the latest year for which complete data were available. Although that might seem like a low score, it represents an upturn after three consecutive years of decline.

Seven of the sixteen problems measured for the index showed improvement in 1992: infant mortality, teenage suicide, high school dropout rates, drug abuse, homicide, food stamp coverage, and access to affordable housing.

Another seven problems revealed declines in the latest research: child abuse, unemployment, health insurance coverage, average weekly earnings, health costs for the elderly, poverty among the elderly, and the gap between the rich and the poor. Two of the problems, traffic deaths and the number of children being raised in poverty, were unchanged.

Fordham's Index of Social Health is based on national statistics. But similar statistics are available for states and counties. What is the social health of your community?

---

patterns of fuel use, and acreage of parks and greenbelts. Ecological balance also is described by a variety of population measures, such as the density of the population in various neighborhoods, its age distribution, fertility rates, and death rates. That last statistic alone, death rates, opens the door to a panoply of community reporting. Infant mortality speaks loudly about the well-being of a community. Deaths from a variety of accidents reveals the community's well-being on the street and on the job. Deaths from gunshot wounds localize the national debate about gun control and violence in contemporary American society.

These are just a few aspects of a community. A full portrait will describe numerous aspects of a community's people, organizations, activities, culture and geography. Each strategist will approach these elements differently in the process of creating a game plan. You can expand the list, and you can change the emphasis on various elements. And, of course, each journalist will have his or her own creative interpretation of how the tactical execution of each element in the game plan should be carried out in day-by-day reporting.

The Nine Nations of North America, a highly readable and imaginative reporting plan, was created by *Washington Post* editor Joel Garreau. His purpose was to help reporters see and understand the patterns in the news. Garreau's perspective is based on a rich view of North American regionalism—he identifies nine regions in all—stretching beyond the boundaries of the United States to encompass Canada, the Caribbean Basin, and part of northern Mexico.

> Each has a peculiar economy; each commands a certain emotional allegiance from its citizens. These nations look different, feel different, and sound different from each other, and few of their boundaries match the political lines drawn on current maps. Some are clearly divided topographically by mountains, deserts, and rivers. Others are separated by architecture, music, language, and ways of making a living. Each nation has its own list of desires. . . . Most important, each nation has a distinct prism through which it views the world.

The differences in these "national" settings explain their varying perspective on many issues in the news, everything from energy policy to gun control. Debates about the distribution of federal funds to state and local governments regularly pit the Frostbelt against the Sunbelt. On a more mundane level, it is bratwurst versus tacos. Almost every topic in the news, from poll results identifying the most important problem facing the country to regional variations in lifestyle, can be

A reporter broadcasts the local news from the streets of Chicago. Courtesy NBC, Chicago.

creatively analyzed and explained from this regional perspective. This is a strategic view that, even if applied in only a single region, yields endless tactical variations. There are Texans who contend that their state itself is seven distinct "nations." Other observers advocate splitting California into two states because of strong regional differences that undergird debate on a wide variety of public issues. What are the regional patterns in your area that help to explain the daily news? Where are the lodes of statistics and other information that detail these differences?

Game Plans for Local News

Analogous to the regions of North America or the regions of Texas and California are the neighborhoods in your local community. In the United States most news organizations concentrate on local news. That is true for virtually all weekly and daily newspapers, most television stations, and even some magazines. Translate the ideas and concepts that other journalists and scholars have developed for nations and regions into a game plan for covering your local community. In this situation there is a special opportunity to make the resulting news stories very personal messages to the members of your audience. Not only is this information about their community, it can be focused specifically on their neighborhood in comparison to other local neighborhoods.

This neighborhood emphasis in your reporting can be greatly enhanced through the use of maps that are coded to reflect differences across the community, differences in everything from the value of homes to the incidence of medical problems. Earlier in this chapter we looked at a map run by the *Austin American-Statesman* that defines the areas of the city for which crime statistics are available by phone from the newspaper's computer. An alternative approach would be to publish this map weekly or monthly with the actual statistics color-coded by neighborhood.

Computer graphics have developed to the point that detailed maps of cities, states, or the nation can be constructed on the basis of almost any kind of statistic. Nearly all news organizations use these maps both before and after an election to show the pockets of strength and weakness for the winner. It is much easier to comprehend patterns of voting from a map than from a long list of voting statistics organized by precinct, county, or state. The same is true for many of the other patterns on which your game plan will focus.

Even back in the days before the software for mapping local communities was widely available, University of Texas researcher Lorna Monti produced a comprehensive set of social maps of Austin, Texas. At that time, the mid-1970s, the city was in the early stages of major growth, and its maps revealed distinct differences across the city in gains and losses of population. Some neighborhoods were stable, others showed sharp declines, and a few displayed explosive growth. In tandem with other maps displaying the patterns across Austin in income, education, quality of housing, and health, Monti's pioneering use of census data to construct a picture of the local community and its neighborhoods was a comprehensive preview of what the next ten years would bring. Chapter 10 discusses the use of census data in more detail, including the use of some new software that the U.S. Bureau of the Census distributed in 1990 that enables any journalist or researcher to construct similar neighborhood maps from this rich lode of data.

There is useful background on the construction of maps to enhance your local reporting in Mark Monmonier's *Mapping It Out*, a detailed handbook on how to enhance your prose with visual displays of information. An earlier book, *Maps with the News*, which looks specifically at the historical evolution of maps in journalism, will take you deeper into the strategic and ethical questions of journalistic map making.

The statistics on which many of these news maps—like those Monti constructed to compare Austin neighborhoods and the one in figure 3.3—are based are examples of information that social scientists call *social indicators*. Just as beat reporters have a period of initiation during which they learn the jargon and specialized terms of the news sources on their beat, reporters who want to mine the wealth of social indicators that are available for their community and their region also have to learn some new terms and techniques. Two helpful sources for this initiation are:

- Ian Miles, *Social Indicators for Human Development*. London: Frances Pinter, 1985
- Robert Rossi and Kevin Gilmartin, *The Handbook of Social Indicators. Sources, Characteristics and Analysis*. New York: Garland STPM Press, 1980

Expanding the Game Plan

The number of ways in which communities can be described is unlimited. Part of your task in constructing a game plan is to decide which of these elements are the most important for your news coverage. That requires a value judgment on your part—a necessity because there will never be time enough to cover every aspect of the community for which there is available data. It also is necessary if your news organization feels any sense of social responsibility.

Increasingly, journalists have taken a proactive stance in local reporting. The *San Antonio Light* advocated a community agenda focused on children's issues and followed through with a year of extensive news coverage. The *Shreveport Times* reported extensively on the quality of housing in that Louisiana city and brought a neglected area of concern onto the agenda of subsequent local elections. As mentioned earlier, a number of newspapers have designed campaigns to encourage more public dialogue during presidential campaigns.

One goal for a game plan is a comprehensive description of the current state of affairs in the community. Another goal is to organize systematic information about what people want in the future. Survey research, one of the newer modes of reporting, can enhance both of these goals because it can add a rich variety of information, both about how people assess their current situation and about what they desire for the future.

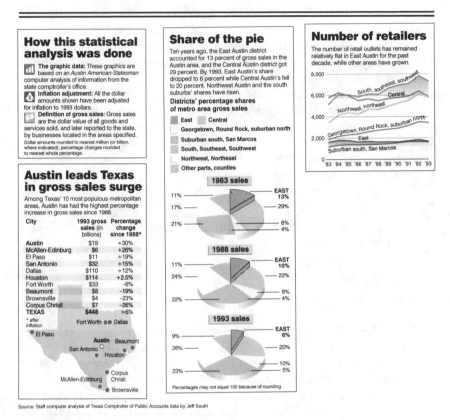

How this statistical analysis was done

The graphic data: These graphics are based on an *Austin American-Statesman* computer analysis of information from the state comptroller's office.

Inflation adjustment: All the dollar amounts shown have been adjusted for inflation to 1993 dollars.

Definition of gross sales: Gross sales are the dollar value of all goods and services sold, and later reported to the state, by businesses located in the areas specified.

Dollar amounts rounded to nearest million (or billion, where indicated); percentage changes rounded to nearest whole percentage.

Austin leads Texas in gross sales surge

Among Texas' 10 most populous metropolitan areas, Austin has had the highest percentage increase in gross sales since 1988.

City	1993 gross sales (in billions)	Percentage change since 1988*
Austin	$19	+30%
McAllen-Edinburg	$6	+26%
El Paso	$11	+19%
San Antonio	$32	+15%
Dallas	$110	+12%
Houston	$114	+2.5%
Fort Worth	$33	–6%
Beaumont	$8	–19%
Brownsville	$4	–23%
Corpus Christi	$7	–26%
TEXAS	$448	+6%

* after inflation

Share of the pie

Ten years ago, the East Austin district accounted for 13 percent of gross sales in the Austin area, and the Central Austin district got 29 percent. By 1993, East Austin's share dropped to 6 percent while Central Austin's fell to 20 percent. Northwest Austin and the south suburbs' shares have risen.

Districts' percentage shares of metro area gross sales

- East
- Central
- Georgetown, Round Rock, suburban north
- Suburban south, San Marcos
- South, Southeast, Southwest
- Northwest, Northeast
- Other parts, counties

Percentages may not equal 100 because of rounding.

Number of retailers

The number of retail outlets has remained relatively flat in East Austin for the past decade, while other areas have grown.

Source: Staff computer analysis of Texas Comptroller of Public Accounts data by Jeff South

Figure 3.3
How the economic boom bypassed part of a Texas city
Reprinted by permission of *Austin American-Statesman*.

When a game plan combines factual information with creative polling of its community, the result is an in-depth assessment of the quality of life enjoyed by local residents. It also is an innovative game plan that combines what have been called the "old" and "new" perspectives of journalism. The old, established tradition relies heavily upon official sources for statements and statistics. A new tradition in journalism emphasizes the community itself as a source of news. Survey research based on representative samples of the community can be a major source of news. Part III of this text discusses the techniques involved in doing survey research. For some ideas on interesting topics for survey research, a good starting point is Ramkrishna Mukherjee's *The Quality of Life: Valuation in Social Research*.

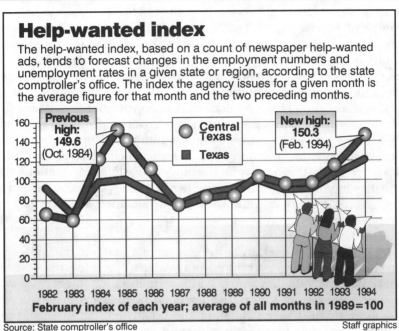

Figure 3.4

An economic forecast based on help wanted ads

Reprinted by permission of *Austin American-Statesman*.

A good game plan ensures an exciting and productive future for a news organization. There also is another, more immediate by-product of strategic planning; it creates ways to evaluate current coverage and to deploy reporters and resources to cover sources of news. For example, some years ago a poll in the Maryland suburbs of Washington, D.C., asked people: "Who are the leaders here in your community?" Responses to this question were compared with the results of a content analysis of the news sources cited in the Maryland news section of the *Washington Post*. Like most newspapers, the *Post* relies heavily upon "official" sources, especially those in government. But these political leaders and public officials were perceived as only a tiny part of the community leadership by the general public. Clergy, for example, who were cited in the poll as a significant segment of the community leadership, almost never are used as news sources. In this instance, the basis of the evaluation of coverage was a simple descriptive portrait of community leadership.

There are many ways to organize a scorecard for evaluating your news coverage. Several times a year the *Gallup Poll* asks a national sample of Americans: "What is the most important problem facing this country today?" Compare your news coverage to the issues cited in this poll. Or, better yet, conduct a local poll on this question: "Is your newspaper or television station providing relevant, timely news about the salient issues of the day?"

There are other, even simpler, sources on your desk right now that can be used to organize an evaluation of coverage. Did you ever read the Yellow Pages as a profile of your community? The number of listings, or simply the amount of space, for each category in the Yellow Pages identifies the relative importance of various occupations and activities in your city. And the number of listings in some categories changes radically over time. Other easily scanned sources that are available every day in your newspaper are letters to the editor and the classified ads.

All of this is feedback from the community that any journalist can tap, both to evaluate current coverage and to plan future coverage. These become valuable sources of information for journalists who develop a sensitivity to the world around them, for journalists who rely more upon their imagination and creativity than upon the rote application of time-worn techniques and perspectives.

Box 3-2
The Yellow Pages as a Source

If the success of check-cashing is any barometer, Austin banks may not be doing a good job with basic payment services.

One check-cashing store was listed in the Austin yellow pages a decade ago. Today there are 54, clearly the fastest growing segment of the financial system in Austin.

"I have the feeling from living in Texas and traveling around the country that a lot of people feel abandoned by banks and thrifts," said Bill Ferguson, president of Irving-based Ferguson and Co., a national financial data publishing and consulting company.

"Maybe not intentionally, but I think they are made to feel they are more of an imposition than they are of a value to a bank or thrift."

Further consolidation of banks and thrifts in urban areas such as Austin will fuel even more check-cashing outlets, Ferguson said. . . .

Excerpted from Earl Golz, "Checking Out," *Austin American-Statesman*, March 7, 1993. Reprinted by permission of *Austin American-Statesman*.

This book will teach you about techniques for honing and analyzing the information that you collect. However, the basic value of that information depends upon your sensitivity to the community your news organization serves.

Three Major Steps

The process of news reporting in journalism can be summed up in three major steps:
- Observing
- Interpreting
- Presenting

Out of all the events that could be observed on any particular day, journalists can select only a few for attention. The great utility of news values, the event orientation of journalism, and the substantive hypotheses of journalism and social science—especially when they are organized into a game plan—is that they reduce this first step, observing, to manageable proportions. Otherwise, each day journalists would find themselves facing the buzzing, blooming confusion of an unorganized world. These perspectives and specific hypotheses do more than guide our observations. They assist us in the interpretation of our observations, helping to convert raw facts into organized patterns of information. How odd it is, remarked Albert Einstein, that not everyone can see that every observation must be for or against some hypothesis. Finally, the information gained through observations must be presented to an audience. Preparing you for these steps is the purpose of this book.

References

Babbie, Earl. *Observing Ourselves: Essays in Social Research*. Belmont, CA: Wadsworth, 1986.
———. *The Practice of Social Research*, 6th ed. Belmont, CA: Wadsworth, 1992.
Barsamian, David. *Stenographers To Power: Media & Propaganda*. Monroe, ME: Common Courage Press, 1992.
Breslin, Jimmy. *He Got Hungry and Forgot His Manners*. New York: Ticknor & Fields, 1988.
———. *How the Good Guys Finally Won*. New York: Viking, 1975.

Cohn, Victor. *News & Numbers: A Guide To Reporting Statistical Claims and Controversies in Health and Related Fields*. Ames: Iowa State University Press, 1989.

Gandy, Oscar H. Jr. *Beyond Agenda Setting: Information Subsidies and Public Policy*. Norwood, NJ: Ablex, 1982.

Hempel, Carl G. *Fundamentals of Concept Formation in Empirical Science*. Chicago: University of Chicago Press, 1952.

Lippmann, Walter. *Public Opinion*. New York: Macmillan, 1922.

Mauro, John. *Statistical Deception At Work*. Hillsdale, NJ: Lawrence Erlbaum Associates, 1992.

Meyer, Philip. *The New Precision Journalism*. Bloomington: Indiana University Press, 1991.

Monmonier, Mark. *Mapping It Out: Expository Cartography for the Humanities and Social Sciences*. Chicago: University of Chicago Press, 1993.

———. *Maps with the News: The Development of American Journalistic Cartography*. Chicago: University of Chicago Press, 1989.

Monti, Lorna. *Social Indicators for Austin, Texas. A Cluster Analysis of Census Tracts*. Austin, TX: Bureau of Business Research, Graduate School of Business, University of Texas at Austin, 1975.

Mukherjee, Ramkrishna. *The Quality of Life: Valuation in Social Research*. Newbury Park, CA: Sage, 1989.

Nussbaum, Martha and Amartya Sen, eds. *The Quality of Life*. New York: Oxford University Press, 1993.

Paletz, David, Peggy Reichert and Barbara McIntyre. "How the Media Support Local Governmental Authority." *Public Opinion Quarterly* 35: 80–92. (1971)

Royko, Mike. *Dr. Kookie, You're Right*. New York: E.P. Dutton, 1989.

———. *Like I Was Sayin' . . . .* New York: E.P. Dutton, 1984.

Sigal, Leon. *Reporters and Officials: The Organization and Politics of Newsmaking*. Lexington, MA: D.C. Heath, 1973.

Sullivan, Michael J., III. *Measuring Global Values: The Ranking of 162 Countries*. Westport, CT: Greenwood, 1991.

Terkel, Studs. *The Great Divide. Second Thoughts on the American Dream*. New York: Pantheon, 1988.

———. *Race. How Blacks and Whites Think and Feel About the American Obsession*. New York: New Press, 1992.

Thompson, Hunter. *The Curse of Lono*. New York: Bantam, 1983.

———. *Generation of Swine*. New York: Summit Books, 1988.

———. *Hell' s Angels: A Strange and Terrible Saga*. New York: Random House, 1967.

PART II

BEATS, INTERVIEWS, AND SOURCES

Chapter Four

BEATS

Students may aspire to write for *Sports Illustrated* or to direct corporate communications for AT&T, but they must first learn about covering city hall, the courthouse and the police beat, among other areas of public affairs.

—George M. Killenberg
Public Affairs Reporting

News media develop strategies to cover communities that meet the expectations and needs of audiences. News media produce important information on a regular basis. One way they do this is by using regular news sources. The term "beat," probably originating from the regular routes walked by nineteenth-century London police, is used to describe a set of regular news sources. Many journalists become regular beat reporters.

A news editor can organize beats in any way he or she likes, but usually editors organize them either by location or by subject interest. For beats organized by location, such as a city beat, several sources can be covered conveniently. For beats organized by subject interest, such as the courts or law enforcement, a journalist can follow cases and develop working relationships with sources. This pattern has been used since the earliest days of the modern daily, and broadcast journalism generally follows the same pattern.

The assumption is that such information is both interesting and important. In the nineteenth century, for example, one of the first regular beats was established by the *New York Sun* to cover the city's courts. This provided a dependable supply of news each day. On most days the courts met from early morning to late in the evening. Reporters were able to highlight poignant or funny stories, often with quotes, as evidenced by the story (quoted by press historian Frank Luther Mott) that appeared during the first publication year of the *Sun* (see box 4-1).

Box 4-1
New York City Beat

William Luvoy got drunk because yesterday was so devilish warm. Drank 9 glasses of brandy and water and said he would be cursed if he wouldn't drink 9 more as quick as he could raise the money to buy it with. He would like to know what right the magistrate had to interfere with his private affairs. Fined $1—forgot his pocketbook, and was sent over to Bridewell.

Patrick Ludwick was sent up by his wife, who testified that she had supported him for several years in idleness and drunkenness. Abandoning all hopes of a reformation in her husband, she bought him a suit of clothes a fortnight since and told him to go about his business, for she would not live with him any longer. Last night he came home in a state of intoxication, broke into his wife's bedroom, pulled her out of bed, pulled her hair, and stamped on her. She called a watchman and sent him up. Pat exerted all his powers of eloquence in endeavoring to excite his wife's sympathy, but to no purpose. As every sensible woman ought to do who is cursed with a drunken husband, she refused to have anything to do with him hereafter— and he was sent to the penitentiary.

New York Sun, July 4, 1834

About the same period, James Gordon Bennett, founder and publisher of the *New York Herald*, systematically added beats, such as the young federal government in Washington, D.C., certain European capitals, and sports. Bennett himself covered financial developments on Wall Street, already becoming an economic power, and wrote a widely read column.

Over time, these beats remained, while others were added. News media today have beats organized around the environment, lifestyle, and public health. These beats sometimes displace and sometimes run side by side with such older beats as the mayor's office and city council, police and law enforcement agencies, courts, education, business, and many other types of beats.

Traditional Beat Organization

However organized, beats provide windows through which readers/viewers peep at communities. The ways beats are organized are very closely related to the ways in which readers, listeners, and viewers see their community. Audiences have few alternatives for learning about the world. What they know comes from newspapers, magazines, radio, television, books, films, and other people.

Newspapers make sure beats cover the key social institutions: local government, courts, law enforcement agencies, schools, hospitals and health agencies. Larger, more complex news media, such as the *New York Times,* add regular beats to cover entertainment, the arts, sciences, lifestyle features, labor-management relations, books, and many other areas of our public and private lives. For example, the *Times* has several beats devoted to various aspects of the arts, opera, and contemporary painting. A number of *Times* reporters work in the health field. If a news medium is smaller, it is likely that beats will be organized around city agencies and that other beats, such as the arts or science, will be covered only occasionally by regular reporters.

These arrangements reveal what the news media regard as important. For the most part beats are built around established power structures and social order. This makes sense in a democracy where citizens are relatively free to elect new officials or even change the structure of the government. Simply because reporters check with the mayor's office nearly every day, mayors are more often quoted than are those challenging the mayor's policies. Police are more often quoted than criminals.

One recent study found that ABC *Nightline*'s Ted Koppel, an expert journalist, overwhelmingly interviews those in, rather than those out of, power. Koppel defends this as quite logical. Those in power are in a position to shape policy, while those out of power are not yet in a position to do so. (Of course, without some press attention, it is hard to get into power.)

Beats also reinforce social values. The social values of a community are protected in their evolution, because the values are embedded in key institutions, and the press reinforces these values by concentrating most closely on these institutions. For example, education almost always is a busy beat. Battles over funding levels, education styles, and social values are fought continually in this arena.

Departing from Tradition

Reporters should be sensitive to new ways of seeing communities, new patterns. The media should constantly be seeking sources who provide different perspectives as well as be aware of issues that are important to community members. Different perspectives provide new ways to see old problems. Just as television networks provide time to the political party that does not occupy the White House to present alternative views of national problems after a presidential address, news media could allow many kinds of people to present differing views about social issues. For example, labor union members, people with AIDS, homeless people, and unemployed people, among others, would provide a variety of perspectives on community issues.

News media can experiment with completely new ways of organizing beats. What if a news medium established a beat around the issue of AIDS? One can imagine that reporters would write stories about victims, medical research, drugs, social costs to employers and public agencies, as well as ethics and equity (Is AIDS research drawing funds and attention away from, for example, the study of breast cancer?). In 1993, *Time* magazine devoted a story to the major influence AIDS has had on the American arts community.

One could organize a beat around the issue of poverty. Reporters no doubt would write stories about housing, jobs, education, health, opportunity, family relations, and children. Several years ago a newspaper in San Antonio, Texas, selected the topic of children for a special emphasis over a one-year period. According to *Presstime* magazine, the newspaper asked reporters on all beats to be alert to relevant stories and made the topic the subject of an ongoing editorial campaign.

In 1996, the *Daily Tar Heel*, at the University of North Carolina, Chapel Hill, ran a series of articles that exposed an interesting issue to readers within the UNC community. The articles take an in-depth look at "salary compression," which occurs when professors and others are hired at salaries higher than salaries of those who were employed in earlier years to do the same job. The stories, written by journalism students who used a database to compare full-professor salaries, also contain graphics. (See box 4-2 for an except from one of the articles in the series.)

Box 4-2
Salary Compression

Some fans were outraged at Charlotte Hornets owners for letting Alonzo Mourning go to the Miami Heat after a salary disagreement last year, and the Hornets performance soon showed what happens when a star leaves.

Less publicized is the free-agent system that has penetrated academic life, as young or established scholars demand big money to come to the University, surpassing in salary those who faithfully toil in the ranks.

A study by UNC journalism students found evidence of serious salary compression among full professors, with recently hired professors making higher salaries than veterans. The study showed that professors hired around 1960 now earn an average salary of $71,385, while those hired since 1993 earn an average of $83,055.

Salary compression occurs when new workers are hired at salaries higher than those already employed who have comparative merit and assignments. It is a reversal of a salary structure where those who hold a higher rank earn the most. . . .

NEW PROFESSORS MAKE MORE

University professors hired around 1990 make more money than professors hired in any other year. Because new professors can attract more money, UNC has difficulty bringing other salaries up to the same level of these "super-hires."

AVERAGE SALARY BY YEAR OF APPOINTMENT

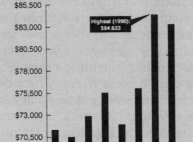

Excerpted from Gretchen Parker, "New Hires Attracted by Bucks," The *Daily Tar Heel*, June 20, 1996, p. 5.

We do not suggest these are the most important beats, although they could be of significant interest to readers. We suggest reporters and editors need to be open to new ways of seeing old information. The older ways of organizing information clearly are not meeting audience needs the way they once did. In terms of market penetration, newspapers have been in decline since the 1920s, when about 1.5 newspapers circulated per household, compared to the 1990s, when the number dropped to about 0.5 per household. Network television has experienced the same decline in market penetration since the early 1980s, national radio since the 1950s, and even mass magazines such as the old *Life* and *Look* since the 1970s.

Most producers in a declining market adjust the product to the changing needs of the audience, or they change the product altogether. Experimenting with the ways that beats—not occasional stories, but day-to-day beats—are organized is one way in which the news media might better fit the product to the changing audience.

A Strategy for Covering Beats

Journalists should plan a strategy to cover a beat in the same way that a news medium designs beats to fit the informational needs of an entire community. In order to implement the strategy, journalists, like other professionals, may have to learn the specialized language of a particular beat or of many beats. They do this by picking up the jargon while on the job, from study, and from advice. Courts, taxes, budgets, and many other community activities are complicated to understand and to explain. If you understand specialized language you can understand the specialized perspectives of your sources.

One of the first phases of implementing a strategy can be centered around money. Where does it come from? Where does it go? These two simple questions apply to every public agency and every private home. Sometimes it is easy to get answers, and sometimes it is difficult. Private agencies, such as the Boy Scouts or United Fund, do not have the same obligation to share budget information as do tax-supported agencies.

Recently, journalists have shown more interest in the amount of money that public service organizations allocate to administrative costs versus actual program activities. Many view this as one perspective on whether agencies are committed to make programs work

The mayor of Chicago is interviewed by a political journalist on a Sunday morning news program. Courtesy NBC, Chicago.

for the public or are used as a sort of front for gaining personal wealth or perks. In 1993, many were shocked when a journalist was able to determine that the head of the United Fund drew what many considered an exorbitant salary and flew regularly on the Concorde—all while raising substantial funds for the agency. Amid the publicity surrounding this story, the agency head resigned and was later convicted for misuse of funds.

The budgets for cities and counties are public information. Usually they are published both before and after final adoption. One can determine how much of any budget comes from property taxes, local sales taxes, fees, and reimbursement from the state or federal government. You can determine how the money is spent. Figure 4.1 shows where the money came from and where it was allocated in Chapel Hill, a small city in the middle of North Carolina.

Budgets can be very revealing and can reflect the soul of an organization or the community. One can think of budgets as a formalized set of priorities. As with the federal budget, much is fixed, yet there are choices on how money can be allocated. Reporters can deepen any look at budgets and organizations by asking what values are represented. For example, if a community allocates substantial amounts of

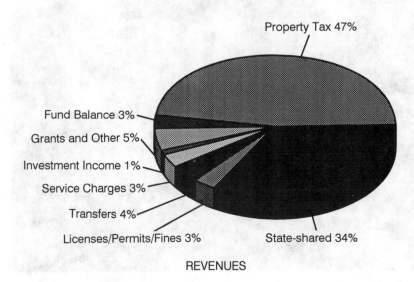

GENERAL FUND SUMMARY 1995–96

Property Tax 47%

Fund Balance 3%

Grants and Other 5%

Investment Income 1%

Service Charges 3%

Transfers 4%

Licenses/Permits/Fines 3%

State-shared 34%

REVENUES

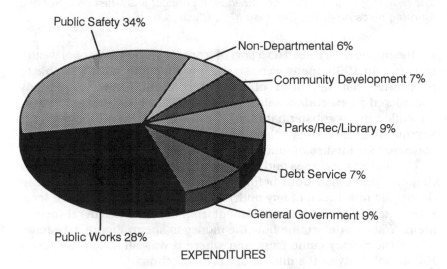

Public Safety 34%

Non-Departmental 6%

Community Development 7%

Parks/Rec/Library 9%

Debt Service 7%

General Government 9%

Public Works 28%

EXPENDITURES

Total General Fund: $24,875,890

Figure 4.1
The pie charts represent total income and outflow in the $25 million general fund approved by the Chapel Hill (NC) Town Council for the 1995–96 fiscal year. The chart appeared in the town's annual budget report.

money for police, this is a statement of the perception of needs by those in power. This may not be evident in the budget of a single year. You can look at trends over time by looking at the budgets for the immediate past years. You can compare your community with communities of similar size. One newspaper found that expenditures for police were associated with the numbers of minority citizens in the community, even though communities with more minority people did not have higher levels of crime. The budget reflected white fears. The same kind of examination of values exists within the budgets of every organization.

In addition to examining budgets, journalists can look for patterns in many other ways on beats, such as by looking at the type of people employed. Is there a demographic match between the numbers and types of people working in a particular agency and the community at large? For many reasons, no organization would match perfectly. Yet the complete absence of minorities or women or those with handicaps suggests patterns of employment that do not fit the ideals of our democracy.

Society as a System

Journalists should be aware that communities function as a connected system. A change in one part of the system eventually affects another part, or even the whole. For example, if a community decides to spend more money on education, then there is less for police protection—unless the community is willing to increase taxes or can obtain funds from other sources, such as state grants.

Communities function as families. If a family with two parents and three children has one child in college, the entire family may have to adjust its lifestyle to help support that child in college. It is unlikely that family income will increase radically, even if the child in college wins a scholarship or works part time. A family dealing with a family member who is an alcoholic might change its allocation of money and attention to accommodate the alcoholic's treatment.

If an individual decides to spend his or her money on popcorn rather than lettuce, that is a choice that, if done too much, could affect the health of the individual. Individuals, communities, and nations function as parts of systems. Journalists should explore the implications beyond a single event, budget, or social action.

Some news media have designed beats that fit the systematic nature of communities. Environmental beats, for example, examine relationships between the agricultural use of fertilizers and (1) crop production, (2) farms' operational costs, and (3) rainfall causing fertilizer run-off into streams and lakes. There are many other effects, but reporters look for how one thing influences another. One can examine the process of tree cutting to see how it (1) affects local economies, (2) influences U.S. international trade relationships, (3) endangers local wildlife, and (4) relates to the preservation of natural resources for future generations.

If you think about effects, all stories qualify for a consideration of patterns. If the president of a local company dies, then one might want to know if there will be a smooth transition of leadership, if the company will change directions, if there will be any increase or decrease in local employment, or if the company will decide to use the "opportunity" to locate to another community.

Reporters use systematic thinking on any beat. The police beat is a traditional beat with daily stories of car accidents and arrests on various charges. One might ask if there is a relationship between high crime and lower business volume. There might be a relationship between crime and the average amount of rents. If the community has many auto thefts, there may be many businesses that specialize in replacement of auto window glass (as there are in New York City). The very nature of the crimes might dictate the need for certain types of businesses. With a little thinking, you can discover many other relationships on the police beat, or on any other type of beat.

Leaders as News Sources

Reporters need to be sensitive to the changes that prominent news sources undergo while they remain in power. News sources go through at least four distinct stages, and as they do so, it becomes more challenging for reporters to find and present alternative points of view. The following section outlines these four stages of the decline of leadership.

Stage 1: I am indispensable. A leader, after a period in office, gains confidence and assurance with each successful passing day and, finally, concludes: I can do this job; in fact, *I am indispensable. No one else can do this job like I can.*

Reporters find that these news sources make available all required documents but generally are offended or hurt if stories include quotes that are not completely supportive of the news sources, who believe they are indispensable. Stage 1 does not happen to all news sources, but it does happen to many of them, usually after about three to four years on the job. Then they often evolve to Stage 2.

Stage 2: I have THE Plan. As leaders become completely confident of their jobs, news sources naturally develop plans for their organizations and, in time, decide: My plan is an excellent plan for the organization. *In fact my plan is THE Plan for the organization.*

At this point, news sources may actually be harming the organizations that initially benefited from the evolution of a self-confident leader. Stage 2 leaders seem to quit listening to advice from within the organization because such leaders believe they are indispensable, and they now have *THE Plan.*

Reporters find resistance to providing any but the most flattering quotes in support of the organization in the way that the leader sees the future of the organization. Such leaders may evolve to Stage 3.

Stage 3: Dissent is subversion. Leaders, especially strong leaders, often become impatient with slow changes in the organization and become completely focused on their plan—which is, after all, *THE Plan.* When this happens, these leaders are seldom—if ever— aware of their own evolution because, in their own minds, they are indispensable and they have developed THE Plan for the organization. They conclude: *Dissent to my plan is, in reality, subversion of the organization.*

At this point, the organization, whether a public department or private company, is in trouble, although it may not be evident to outsiders. Morale is harmed because these Stage 3 leaders are actively hostile to points of view other than their own, which from their perspectives are subversion.

Reporters often will find some Stage 3 news sources all too ready to reveal inside information, if they can get away with it, as one way to try to shape the organization or at least get back at it. However, reporters need to be careful. The major news leaders may have a change of heart, decide they do not like the stories, and blame the reporter, making it difficult to obtain even regular documents by, for example, making them available only at awkward times.

Stage 3 leaders often see themselves as imperiled by an unappreciative world that refuses to recognize that they are indispensable and have developed *THE Plan* for the organization, which could be smoothly executed if organizational traitors could be silenced and the world not alerted by unwanted and intrusive journalists. Objective observers might see such leaders as dictatorial or even sick, although the news sources seldom see themselves as anything other than bold, indispensable, brilliant, and creative leaders, which they were, long ago, before they evolved into Stage 3 leaders.

Stage 3 news leaders are the most challenging for reporters. One thinks, for example, of longtime FBI leader J. Edgar Hoover, who attempted to prevent circulation of any but favorable views of the Federal Bureau of Investigation while he fixed his own vision of the agency into its historical fabric. Hoover collected files on various presidential leaders, thereby assuring that he would be reappointed director for life. He held the office for 48 years through eight presidencies. Hoover did not allow homosexuals to become FBI agents, although Hoover may have been homosexual himself and, according to a recent PBS program, was even viewed in the 1930s holding hands with a special friend at New York night spots. The special friend held a high office in the FBI.

There are many Hoovers—news sources who control their organizations with the idea that they are indispensable and have THE Plan for their organizations, and that those who disagree are, in a sense, simply traitors (to the leader). That includes reporters who in any way publish material not considered favorable to the news leader's vision of the agency. Sometimes these news sources evolve to Stage 4, which can, finally, get them into trouble.

Stage 4: I am above the law. Some news leaders, finally, trespass the law in directing their own organizations. These leaders, without realizing it, convince themselves that they (1) are indispensable, (2) have THE Plan for their organizations, and (3) have confronted subversion (i.e., other views), so they conclude that (4) *I am above the law*.

These news leaders head organizations that are in trouble. The trouble might be as simple as maintaining loose travel records because the agency's work is too important for staff to be bothered with such paperwork. The trouble might be that procedures are inefficient and costly but cannot be changed because no one challenges the news leader. Hiring procedures might become illegally racist or sexist because of blind spots in the perspective of the leader, but no one confronts the leader.

Journalists should assess agencies and leaders on a regular basis. You could even create a private "score" to measure leaders. For example, news leaders who conclude they are indispensable (Stage 1) would be given a score of 1. Organizations and agencies with such leaders are often skillfully led. That is true even when—or if—the leader decides his or her plan is the only plan for the organization (Stage 2), and reporters could score these leaders as a 2. A score of 3 would be given to leaders who discourage, shun, or crush dissent (Stage 3), and a score of 4 to those leaders who are actually brushing against illegal procedures and acts (Stage 4). (This scoring system is for private guidance only.)

Most reporters can "score" the leaders of the organizations they cover. If a news source has led an organization for a long time, he or she is most likely to earn a score on our mythical scale of between 2 and 3.

Yet for leaders who have been in the same job for more than eight to ten years, reporters should be careful to see if leaders have, in their self-assurance of power and impatience to put their own stamp on the organization, evolved to a score of 3 or even 4. It is rare for leaders who hold the same job for more than ten years to be flexible, responsive, democratic leaders of their organizations. Stage 4 news sources are challenging for reporters because they seldom, if ever, realize their own perspective is not the same as the perspective of the world at large. They will view your efforts the same as they view those of any other "traitor."

There are few Stage 3 or Stage 4 news leaders who react like the British colonel in the film *The Bridge on the River Kwai*: When the colonel finally realizes his efforts to maintain firm British morale among his fellow World War II prisoners has, in actuality, helped the Japanese build a fine resupply bridge, the colonel (played by Alec Guinness) in a final scene says something like "What have I done?" as he staggers over to fall on the dynamite detonator, blowing up his precious bridge. Journalists will find few news sources with the colonel's kind of insight, and fewer still who would admit it, or even participate in correcting the damage they have inflicted. Nearly always such news leaders, if finally forced from office by retirement or other means, blame others for failures, as Adolf Hitler blamed the Germans for Germany's defeat in World War II. Stage 4 news leaders, after all, are indispensable and, in their own minds, after them necessarily comes the deluge.

Tapping Other Information Sources

Government agencies are computerizing records and, after an interval of time, destroying the paper records. In some cases, agencies allow private, profit-making companies to computerize the records, which means that citizens and reporters have to pay a fee to access records. This can force taxpayers to pay three times for public records. First, citizens pay for the records to be gathered. Second, they pay for them to be put into databases. Third, citizens pay when information is requested from a private vendor. This is an excellent deal for the private companies. Many reporters are disturbed by this trend.

As a reporter you need good strategies to obtain beat information. Learn the roles, names, and positions of those on the beats, from agency head to secretaries. Be sensitive to organizational politics. Find the routine records and assume that records provide the basic facts while people provide the quotes to support (or refute) the facts.

You should base stories on facts with a few quotes, rather than upon quotes with a sprinkling of facts. If beat stories are based solely on quotes, they probably are not worth publication, unless you are interviewing a rape victim or the president or someone whose quotes are important or unusual. Beat reporters too often put together stories based on quotes gained from a quick telephone call. Such stories waste space as well as audience time. If a beat story is based mostly on quotes, you have not done enough research.

Most beats require that you attend meetings. Organizations present a happy face to the world, so they sometimes resist allowing reporters to attend meetings. Most states have open-meetings laws that require that the public be notified of meetings and allowed to attend. The press is both part of the public and a representative of the public.

There are some meetings from which reporters can be legally excluded. In North Carolina, for example, meetings to discuss personnel matters (such as hiring and firing) are judged too sensitive for public scrutiny. On the grounds that public disclosure would cause the price to escalate, reporters also can be legally excluded from meetings that discuss the acquisition of property. Other specific exemptions for closed meetings include: matters involving criminal accusations against or formal censure of any person; law-enforcement investigations; bank regulation; or civil lawsuits or subpoenas.

If you are excluded from a meeting, you should protest and ask that your attendance be reconsidered. Some news media organizations have developed wallet-size cards that contain information you can use to ask the chairperson to keep the meeting open, at least until you can call your organization's attorney. Some cards provide carefully crafted legal statements that you can read verbatim. Check with your own state press association.

Using Some Common Sense

Like automobiles, reporters come in a variety of colors and models, some newer, some older. No single personality ensures success on a beat. There are helpful guidelines, however.

1. You should keep regular contact with your beat sources. If you cannot get around every day, you can use the telephone to keep in touch.

2. Realize that the power of organizations is often diffuse. You may find that secretaries are important preliminary sources for major stories. Assume everyone is important—everyone is.

3. Develop a sense of the organizational culture and the "score" of the organization's leader. Some leaders are more open than others. Be constantly prepared to use the Freedom of Information Act or the open-meetings law of your state.

4. Devise strategies that enable you to present a mix of current, ongoing news as well as longer trend stories. Knowledge of databases will enable you to reach beyond the trends evident in the annual reports. Reporters should fit strategies to the beats rather than simply be reactive to the news occurring on the beat. These strategies may require that you be reasonably aggressive. No one likes to go out of his or her way in organizations; therefore you have to push to acquire new sources or even to make old sources respond in new ways. Most organizations get used to doing things in a certain way and, thereafter, that becomes "right," despite changes in record-keeping technology or even changes in the company's mission.

5. Look for ways to combine information from your beat with information from other beats for creative new mixes of stories. Push the news editor to develop creative teams of reporters across beats to pursue important community stories that stretch across more than a single beat, as most important stories do.

6. Develop themes within your beat and pursue them for considerable periods when you can. Communication research

shows that the press has some power to set the agenda of topics that people discuss and consider, and you have that power within your beat if the topic is mentioned consistently. Three front-page major stories during a year are not as important as twelve smaller stories, one each month, according to agenda-setting research. In terms of news emphasis, the tortoise of consistent reporting usually outruns the hare of occasional but major-emphasis reporting.

7. Be professional. Doctors and lawyers represent individual clients but also have an interest in a community's public health and legal systems. Journalists have an interest in community systems and, through these systems, the individual citizen. Sometimes journalists champion individual citizens or groups of citizens, such as the homeless or those with AIDS.

Journalists aren't required to pass a tough examination as are lawyers, doctors, or accountants, and journalists are not traditionally considered professionals. Anyone can be a journalist if he or she can observe well, is fair, and writes well. But a good journalist is something beyond an observer and writer. To excel in the profession, a journalist must be a strategist who plans for the most effective ways to gather, organize, analyze, and present information. Journalists have to be thinkers and thoughtful planners to find patterns woven into the daily news of their beats.

References

Killenberg, George M. *Public Affairs Reporting: Covering the News in the Information Age*, p. vii. New York: St. Martin's Press, 1992.

Mott, Frank Luther. *American Journalism, A History: 1690–1960*, p. 223. New York: Macmillan Co., 1962.

Cisneros, Henry G. "A Cry for Leadership from the Urban Apocalypse." *Presstime* 14 (June 1992): 42–43.

Shaw, Donald L. "The Rise and Fall of American Mass Media: Roles of Technology and Leadership," Roy W. Howard Lecture presented April 4, 1991, at Indiana University, Bloomington.

Chapter Five

PERSONAL INTERVIEWS

Reporter from the *Daily Thunderstorm*: I've come to interview
you. . . .

Mark Twain: What do you do it with?

Reporter: . . . It ought to be done with a club in some cases; but
customarily it consists in the interviewer asking questions and
the interviewee answering them. It is all the rage now.

Q. How old are you?

A. Nineteen, in June.

Q. Indeed. I would have taken you to be thirty-five or six. Where
were you born?

A. In Missouri.

Q. When did you begin to write?

A. In 1836.

Q. Why, how could that be, if you are only nineteen now?

A. I don't know. It does seem curious, somehow.

Q. It does, indeed. Whom do you consider the most remarkable
man you ever met?

A. Aaron Burr.

Q. But you never could have met Aaron Burr, if you are only nineteen years—

A. Now, if you know more about me than I do, what do you ask me
for?

—Mark Twain, "An Encounter with an Interviewer"

Fortunately, most interview subjects are not that hard to tackle.
Unfortunately, however, few interview subjects are able to infuse a

question-and-answer session with much wit either, yet the interview remains a key technique in the reporter's repertoire. The message of this chapter can be simply stated:

•Know when an interview is appropriate.

•Know how to do one correctly.

The first advice regarding an interview is to know when it is not the right thing to do. Interviews, for instance, are not the best way to gather purely factual information, but interviews are an excellent technique for getting opinions. For facts, you're better off looking at the written record. People often forget, misrepresent, or incorrectly recall names, dates, or figures. Do not use an interview to obtain factual information that you can get more quickly and reliably somewhere else.

A second important warning about the interview situation is to remember that you and your subject do not share the same goals. Journalist Thomas Morgan said: "I want the truth; they want to be beautiful." Even a source who attempts to be honest or candid is likely to be at least subconsciously measuring his or her words, knowing they will be in print or on the air. A source has a point of view that will color the content and tone of the information you get from the interview. In fact, that point of view usually is one of the things that you are seeking in the interview.

With this preface about the disadvantages of interviews, here are some guidelines for making an interview as useful, complete, and valid as possible.

Getting the Interview

Beginning journalists often are afraid to approach people for an interview, especially prominent people in "high" positions. Yet the simple, direct approach is often the best way. The Washington bureau chief of the *New York Times* once got an exclusive interview with Harry S. Truman that made the rest of the press corps apoplectic. How did he score his beat? He asked the president for the interview at a dinner party! Harrison Salisbury, also of the *Times*, recalled that author George Bernard Shaw didn't give many interviews. Nonetheless, "One of our reporters just went down to that little house he had in Hertfordshire and walked in on him one day and got a hell of a good story."

Moral: If you don't ask, you'll never get an interview. Ask.

Box 5-1
The Ten Stages of a Typical Interview

1. Defining the purpose of the interview
2. Conducting background research
3. Requesting an interview appointment
4. Planning the interview
5. Meeting your respondent, breaking the ice
6. Asking your first questions
7. Establishing an easy rapport
8. Asking the bomb (potentially sensitive questions, if any)
9. Recovering from the bomb, if necessary
10. Ending the interview

Ken Metzler, *Creative Interviewing: The Writer's Guide to Gathering Information by Asking Questions*, 2nd edition, p. 19.

Generally—almost invariably with prominent people—you need to make arrangements in advance. The late Isaac Marcosson, a prominent journalist in the early twentieth century, interviewed Presidents Woodrow Wilson and Theodore Roosevelt, British Prime Minister David Lloyd George, Russian revolutionary Alexander Kerensky, actress Ethel Barrymore, writer Mark Twain, and tycoon J. Pierpont Morgan. Marcosson offered this advice:

> Interviewing outstanding personalities is in the last analysis merely a piece of glorified salesmanship. . . . Just as the salesman must eventually convince his prospect that he needs and is able to buy the product under discussion, so must the interviewer persuade any world figure that an interpretation of personality or a wide publication of his utterances is vital or opportune to the moment and the cause in which he is enlisted.

The job of salesmanship can be difficult when would-be sources have reason to believe you are investigating something unpleasant about them. But even then you can make the pitch that any story will be more fair and accurate if it has their point of view in it.

Occasionally, catching people unexpectedly will work as it did with George Bernard Shaw. Working on their Watergate stories about the Nixon Administration, *Washington Post* reporters Bob Woodward and Carl Bernstein would knock on people's doors at home in the evening with no advance warning. "Nine times out of ten, people wouldn't let us in the door," said Bernstein.

> But sometimes it worked. The theory was that there were a lot of people who worked in places where the last thing in the world they would want was a visit from somebody named Woodward or Bernstein. And if you call them on the phone they're gonna say no. . . . But instead you show up at their homes. . . .

When you catch people off guard before they have a chance to erect their defenses and hedge their answers, you may obtain honest, straightforward replies. This practice is more defensible when dealing with public figures who are accustomed to reporters' queries than it is when interviewing private persons thrust into the limelight by an event. Nonpublic figures should be asked to give their informed consent before the interviewer begins his or her questions.

The Interviewing Process

After you have achieved success in getting your interview, you will be on course to get the information you need. However, before you actually ask the opening question, considerable advance thought and planning are necessary.

Be Prepared

If an unprepared subject is the dream of any interviewer, the unprepared interviewer is the bane of the subject's existence. On occasion, however, a reporter will be thrown into an interview situation with no time to prepare. A city editor might say, "Dr. Ernest Grinchfink, the famed world expert on geonuclear sociographics, is in the conference room for his interview, and the science writer just called in sick with the flu. Go interview him." The best you can do in a situation like this is to wing it. Honesty is often the best policy up front, coupled with a devout effort to listen intelligently and understand what the subject has to say. Listening carefully is always the key to a good interview.

Usually, you'll have time to prepare yourself properly. Learn as much about the person and situation as time permits. Don't ask a United States senator questions regarding length of time in politics, party affiliation, or the name(s) of the committee(s) he or she sits on.

You waste interview time gathering information you can more easily obtain elsewhere, and you let the subject know that you haven't done your homework. Use your newspaper's library or the public library. A source who feels you are unprepared or not knowledgeable may feel free to give only vague, ambiguous, or half-true answers. If you are unaware of the subject's background, you won't be able to detect inconsistencies, and you may miss some real news.

Put yourself in your audience's position. Ask yourself what readers or viewers would ask this person if they could. Having enough questions on varied topics prepared in advance can help move even the most floundering interview along.

Tips for Interviewing

1. *Type or write out your questions in advance to make sure you cover all the topics you want to cover*. However, do not be rigid. If an interview heads down a promising path not covered by your questions, don't rein in the subject and force him or her back to a question on your list. Often the unanticipated angles produce the most newsworthy results.

2. *Consider the appropriate time to ask specific questions*. Specific questions produce more usable materials for journalists than do abstract or hypothetical inquiries. Although a general question can provoke a useless answer filled with platitudes, some journalists, such as free-lancer Edward Linn, do like to start with some broad questions. If you ask *only* questions that are specific and narrow, you risk putting your subject in a straitjacket of your making. Toss in a few broad "softballs," too, and you may obtain some serendipitous responses.

   In *The Craft of Interviewing*, John J. Brady offers some good advice: "Generally, if your subject is at home with words and ideas, lead him out with an open, general question. If he is ill at ease, make him comfortable with a question about the concrete, the easily explained."

3. *Avoid "leading" questions that are so pointed they steer the subject into a predetermined answer*. This is just as true for journalists as it is for lawyers in court.

4. *Ask just one question at a time*. Avoid "double-barreled" queries, such as, "Do you like your car, and is it economical?" They generally produce only single-barreled answers

and much confusion as well. Too frequently it is unclear which question is being answered.

5. *Don't make speeches.* Avoid overlong questions. The following excerpt from a presidential news conference illustrates both points 4 and 5:

> Mr. President, I have a two-prong question on the NATO nuclear force. First, can you tell us how goes the Merchant Mission? [Livingston Merchant was envoy to NATO.] Secondly, in view of the lack of enthusiasm, if we can believe the press, reflects a certain amount of public opinion in Europe as to the Polaris armed surface force because of its alleged greater vulnerability as compared to the atomic submarine. Why haven't the proposals for a conventionally powered submarine force been put forth, a proposal which would not apparently annoy Congress as much as an atomic submarine and would cost about half as much as the atomic submarine?

6. *Use a clean-up question to sweep up the loose ends when you finish.* "Is there anything about this subject that is important that I haven't asked you about?" If you have established rapport with your interviewee, you may be pleasantly surprised.

Establishing Rapport

You are not going to get much out of an interview if you don't establish some level of rapport at the outset. There is no foolproof system for doing this. Each reporter develops his or her own style over time. Shirley Biagi, in *Interviews That Work*, for example, offers this advice:

> At the beginning of an interview, a person wants to hear your voice and get a chance to decide whether you're likable and trustworthy. Be prepared for a few minutes of casual introductory conversation.

But she also adds the admonition of a *New Orleans Times-Picayune* journalist:

> One central lesson that all interviewers should learn is to "shut up," according to Kristin Gilger. "Reporters talk too much." . . . Let the interviewee talk.

Harrison Salisbury of the *New York Times* came to similar conclusions about establishing rapport:

> In the early days it was much tighter and I had a series of very sharply
> defined questions and I was in a great hurry to put them across, bing,
> bing, bing. As the years went on I've taken a much more relaxed tech-
> nique which I think is more effective, of letting the interview develop its
> own pace and establishing a sort of a mood of interchange before
> bringing in the sharper questions.

The conversational, soft opening, however, can fall flat too—especially
if you try to break the ice by emulating the jargon or presumed speech
style of the person you are interviewing. George Killenberg and Rob
Anderson report the misstep of an experienced and well-known
television interviewer:

> Phil Donahue committed a gaffe when he referred to a biker's wife as
> "your old lady." The biker sternly corrected Donahue. "She's not my
> 'old lady'; she's my wife." Presumptuousness in your greeting or man-
> ners may offend.

In the final analysis, although everyone agrees about the worth of
achieving rapport, the absence of it does not necessarily doom an
interview. Author Alex Haley once made an appointment to interview
American Nazi boss George Lincoln Rockwell for *Playboy*. When they
talked on the phone, Rockwell asked him, "Are you a Jew?" Haley
said no, but did not volunteer the fact that he was black. The interview was set up, Haley arrived, and there was a good deal of embarrassment all around.

"He [Rockwell] said: 'I see you're black, and I'm going to be very
honest with you right now, that we call your kind "niggers" and we
think you should all be shipped back to Africa,'" Haley remembered.
"And I said: 'Well, sir, I've been called "nigger" before. But this time
I'm being paid very well for it, so now you go right ahead. . . .'" In time,
Haley said, "he and I became quite garrulous together," and later carried on a correspondence. Professional survey organizations and the
news media commonly try to minimize the chance of this sort of thing
happening by making at least a rudimentary match between interviewer and subject.

Some journalists suggest establishing rapport before pulling out
your notebook or tape recorder. Others say that drawing your note-
taking weapon after you have begun chatting can change the mood in
mid-interview, make the subject wary, and destroy any rapport that
you have established.

Eventually, you must move away from the initial pleasantries. With
a talkative source in the mood for just passing the time of day, this
can be tough. A reporter once got an appointment to talk to the gov-

ernor of Hawaii about a specific topic for a specific story. It was the end of the day. The governor was relaxed and talkative. Try as he might, the reporter was unable to direct the governor's attention to what the reporter needed. Ultimately, after 90 minutes of very pleasant but not very journalistically productive discussion, the governor's secretary came in and reminded the governor of a dinner engagement. Under that pressure of time, the governor switched gears, cut out the small talk, and gave the reporter all he needed—and more—in about 10 minutes.

There are no panaceas for such situations. Few reporters are very good at walking out on rambling governors, especially if the reporter hopes to get an appointment for an interview again. For a regular "beat" reporter, such sessions can foster lasting rapport that goes long beyond that one situation. Cheerfully bantering your way through a chat like that can help the source see you as another human being and not just as a journalist. It can pay dividends in the long run.

Interviewer Role Playing

At times you can continue a friendly rapport throughout an interview. At other times, as in clearly confrontational situations, you may need to change posture and mood. You can choose among roles ranging from "ignorance" through "knowledgeability" to an "I-know-more-than-you-think-I-do" bluster.

Feigning ignorance sometimes elicits useable quotes. You can get explanatory matter in quotable, attributable form, so you won't have to say something in a story on your own. You get your source to say it. Sometimes, you don't need to feign ignorance because you really *are* ignorant about the topic. Usually, the source does know more about the topic than you do, or you wouldn't be doing the interview. If you don't understand something, stop and clear it up. Which would you rather do—expose your ignorance to a source, or try to explain to your city editor or news director that you don't understand the story you just turned in?

Most interviews go more smoothly when the interviewer has some knowledge of the subject at hand. Pulitzer Prize winner Clark Mollenhoff provides some good advice:

> It may occasionally be wise strategy to play ignorant. But it is never an advantage to be ignorant about the facts, the specific terminology, or the relevant law when interviewing a subject.

If you seem a little knowledgeable, the source may be more at ease. Legendary journalist A. J. Liebling once interviewed jockey Eddie Arcaro. "The first question I asked was, 'how many holes longer do you keep your left stirrup than your right?'" Liebling later commented: "That started him talking easily and after an hour, during which I had put in about 12 words, he said, 'I can see that you've been around riders a lot.'" Liebling had not been.

At the far end of the spectrum is the use of a bluff—encouraging the subject to believe that you know everything anyway so it is best to come clean. In such situations, the source may open up, confirming things that you only suspected, or may not even have guessed at, but about which you didn't know enough to write a solid story.

A *Wall Street Journal* reporter used a bluff to get a source to admit that he had invested in a particular project. Although the reporter's research indicated that the man invested $77,000, the reporter wasn't sure this was true. What the reporter asked was, "How did you happen to invest $77,000 in the XYZ project?" The man assumed the reporter knew about it, so he explained. If the reporter had asked, "Did you invest?" the man could have denied all. Even if the $77,000 figure was wrong, the source might have answered, "It wasn't $77,000, it was. . . ."

One time, Honolulu's symphony orchestra was preparing to announce the selection of a new conductor from among three candidates. *Honolulu Advertiser* reporters went from source to source in the symphony hierarchy saying, "Why was 'A' considered the best choice?" As it turned out, "A" wasn't, but the paper was able to pin down which of the three men was chosen.

Note Taking

Eventually, the interviewee's comments must be turned into a story. That means you must keep track of what was said—by taking notes, taping the interview, having a good memory, or some combination of these. Different interviewers have different styles.

Most reporters take at least some notes during an interview, even when they are simultaneously taping it. The notes can refresh your memory for key points when you listen to the tape. Some form of shorthand or speedwriting is important if you hope to have fairly complete notes. Many reporters have benefitted from a course in Gregg shorthand, although you must use it fairly frequently or you will get rusty. Speed in taking notes is necessary if you are to avoid those awkward moments in an interview when the subject has finished talking but sits in silence, waiting for you to finish writing.

Note taking reassures some subjects that you are interested in what they have to say and are making an effort to get it down accurately, but it makes other subjects nervous because it continually reminds them that their words may wind up in print, and that inhibits them. You need to know when to start taking notes. Flipping out your notebook right at the start of an interview scares some subjects. One excuse for bringing it out is to offer a bit of admiration for some observation that your subject has just made—"Say, that's good. I want to be sure I get that down just right."

Some interviewees will watch your note taking for indications of what you think is important. When you're not taking notes, it signals them that they're into some bland or irrelevant area. Some subjects get offended when you stop writing. Others use this as a clue to change course.

Taking notes can have the unintended side effect of turning off the spigot just when the flow is beginning. A subject who is trying not to say anything striking or newsworthy will become alarmed if you begin to rapidly take notes. To avoid making a subject nervous or irritable, some reporters have perfected the technique of asking an innocuous follow-up question after their source has just let fly with some blockbuster quote. They scribble notes on the blockbuster while the source is answering the unnoteworthy follow-up question. It is important not to overreact when you do get a blockbuster. You should just quietly continue asking questions and taking notes, or perhaps change the subject to something insignificant. Otherwise, your subject may have second thoughts and will beg you not to repeat what he has said, leaving you with a tough decision or an angry interviewee.

There is evidence that excessive note taking diverts the interviewer's attention from the thread of the conversation. In an effort to write down each word precisely, you may pay too little attention to the broad sweep of things. In taking notes, as in asking questions, be prepared to change course and follow a promising lead when it arises. If you are in the middle of transcribing one quote and a better one comes along, abandon the first one.

Sometimes you want to take notes but can't. Gail Sheehy describes one such incident in *Hustling*, her book about New York City prostitution:

> We arrived at David's [a pimp's] penthouse in full dress but without a scrap of paper or pencil between us. Every fifteen minutes I had to excuse myself and dash for the bathroom to make notes with an eyebrow pencil on the back of a checkbook.

Relying on Memory

Some writers are able to regurgitate key passages of an interview verbatim with no notes to work from. When Truman Capote was researching *In Cold Blood*, an account of a vicious multiple murder, he found that many of his prospective sources tensed up when he tried to take notes.

> If you write down or tape what people say, it makes them feel inhibited and self-conscious. It makes them say what they think you expect them to say. . . . I taught myself to be my own tape recorder. What I'd do was have a friend talk or read for a set length of time, tape what he was saying, and meanwhile listen to him as intently as I could. Then I'd go write down what he had said as I remembered it, and later compare with what I had with the tape.

At the end of a day of interviewing, Capote would go back to his motel room and transcribe the remembered quotes. Few reporters have mastered the art as well as Capote did.

Mining for Gems

Interviewing is like pulling teeth if you come across a reluctant witness who only gives you unadorned yes-and-no answers, or speaks in generalities and platitudes. When this happens, you need to pull tricks from your repertoire to get usable quotes and colorful anecdotes to illustrate the generalities. If you are dealing with a weighty topic, anecdotal material especially can make the difference between dull writing and sprightly prose.

Some ways to "probe" with an interview subject:

Silence. If you get a short, noninformative answer where a long one was expected, just sit quietly and wait. Your subject probably will become uncomfortable and try to fill the empty space.

Encouragement. "That's interesting." "Good." "Uh-huh." Short, encouraging phrases will let your subject know that you are listening, are impressed, and would like to hear more.

Repetition. Repeat the subject's answer in his or her own words. If you've misunderstood, the subject can clear it up. In any event, this technique inspires elaboration.

Examples. Asking for examples can generate anecdotes.

Box 5-2
The Useful "Mm-humm"

How do you get long, detailed answers to your questions? One answer found by scholars who have spent their careers studying interview situations is that long questions tend to produce long answers. But an even simpler method was discovered by Joseph Matarrazo, who investigated the impact on an interview of an "mm-humm."

Lo and behold, it made a difference. Interviewers who asked questions lasting 5–6 seconds typically obtained responses in the range of 30–40 seconds. But when an interviewer spiced up his interview with "mm-humm's," the answers got longer—up in the 50–60 second range.

To obtain greater detail from your respondent, try for the "mm-humm" effect. It is likely to keep your subject talking. Meanwhile you can think up the next question.

"Why?" Get at the reasons behind what the subject has just told you. Getting answers to the questions "Why?" and "How?" are journalists' greatest challenges.

Longer questions. Researchers have found that longer questions produce longer answers—up to a point, after which your questions will become convoluted and unintelligible. This theory has been tested with presidential press conferences, job interviews, doctor-patient interviews, and even communication between astronauts and ground control, and it has been consistently confirmed.

Handling Bombshells

Some news interviews require you to ask tough, embarrassing questions. Beginning interviewers find this the hardest part of doing an interview. There are a number of methods that can be used to minimize the discomfort:

Attribute the question to someone else. Create the impression that it isn't really your opinion, but you need to ask anyway because "other people" are saying things. When Barbara Walters interviewed the Shah of Iran, she said: "Your majesty, there are people who say you are a dictator, a benevolent dictator, perhaps, but a dictator all the same. I know you have heard these criticisms. This is your opportunity to answer them."

Use a nonbeat reporter for a tough interview, so that the beat reporter's rapport with a regular source is not destroyed. A variation of this is to double-team a subject, using a "good cop-bad cop" approach in which one reporter is "sympathetic" to the subject, while the other one bores in with more accusatory, confrontational language.

Ease into it gently. Very few interviewers would begin their conversation with a victim of child abuse by blurting out, "Tell me about being abused as a child." Most likely the interview would begin with general details of the person's biography. You will sense when the time comes to ask about the details of this person's experience. Many times the interviewee may bring it up himself or herself.

Wait until late in the interview. In public opinion polling, it is common to put the more personal items—questions about family income, attitudes about sex, and so forth—at the end of the interview. This also works for journalistic interviews. By the end of the interview, you should have established rapport and, even if the questions provoke anger or cause the interviewee to break off the conversation, you have gathered all the other information you need and stand to lose very little. Even so, try not to embarrass, provoke, or anger your source. It is unprofessional.

Mary Anne Pikrone, who wrote for the *Rochester Times-Union*, recalls interviewing a former nun:

> One of the first things I wondered was, does she date and what does it feel like to be in the arms of a man and be kissed again, after 10 years in the convent? I finally got that question out about two hours into the interview, and by that time we were communicating so well that she answered it without hesitation. Don't be afraid to ask what you're wondering.

After asking the tough questions, you can throw in a couple of final, easy questions. That will leave the subject in a little better frame of mind and make it easier for you to come back for information later if you need to. But don't avoid the tough questions. People can be more forthright than you would expect, even about such topics as sex, money, or religion.

Box 5-3

How to Ask a Simple Question

Allen H. Barton's classic tongue-in-cheek guide to asking embarrassing questions in nonembarrassing ways applied to the question, "Did you kill your wife?"

1. *The Casual Approach*: "Do you happen to have murdered your wife?"

2. *The Numbered Card Approach*: "Would you please read off the letter on this card that corresponds to what became of your wife?" (Hand card to respondent)
   a. Natural death
   b. I killed her
   c. Other (what?)

3. *The Everybody Approach*: "As you know, many people have been killing their wives these days. Did you happen to have killed yours?"

4. *The "Other People" Approach*:
   a. "Do you know any people who have murdered their wives?"
   b. "How about yourself?". . .

Excerpted from Allen H. Barton, "Asking the Embarrassing Question," *Public Opinion Quarterly*, 1958

The Final Scene

Do not overstay your welcome. If your subject has agreed to give you a 30-minute interview, get ready to leave at the 30-minute mark. Often, you'll be asked to stay anyway. If not, it will be easier to get a follow-up visit if you have shown that you won't try to monopolize your source's time.

Do not stop listening after you have packed up your notebook and recorder. Some journalists have obtained their best anecdotes and most pointed quotes when the source has relaxed and is making pleasant conversation at the door. Usually, it's better not to restart your recorder or pull out your notebook at this point, but you should pay close attention and then make notes as soon as you depart.

Telephone Interviews

If there is time, you are better off doing a face-to-face interview rather than talking by phone. It is easier to establish rapport, and you are better able to draw cues from the expressions and moods of an interview subject. Feature interviews or sessions dealing with complex scientific or statistical matter are very difficult by phone. In the case of a feature interview, a phone call gives you no sense of color, setting, personal quirks, or habits, all important elements of the feature interview.

Long treatises have been written about "nonverbal communication"—the twitchings, body movements, facial expressions, and other subconscious clues to attitudes that people give when they talk with one another. You don't need to read the academic literature on the subject to know when someone is uncomfortable with the question or the questioner, when your subject hasn't properly understood the thrust of your questioning, or when a subject is nervous. All of this is invisible over the phone.

Phone interviews also tend to be shorter because they are not as comfortable to do. Interviewees get restless much more quickly. Even so, you may only have time for a phone call as a deadline approaches, and a call is better than nothing.

Taping phone conversations is an effective way to get a verbatim account, and this procedure can provide backup if you later are accused of a misquote or sued, but is it legal? In most states, it is legal to tape phone conversations without the knowledge or approval of the other party. In some newsrooms, phone conversations between reporter and source are routinely and clandestinely taped. Elsewhere, the practice is banned or at least requires the approval of senior editors. With the continuing changes in telephone technology, the laws are in considerable flux. Find out what the current laws are in your state.

Is taping phone conversations ethical? Journalists disagree with each other. Frederick Taylor, executive director of the *Wall Street Journal*, has argued, "If it is okay to take written notes, even in shorthand, certainly it is okay to take notes on a typewriter. And if it is okay to take notes on a typewriter, it is okay to take notes on your CRT. . . . Why does one step further into the electronic age cause such shudders?" Yet the *Wall Street Journal* forbids taping a phone call without permission from the other party, unless the bureau chief and managing editor are notified and give permission.

Jim Hoge, former publisher of the *New York Daily News*, said: "I favor informing interviewees when it [taping of phone interviews] is done." "It's all just notes, a collection of words or bleeps or electronic impulses that a reporter uses to do the job," said Minnesota newspaper editor Jan Mittelstadt. "What's the big deal?"

A. M. Rosenthal, executive editor of the *New York Times*, said, "It doesn't sit well in the stomach to tape someone and not tell them you're doing it. It's not honest. It's not fair. Period." Gilbert Cranberg, former Des Moines editor and now a University of Iowa journalism professor, pointed out that the American Bar Association forbids taping by attorneys without consent of all parties. "Journalists should not settle for a lesser standard of conduct than lawyers," Cranberg argued.

The *Los Angeles Times*, *Boston Globe*, *Philadelphia Inquirer*, and others forbid or restrict secret taping. Consider your choices. First, you must decide whether secret taping violates your own personal ethical standards. If not, find out whether taping violates either a newsroom policy or a state law. Of course, all this concerns taping without telling. Hardly anybody sees a problem with taping when all parties to a conversation have consented.

Source Attribution

There is often a question of whether or not a source wants the information he or she divulges to be be printed or broadcast. The dilemma of obtaining information but not having the privilege to use it is frustrating for all journalists. Possibly one way to avoid this problem is to discuss with the interviewee before conducting the interview the *options* for handling potentially restricted information. Although "grey" areas may still surface, you might be able to discover or eliminate barriers from the start. If you feel this strategy would not be beneficial, you might prefer to handle the problem spontaneously. In any event, you should be aware of some of the concerns regarding source attribution that may surface during an interview.

Off the Record

Q. When were you born?
A. Off the record?

It is seldom that bad, but the off-the-record syndrome has reached ludicrous proportions in journalistic interviews. Should you accept off-the-record information? Sometimes, you probably should, but usually not. The first hurdle to cross is to define exactly what off the

---

Box 5-4
Guidelines on Use of Sources

1. Try to get sources on the record.
2. Don't rely totally on unnamed sources. Use sources as tips to find someone who will talk on the record or to uncover independent confirmation, such as from records.
3. Distinguish between "leaked facts" and "leaked opinion."
4. Talk to an editor about any promise of confidentiality so the two of you can "share the burden of trust that such a promise carries."
5. Reveal your source to an editor.
6. Do not use such words as "key officials," "well-placed," or "informed" sources. Provide the fullest possible identification, such as "an official in the city manager's office." (Jeff Portnoy, a Honolulu attorney who represents several news media clients, has similar advice a legal perspective: "Try not to use the word 'source' in a story. Use some other word which means the same thing, but does not carry the same emotional tag.")
7. Don't allow an unnamed source to demean, attack, or vilify a named person or institution except under extraordinary circumstances, and if then, with permission of a senior editor only.

Roanoke Times and World-News

---

record means. Journalists themselves disagree on the fine distinctions made between several types of restricted information:

Off the record "usually means that nothing in the conversation may be used," states George Killenberg and Rob Anderson in *Before the Story.* Off-the-record interviews are a means of briefing a reporter, nothing more. "You can't use it, even if you don't use my name."

Journalists differ on whether they are allowed by the off-the-record ground rules to search for ways to get the same information on the record. Of course, if you do track down the same information elsewhere, your off-the-record source may never believe you and just assume you broke a confidence. For this reason, some journalists bring an interview to a screeching halt whenever a source says, "Off the record," because they prefer not to have their hands tied.

Deep background, a version of what "off the record" means, came into popular prominence in Bob Woodward and Carl Bernstein's investigation of Watergate during the Nixon Administration. Here is how their book, *All the President's Men*, defines a deep background agreement with Woodward's favorite source, Deep Throat:

> He [Woodward] would never identify him or his position to anyone. . . .
> He agreed never to quote the man, even as an anonymous source.
> Their discussions would be only to confirm information that had been
> obtained elsewhere and to add some perspective.

In Washington, another version of deep background is the so-called Lindley rule, named after Ernest K. Lindley of *Newsweek*. This allows the reporter to print what he or she gets, but without any quotation or even a veiled attribution to anyone.

To Mike Feinsilber of Associated Press, the term "background information" means, "I'll agree to talk with you if you agree not to use my name or title." Instead, the writer uses such terms as "an administration source" or "a Pentagon official" or "an aide close to the secretary." But the rules vary. In some cases, background information means that no attribution may be given even to the source's organization.

Not for attribution is similar in meaning to *background*. It generally means, "You can use this, but don't quote me by name. Don't attribute the information in such a way that I can be identified as the source." This is often the only way to get sensitive information. People in touchy situations will not give you this kind of information if they think the leak can be traced to them. On the other hand, the device is also a convenient way for a source to grind an axe without being spotted. An unattributed quote doesn't allow the audience to evaluate the credibility of the source or identify what ulterior motives may be present.

Sometimes when a source says "off the record," what he or she really means is that the information is not for attribution—which is a lot less onerous. You should make the ground rules clear. If you dig in your heels and refuse to accept information on an unattributable or off-the-record basis, the source may give it to you on the record.

Never ask, "Is that on the record?" Asking that question virtually guarantees that it will not be. However, many reporters feel it is necessary to explain to sources who are unfamiliar with the news media that anything they say is considered on the record. They have an ethical concern about taking advantage of a naive source.

Some newsrooms require reporters to obtain permission from a supervisor *before* giving any grant of confidentiality. Some editors and news directors insist on this because they believe that lazy or sloppy reporters overuse anonymous sources when they ought to be working backward more often, using such sources—if at all—only as tipsters and then verifying the information from documents and other on-the-record sources. *USA Today* never uses anonymous sources.

Other editors feel it is unrealistic to expect a reporter to stop an interview and contact a superior before continuing a conversation on a confidential basis. Ultimately, the supervisor must decide whether to print or broadcast information obtained in confidence. Because this provides a final "filtering" of the story before it becomes public, some editors and news directors ask, why tie a reporter's hands at the fact-gathering stage?

Sometimes a source may try to impose an ex post facto censorship on an interview by asking that you show him or her the story before it is printed or broadcast. Few reporters concede to such requests. However, some journalists do feel more comfortable when dealing with complex technical or statistical subjects if they check back with the original source—with the understanding that the source does not get to "edit" the story, only to suggest corrections in fact or perspective.

Another common ploy used by sources is to complete the interview and then make a belated "off-the-record" demand because of their concern that something explosive has been said. Few reporters grant such requests, contending that any deals about confidentiality should be struck in advance—after all, the source knows he or she is talking to a reporter and that reporters interview people to get information to publish or broadcast.

Above all, play fair with sources. Cutting corners on the confidentiality rules to get a story is usually a hollow victory followed by penalties and regrets afterward. You don't want to be known as a reporter who backstabs sources. If you gain that reputation you soon won't have any more sources.

The Ethics of "Sourcery"

"Where I come from in journalism, the magic word is 'attribution.' When I decide to protect a source, I stick to it as a matter of principle. But I don't make such decisions casually," said Peter Bridge, editor of *The Observer* in Kearny, New Jersey. Bridge did make such a decision in connection with a story about an alleged bribe to a Newark housing official and later spent three weeks in jail for refusing to testify about his confidential source before a grand jury.

Even Bridge says there ought to be limits on anonymity:

> I'd much prefer to write, and read, articles in which information is connected with an identifiable and identified source. Attributing facts to real people or documents fortifies credibility. Conversely, attribution to "unidentified sources" detracts from credibility.

Richard Smyser, editor of the *Oak Ridger* in Oak Ridge, Tennessee, says journalists need to distinguish between two types of sources. First, there are the invaluable sources who need to be "cultivated, appreciated, protected." They tend to be lower-level people, "real whistle-blowers. People who are genuinely upset when they see wrongdoing and want to do something to right it, but have themselves, their jobs, their families, to think of, too." And then, says Smyser, there are

> "sourcerers" [who] tend to be big-time folks—presidential aides . . . aides to presidential hopefuls during primary campaigns; negotiators—both management and union—at intense bargaining times; members of Congress and their staffs during heated congressional battles. People on the make, mostly.

> Do they want the public to know the truth? Do they want to right a wrong? . . .perhaps, but don't count on it. Most "sourcerers" are out to win an election, pass a bill, trash an opponent or make a buck. And if leaking on someone or something might help, they'll do it. And with our help, they do it all too often.

Cleaning Up Quotes

> On the other side, these attacks that are coming on the other side of the aisle, on the defense spending, incidentally, in the figure that we've submitted in the budget, we ourselves and the Defense Department, under the secretary, reduced that budget by $16 billion before it was submitted by taking things out that would have been worthwhile, would have increased our security ability, but which we believe we could do without for a time, and settled on this particular thing.

His image was the Great Communicator. But this contorted sentence was spoken by President Ronald Reagan at a press conference. If experienced public figures talk this way, think how the statements of ordinary people will look when you put them in writing. You need to decide how much to "clean up" the quotes of your sources in writing a story. Simple written sentences usually have a subject and a verb and make a single point before they reach a period. When people talk, however, they often intersperse their words with "uh" and "ah" and "you know." They tend to ramble around before stopping for breath. The syntax is garbled, even though the meaning may come through.

What should a journalist do? Novelist George Higgins says, "You can't write the way people actually talk, because it's just too difficult to read. You are dealing in a different medium." Many reporters agree that it is better to polish up quotes a bit to help the speaker look literate—so long as (and this is a very important "so long as") the reporter remains faithful to the meaning and intent of the speaker.

When it is too difficult to clean up a quote, do not use quotation marks. Instead paraphrase what was said and attribute the statement to the speaker. When you do use quotation marks, often the use of ellipses is all that is needed to bring sense and order to the words. Eliminate the ramble. Keep the nuggets. Put yourself in the speaker's shoes and see if you would be satisfied with the way something was said.

Special challenges in cleaning up quotes arise when the speaker has a regional accent or a dialect that renders his or her speech ungrammatical. In feature stories, capturing the rhythm and pace of speech illustrates part of the source's personality. However, a long story filled with Southern-accented quotes or Zsa Zsa Gabor-type Hungarian-English makes reading difficult. Also, the overall effect can seem condescending or patronizing to the speaker. You can use a few illustrative and colorful quotes early in a story to convey the impression, then slide back into standard grammatical English for the rest of the story.

Obscenity presents yet another challenge. If a lawyer curses a judge and is held in contempt of court for it, you have a challenge writing the story unless you can tell what was said. Most news media have rules about what obscenity is allowed and what isn't. This is an area where you need to consult with an editor before starting to write the story.

Be Skeptical

"In the case of news, we should always await the sacrament of confirmation," Voltaire wrote to the Count d'Argental in 1760. This remains good advice. Do not put something in a story just because

you have a quote from a news source; it may be wrong. Good writing
sometimes can be irresponsible reporting.

Your responsibility to the audience doesn't stop at the end of the
interview. Double-check your facts and observations with other people, by referring to documents, or by any of the other techniques discussed in this book. Never rely on one interview with one person to
capture the essence of a complex situation. Broaden your base of
reporting to capture the full pattern. Interviews can be an important
part of this effort but normally should not be your only source.

References

Bernstein, Carl and Bob Woodward. *All the President's Men.* New York:
Simon and Schuster, 1974.

Biagi, Shirley. *Interviews That Work*, 2nd ed. Belmont, CA: Wadsworth,
1992.

Brady, John Joseph. *The Craft of Interviewing.* New York: Vintage Books,
1977.

Capote, Truman. *In Cold Blood: A True Account of a Multiple Murder and
Its Consequences.* New York: Random House, 1965.

Donaghy, William C. *The Interview: Skills and Applications.* Glenview, IL:
Scott, Foresman and Co., 1984.

Killenberg, George M., and Rob Anderson. *Before the Story: Interviewing
and Communication Skills for Journalists.* New York: St. Martin's
Press, 1989.

Marcosson, Isaac. *Adventures in Interviewing.* New York: John Lane, 1919.

Matarazzo, Joseph D., Morris Weitman, George Saslow and Arthur N.
Weins. "Interviewer Influence on Duration of Interview Speech." *Journal
of Verbal Learning and Verbal Behavior*, I (1963): 451–58.

Metzler, Ken. *Creative Interviewing: The Writer's Guide to Gathering Information by Asking Questions*, 2nd ed. Englewood Cliffs, NJ: Prentice-
Hall, 1989.

Rafe, Stephen C. *Mastering the News Media Interview. How to Succeed at
Television, Radio, and Print Interviews.* New York: Harper Business,
1991.

Sheehy, Gail. *Hustling: Prostitution in Our Wide-Open Society.* New York:
Dell, 1973.

Chapter Six

DIGGING IN
STUDENTS PURSUE A TRAIL OF HEROIN

> For Americans, the second half of the twentieth century has been
> marked by an unusual amount and type of social change. The
> underprivileged have demanded equal rights, a significant
> portion of the visible political elite has weakened or fallen, and
> many of those in between have been maneuvering for new social
> position and identity.
>
> —Joshua Meyrowitz
> *No Sense of Place: The Impact of*
> *Electronic Media on Social Behavior*

Telling a big story in a way that will appeal to readers takes more
than gathering statistics and writing about them. It takes cooperation
among writers, editors, photographers, and designers.

In the mid-1990s, heroin use was on the rise across much of the
nation. State law enforcement officers knew that North Carolina was
no exception; in the first eight months of 1994, heroin-related deaths
in North Carolina surpassed those from cocaine. It was a story that
needed to be told, and told in more depth than the day-to-day coverage of drug busts and overdose deaths could provide.

In the fall of 1994, at the University of North Carolina at Chapel
Hill, Professor Philip Meyer put his advanced reporting students on
the story. Meyer, who holds the Knight Chair in journalism, enlisted

This chapter was written by Bill Cloud.

93

the help of the advanced editing students in a class taught by Associate Professor Bill Cloud. Associate Professor Mike Williams recruited a photojournalism student and a graphic design student to help.

The students, under the guidance of the professors, produced an eight-page tabloid special section that appeared in the *UNC Journalist*, the twice-a-semester publication of the university's School of Journalism and Mass Communication.

The heart of the project was a Carolina Poll conducted by students in the school, finding out what North Carolina residents knew about drug use and the upsurge of heroin. In addition, students researched supporting statistics about drug use and interviewed law officers and prosecutors, as well as drug-rehabilitation workers. More dramatically, they interviewed people close to victims of heroin, telling the stories of six of the 30 people who died in North Carolina in the first eight months of 1994 after using heroin. And they talked to heroin users, both current and former, producing a devastating tale of a seemingly smart student who, in the eyes of a reformed addict, was falling into the abyss.

Illustrating and packaging the stories required close cooperation among all parties. Designer Mario Garcia of the Poynter Institute* and others espouse the "WED" concept, the idea that writing, editing, and design are integrated. Implicit in the concept is the inclusion of photojournalists, photographers who know how to tell a news story with pictures.

More and more frequently on a newspaper, a team would be established to plan and carry out the project. At the university, the planning started with a suppertime gathering of the involved students and faculty members.

Because the classes met at different times and because so many students were involved, Melissa Twomey, a graduate student in the editing class, and Julie J. Thompson, a graduate student in the reporting class, worked as news editors, helping to coordinate the class's efforts. Joining the team were photojournalist Candice Cusic and Alison Shepherd, who met with the reporting class and discussed graphics possibilities

One problem soon became clear: Drug users might be willing to talk to reporters, but they didn't want to be photographed. In some such cases, "photo illustrations," or pictures staged to illustrate the

---

*The Poynter Institute for Media Studies, located in St. Petersburg, Florida, studies contemporary issues in newspaper journalism and conducts regular workshops for journalists.

story, are used, as long as the photos are clearly labeled. However, in this instance staged photos were rejected; our main criterion was honesty with the reader.

Cusic's contribution to the project was valuable: supplying pictures of drug counselors and drug enforcement officials doing their jobs. Shepherd showed her artistic skills in the gripping illustrations she provided for reporter Terry Hominid's interview with "Charlie," a heroin-using college student who considered himself a "professional" drug user seeking a "higher mentality." Hammond contrasted Charlie's words with the comments of "Paul," who is 20 years older than Charlie and saw his life nearly destroyed by drugs.

Shepherd also helped illustrate reporter Holly Ramer's fact-laden story reporting on the poll results and other statistics, revealing among other things that 18 percent of the 18- to 24-year-olds surveyed said they knew heroin users. Shepherd prepared charts illustrating drug use among those aged 18–29 and vividly showing how 93 percent of those dying from heroin were males.

The editing class brought things together. Twomey worked with Sharon Baldwin, Jennifer Hamby, David Hathaway, Marty Minchin, Chris Nichols, Steve Roblee, and Kathryn Sherer at the editing stage. Besides smoothing out wording and repairing grammar, the editors worked hard to eliminate repetition and inconsistencies, such as making sure they all agreed on the current street price of heroin, among the stories.

Roblee and Sherer both read Hammond's 3,000-word story of Paul and Charlie, working with Hammond and coming up with many suggestions. Roblee, Sherer and the other editors wrote headlines for the main and sidebar stories that captured both the emotion and the facts of the stories. In the two longer pieces, they inserted subheads to create entry points and break up the gray of the type. They also chose quotes to be set in larger type as tools to draw readers into the story package. In addition, their suggestions led to another element in the eight-page package: a glossary of the jargon of drug use, explaining terms that kept cropping up in the six profiles of victims.

The editors performed much of the layout work, electronically placing the stories on the pages using QuarkXpress layout software and working within the framework of the design prepared by Williams and his students. The seven longer stories and the six individual profiles were illustrated with drawings, graphics and photographs. Besides the illustrations and photos, the design staff created a logo and specified a dark line to be used on every page to give the section a feeling of unity. Design work, reflected in the use of boxes and varying type widths, added interest to the page of victims' profiles, which lacked other forms of illustration. In addition, typefaces were chosen to set the package off from the rest of the *Journalist* and give it the feeling of being a truly "special" special section.

The result was a section that combined strong reporting and writing with an appealing design. The special edition of the *Journalist* was published in the fall of 1994 and was titled "Heroin: It's Back." Portions of the five main stories are reprinted below. (Because the articles have been formatted to fit a 6" x 9" textbook, the newspaper design and other creative elements cannot be replicated. However, you will note that the contents of the stories reflect a group effort and illustrate how an issue that is important to the community can be addressed from different angles to present a gripping tale of reality.)

"A Tale of Two Users"
Terry Hammond

Mainlining heroin is a spiritual experience for this UNC-CH undergraduate. He sees himself as a pioneer of sorts, as someone on a quest for what he calls "higher intellect."

When he was 18 and in Governor's School, he injected opium. "It scared me to death. I had absolutely no idea what I was doing. I did not even smoke dope."

This student, call him Charlie, vowed to stay away from hard drugs from then on. "I said, 'Maybe I'll try marijuana, or I'll try acid, or I'll try LSD, or something like that.'" His resolve didn't last. "After I experienced other, lighter drugs, I felt more confident in my own ability to handle the effects of drugs and to be able to distinguish reality from the effects of the drugs, mentally."

The stereotypical image of a heroin user as a long-haired white rock star or a poor black who hangs out on street corners doesn't fit Charlie. He looks like any other college student raised in white upper-middle-class circumstances. His father works in finance, and his mother is a homemaker. They live in a resort area.

So why shoot heroin? "I think it's a college-mentality thing." Drugs make him more intellectual, Charlie says. "Any gathering of high intellect brings in an association of drugs.

Too Cynical? Too Naive?

When the transcript of Charlie's conversation is read back to Paul, the initial reaction is puzzlement. Paul (also a pseudonym) lifts an eyebrow at the association of drugs and intellect. He knows something about heroin, too. Paul is 20 years older than Charlie.

Charlie and his friends regularly use a variety of drugs. They say they can handle them. "When I am under the effects of drugs, I feel like an enlightened despot," Charlie says. "I will come out with some of the most profound philosophies. When you are on drugs, you have more tendency to interconnect things you normally wouldn't associate as being interconnected."

Paul shakes his head, lights a cigarette and draws in a lungful.

Charlie's face is earnest. He wants people to understand that he and his friends aren't garden-variety drug abusers. "We are constantly looking for new things to read or listen to or talk about while we are messed up," he says. Charlie and his friends consider themselves professional drug users.

"Amateur drug users are the people who are just into getting high or doing drugs just for the sole effect of doing drugs. And professional drug users we term as people who are after a higher mentality. The drugs are a means to an end."

That prompts a snort from Paul, as though he knows something Charlie doesn't.

Charlie says his quest for expanded intellect led him to smoke pot, inject LSD, trip on stamp acid and shoot speed. "I use marijuana quite frequently because that is the most accessible drug on campus right now," he says.

He shoots heroin less often because it is harder to score. Marijuana and alcohol are equally accessible on the UNC-CH campus, Charlie and his friends say.

Charlie knows he's going to have to curtail his drug use. He's interviewing for jobs and hopes to land a high-paying position in New York City. If he finds he can't handle things without drugs, Charlie says, he hopes he'll be "professional enough" to admit it.

Then, he says, he'll "either check into a clinic or try to figure out if there's a happy medium or a way I can continue with the drugs and go on to this goal of having a nice job and . . . a lot of wealth." On the other hand, he says, "Maybe after three or four years in the work force, after I've made a lot of money, then I'll say the money's not everything . . . and I'll want to go back to being a druggie."

"Just like that," Paul mutters. He grinds his cigarette into the ashtray.

Charlie is still trying to explain professional users. "They know where to draw their own personal lines and know when they need help," he says. "They know they're addicted, but they know that addiction does not permeate their social life."

Nothing Left but Crack

But Charlie makes no bones about it. "I'll come flat out and tell you I'm addicted," he announces. His voice is somewhat defiant, perhaps because one of his friends has just announced there's no such thing as addiction.

To what is Charlie addicted? He reels off a list. "To drugs and heroin—to that mentality that I cannot sustain being straight. I have to have the drugs to push myself through that buffer area of day-to-day, grind-it-out living. I have to have the drug to have the mentality or spirituality . . . I can attain when I am on drugs."

In the next breath, however, Charlie insists his addiction doesn't bother him. "I think I am professional enough to know that I can put aside the addiction during classes," he insists, "or around friends or people who don't like drugs, or around family, or when I'm driving a car."

"Yeah, yeah, yeah," Paul mumbles. . . .

"Risking Death for a 'Rush'"
Julie Ross

Heroin users must balance a desire for euphoria with the risks of overdosing and death. Here's how the drug interacts with the body to create that conflict:

Heroin use develops in three phases, according to the American Medical Association's *Drug Abuse: A Guide for the Primary Care Physician.*

For first-time users, the experience is often unpleasant. Nausea and vomiting are common, and the "high" is relatively mild. In the second phase, users develop a physical dependence on the drug, and tolerance increases. They need larger doses to achieve the same euphoria. Some withdrawal symptoms will appear when use is interrupted. When the final phase is reached, the "high" is rarely achieved and users are ingesting heroin simply to fend off withdrawal.

Heroin is derived from the opium poppy plant and chemically altered. It can be very addictive because it readily stimulates the "reward center" of the brain, which is responsible for the feeling of pleasure.

The drug's physical effects, which can vary, commonly include pain relief, drowsiness, euphoria, nausea, constricted pupils, itchy skin, constipation, depression of the nervous system and an eventual decline in sex hormone levels.

With intravenous injection, still preferred by most addicts, the user will immediately feel an intense "rush" in the abdomen, often compared to sexual orgasm. The drug is rapidly converted to morphine once inside the body, and it produces the same effect morphine would once it reaches the brain. After several minutes, the initial "rush" fades, and a state of relaxation sets in that can last three to six hours.

The body eliminates most of a heroin dose within 24 hours. However, withdrawal will begin 6 to 12 hours after a dose wears off and can last seven to 10 days. For addicts, withdrawal can last a lifetime—fever, chills, tremors, sweating, itchy or "crawling" skin, insomnia and vomiting are common symptoms. Some users have even described feeling as if their fingernails were popping off.

But while heroin withdrawal feels bad, it is actually less threatening than withdrawal from other drugs, according to Dr. Robert Gwyther, professor of family medicine and co-director of substance abuse services at University of North Carolina Hospitals. "Withdrawal from alcohol, sedatives and barbiturates sometimes is fatal, and medically it's much more dangerous," he said.

And heroin addiction can be conquered, he said, pointing to the many Vietnam veterans who quit the habit by themselves after returning home. "Most people in addiction medicine believe that cocaine is worse to kick—and nicotine might be worse than cocaine." . . .

"Price, Purity Lead to '90s Popularity"
J. J. Thompson

How do you create a fast-moving market for an almost forgotten product? Increase supply, lower prices and give the product a '90s-type, health-conscious twist.

That formula has succeeded for heroin, which, after a decade-long lull, is experiencing surging popularity among American drug users.

Now, it's as easy to get heroin as it is to "get in the car and go. There's lots of it out there on the streets," said James Goode, coordinator of Wakeview Clinic, a Raleigh methadone treatment center for heroin addicts.

One senior at the University of North Carolina at Chapel Hill who uses heroin said the drug was so prevalent in Myrtle Beach, S.C., where he spent last summer, that "you couldn't get away from it," and even on campus, while it's still difficult to get, "heroin's more available than it was three or four years ago."

In a special Carolina poll, four of the 462 respondents said they used heroin. These four also reported that they had used it within the past 30 days.

Quite popular among drug users in the 1970s, heroin was seldom even talked about during the '80s. One reason is that there was less of it around. American foreign policy directed toward drug-producing countries succeeded in keeping most heroin outside U.S. borders, said Joel Rosch, director of research with the State Bureau of Investigation (SBI).

While much of the world heroin supply still comes from Southeast Asia, the production of poppies—from which heroin is derived—has begun to blossom all over the world in the last decade. South America, led by Colombia, has become the second-largest vendor of the opium-derived drug, supplying about one-fourth of the heroin entering the United States.

When supply goes up, the rule goes, price comes down. So it has been with heroin.

A user would have considered it a good deal to fork over $40 for a bag of heroin only a matter of months ago, Goode said. "Now it's down to $15, and it's stronger."

Stronger, indeed. Heroin purity in the state is as high as 95 percent, said Irvin Allcox, a special agent in the SBI's drug chemistry lab.

Using nearly pure heroin lets users smoke or snort the drug like cocaine to get the heroin's desired mellowing effect. In the past, users had to shoot the heavily cut heroin directly into the bloodstream.

Thus this new, improved version comes packaged without the threat of AIDS.

"Heroin is a drug that you can look at the purity level to see how much is on the streets. A dealer will cut it as much as the market will stand," Allcox said. Right now, there's obviously a good bit of heroin out there because dealers can't get away with diluting it.

Heroin's comeback doesn't give only drug dealers new business. Goode said his clinic is treating more than 80 heroin addicts, compared with 50 to 55 this time last year. He expects to have 100 recovering addicts in the program by early next year.

"Heroin and crack are the most addictive drugs out there," Goode said. Because the body builds a tolerance to heroin, it requires more and more of the drug to satisfy the addiction. Heroin's increased purity only escalates that cycle.

The increased purity also raises the risk of overdoses. . . .

"A Killer Returns"
Holly Ramer

A spiraling tornado called heroin has touched down in North Carolina as it crosses the country in its nationwide resurgence. Twelve percent of adults in a special Carolina poll for the *UNC Journalist* said they know someone who uses or has used heroin.

And 1 percent told interviewers they use heroin themselves.

This year, the number of heroin deaths in the state has surpassed those from cocaine. In 1989, there were 14 who died of heroin, 34 from cocaine. Last year, heroin pulled nearly even.

And in the first eight months of 1994, heroin killed 30 compared with 19 cocaine-related deaths.

The N.C. statistics fit into the pattern of increasing heroin activity in much of the nation. In the Northeastern and Midwestern United States particularly, heroin is readily available, low-priced and purer than ever, according to the Office of National Drug Control Policy, which releases monthly reports about national trends in drug abuse. But the Southeast is not far beyond, with Atlanta treatment providers and police and those who study the drug trade reporting increases in heroin activity.

In North Carolina, heroin activity follows the state's highway system, with the highest concentration of drug use found in the Piedmont.

Heroin traffic starts in Washington on the North Carolina coast and heads westward, with Greenville, Wilson and Durham having the greatest concentrations of heroin users, said Eric Tellefsen, an State Bureau of Investigation narcotics agent.

While about 12 percent of the respondents from both the coastal and Piedmont regions said they knew heroin users, only about 7 percent of those in the western region said they knew of someone who used the drug. . . .

Percentage of N.C. heroin deaths by gender

Figures are from Jan. 1 to Oct. 3, 1994

SOURCE: Carolina Poll   ALISON SHEPHERD

Drug use among N.C. adults, ages 18-29

Source: N.C. Medical Examiner

Figure 6.1 These two graphics appeared in the *UNC Journalist* special edition, "Heroin: It's Back."

"Behind the Scenes of a Drug Bust"
Jacob Stohler

In real life, in Chapel Hill, undercover drug operations involve far less tire squealing than on television. Between surveillance, paperwork and communicating with other police departments, there's little time for acts of drama.

Even a sensational drug bust that catches the media's attention, like a record heroin raid in Durham in September, is just the finale of a long, tedious and quiet performance. Police avoid surprise, especially when drugs and guns are involved.

"There's always a chance of something happening with a narcotics arrest," said a Chapel Hill undercover detective. "You just never know what the bad guy is going to do."

Television is at least right about one thing: Investigations begin with a tip. An informant, an arrest or just a passing patrol officer's observation can trigger suspicions and start an investigation.

First, detectives set up surveillance on the suspected house or person. They try to determine who's in charge, how many people are involved and what, if anything, they are actually doing. Questions of jurisdiction must also be answered at this point—such as whether other police departments, or even federal agents, should be called.

When agents decide they are on to something, they approach the suspect and make a "controlled buy." The exchange is documented and usually is followed by at least one more such buy. No arrests are made.

Agents use these buys to size up the suspect and feel out the operation. Are there guards at the house? Does the suspect operate alone? Are there other drugs involved? Will weapons be part of the equation?

The raid is the trickiest part. A team of agents shows up with a search warrant early in the morning, hoping to find the suspects and the drugs, but not guns.

An early-morning raid on Sept. 3 netted the largest amount of heroin ever seized in Durham—four pure ounces. On the street, that would translate into 5,000 bindles worth about $40 each. A bindle is the equivalent of one hit of heroin.

The six-month police investigation led to charges against a man and a woman for trafficking, conspiracy to traffic and possession. Police said Robert James Story had been buying heroin in New York City and bringing it to Durham stashed on planes and trains.

"This is going to dry up several street-corner drug markets," Cpl. John Mozart, a Durham police officer, said at the time of the arrests. "You're going to have heroin junkies looking elsewhere than Durham for their heroin this weekend." . . .

Reference

Meyrowitz, Joshua. *No Sense of Place: The Impact of Electronic Media on Social Behavior*. New York: Oxford University Press, 1986, p. 307.

PART III

COMMUNITY CONNECTIONS

Chapter Seven

SURVEYING THE PUBLIC

Surveys are excellent vehicles for measuring attitudes and orientations in large populations.

—Earl Babbie, *The Practice of Social Research*

Newspapers have long conducted "man-in-the-street" (citizen) interviews and called them surveys of community opinion. The idea is simple enough—and totally fallacious! Typically, the city editor assigned someone to find out what citizens thought about a city council proposal to raise property taxes, the latest proposal to combat crime, or whatever issue was on the top of the editor's mind at that moment. With a photographer in tow to take the requisite mug shots that traditionally accompany this news feature, the reporter set out to find some people who met the two necessary qualifications for inclusion in this pseudo-survey of public opinion. First, of course, they had to be willing to stop and give their opinion. Second, their answers needed to be interesting. Colorful or provocative responses make far better news copy than the limited, sometimes monosyllabic, answers that are typical responses to questions about public issues. Once the reporter had found a half dozen articulate, quotable people to answer "the question," a story was written about how local residents viewed the issues of the day.

Notwithstanding the long tradition of citizen interviews—and their rebirth, both on TV and in the newspaper, thanks to computer technology—the premise of this news feature is fatally flawed. No project of this sort can give you the foggiest reliable notion about what the community really thinks about "the question." Although many TV stations and newspapers hedge by noting that the results presented are not a scientific survey or poll of public opinion, most members of the general public don't understand the distinction. Broadcasting or publishing this kind of feature is fraudulent and unethical!

In the jargon of survey research, citizen interviews are based on a convenience sample. The people who participate are convenient to interview—all in the same shopping mall or the same supermarket parking lot. Even if the locations of the interviews are scattered over several parts of town, think about those who still are excluded by these locations and by the time of the day when the interviews are conducted. Usually, there also are only a handful of interviews. In short, there is absolutely no basis for inferring that the views voiced by these interviewees are in any way typical of anyone other than that particular handful of persons. They represent themselves and no one else. It is ridiculous to use this reporting method to draw any conclusions about how people think or feel about any public issue or current situation. At best, the information is raw data, a few stray quotes gleaned from a very large pool. At worst, because a news story based on this raw data gives the appearance of being a picture of how the community feels, it is misleading.

The motivation behind citizen interview assignments is laudable. It gets local names in the daily news report, and "names make news." Also, it obtains feedback from the audience about important issues. Most of the space in newspapers and the bulk of the time on TV news broadcasts are used to let our leaders speak to the rest of us. Reporters cover a state-of-the-union address in which the president tells us what he thinks, a state legislative session to listen to lawmakers' remarks, or a Rotary Club speech by the county prosecutor. Nobody would suggest that news media should not do that. In a democracy it is important for all of us to know what our leaders are doing, thinking, and saying. The problem is that virtually all of the daily news is one-way communication—from them to us.

The concern about feedback is an important one for journalists. It fuels much of the contemporary interest in public journalism which entails local newspapers and broadcasters making an effort to create a proactive public forum where the issues that concern the public become the focus of journalists' questions to candidates and of the subsequent news stories. Numerous studies have found that much of the news coverage on election campaigns ignores the issues that the voters think are most important. In other words, public journalism and other strategies for obtaining feedback from the audience are

Feedback from citizens helps pinpoint important issues. Courtesy Chicago Tribune.

efforts to make mass communication more interactive and less of a one-way street.

Fortunately, most news media are now aware that the people who give responses in citizen interviews are neither typical nor representative. But increased understanding of what constitutes good and bad surveys hasn't completely driven this type of survey out of the news market.

Fascination with new computer technologies that can answer the telephone and count the votes has given a new lease on life to surveys based on convenience samples. With computers connected to telephones, the sampling is more convenient than ever. The reporter doesn't have to find anyone. The respondents to the survey volunteer! In the simplest version of these psuedo-polls, members of the audience are invited to phone in their opinion on the question of the day. If they agree, they call one phone number. If they disagree, they call another number. The computer just counts how many phone calls are received at each number. Local television newscasts like this technique because the question can be asked on the regular evening news and the results reported on the late night news. There are even more sophisticated versions in which you phone a computer that is pro-

grammed to interview you. You answer by punching various numbers on your touchtone phone. There can even be open-ended questions in which the computer records your verbatim answer to the question. There are some things to think about:
- Who is most likely to participate in these surveys?
- Do you think some people call in more than once?
- Is this ethical reporting?

Check the TV stations and newspapers available in your community. Are any of them reporting these pseudo-polls?

Surveys: To Believe or Not to Believe

Except in a few newsrooms fascinated with gimmicks and quackery, the citizen interview and its phone-in computer cousins long ago gave way to the public opinion survey, or, as it is sometimes referred to, the scientific poll. As a reporter, you will encounter these surveys on just about every beat. They dominate contemporary political campaigns, are frequently commissioned by interest groups on just about every imaginable topic, are a staple of planning in both government and business, and increasingly are conducted by news organizations themselves.

Box 7-1
Understanding Public Opinion

There is no perfect wording for any question in a public opinion survey. As we have seen, some ways of wording a question are bad because they bias the responses toward a particular answer. But even two very similar versions of a question that lack obvious biases can yield different sets of results.

Fortunately, on most major issues of the day a variety of questions from different pollsters are available to reporters and can be used to develop a nuanced picture of public opinion. By using at least two different questions on the same aspect of an issue, it is possible to triangulate on the realities of public concern.

Here are some examples from the national debate on health care that held center stage during the opening years of the Clinton presidency.

Crisis vs. Most Important Problem

Q. Which comes closer to your view—because of rising health care costs we are headed toward a crisis in the health care system, or even though costs are rising, we are not headed toward a crisis?

79% said we are headed toward a crisis.

CBS News/*New York Times*, 1991

Q. Which do you think is the more important problem facing the country today—reforming health care or reducing the federal budget deficit?

50% said that health care is the most important problem while 44% selected the federal budget deficit.

CBS News, 1993

Quality of Care

Q. [Under the Clinton plan] do you think the quality of the health care for *most Americans* will get better, get worse, or stay the same?

Get better: 39%
Get worse: 29%
Stay the same: 30%

Washington Post, 1993

Q. . . .do you think the quality of health care *you receive* will get better, get worse, or stay the same?

Get better: 19%
Get worse: 34%
Stay the same: 44%

Washington Post, 1993

Role of the Government

Q. Do you think the federal government should guarantee health care for all Americans, or don't you think so?

Yes: 61%
No: 33%

Yankelovich Partners for *Time*/CNN, 1994

Q. For each issue I name, please tell me if you think the federal government can or cannot do much to make it better . . . The health care system?

The government can: 77%
The government cannot: 21%

ABC News/*Washington Post*, 1994

Where these public opinion surveys are concerned, journalists fall along a broad spectrum. At one end are a small group of nonbelievers, who distrust all surveys. They can't accept the idea that Gallup or Harris can talk to 1,500 Americans and accurately represent the views of the entire country or that a local pollster can describe public opinion in a community or state on the basis of 1,000 or even fewer interviews. On the other end of the spectrum are a relatively large group of gullible journalists, who will accept any press release with numbers in it, feeling there must be some magic in those integers.

To find the middle ground, let's talk some ways to avoid being gullible. To start, there are right ways and wrong ways to do survey research. There is more than one way to do a survey "right," but there seem to be even more ways to do a survey wrong—through either ignorance or malice. But, overall, the two most common ways to get it wrong are:

- A biased sample of respondents
- Sloppy or biased question writing

The next chapter will discuss in considerable detail how to get a sample right; how to see if somebody else's sample is a good one; and how to phrase precise, unbiased questions. Right now, let's talk about how some public opinion polls and surveys get it wrong.

Sampling Problems

The most notorious example of a sample gone astray is the 1936 presidential election poll taken by the then-prestigious *Literary Digest*. Their 1936 poll was not the *Digest*'s debut into the field. In the 1920s and in 1932, the magazine had developed a record of successfully predicting presidential winners on the basis of its "straw" polls. Now it wasn't so much that the *Literary Digest* was always on the mark. Its predictions of presidential election winners often were well over 10 percent off the actual election returns. But their straw polls always had the right man in the lead. In 1936, the *Digest*'s polling method generated more than two million responses and predicted that Alf Landon of Kansas would score a 3 to 2 victory over President Franklin D. Roosevelt. As anyone who has ever searched for the name of Landon on a list of presidents knows, the *Digest* missed—and not by just a little. In fact, Roosevelt received 62 percent of the vote and carried 46 of the 48 states.

What happened? Analysis over the years attributes the *Digest*'s erroneous prediction primarily to the fact that the sample was drawn mostly from their own subscriber lists, telephone directories, and automobile registrations—places where, in the middle of the Depression in 1936, you were apt to find more well-to-do (and Republican) people.

Box 7-2
Focus Groups

About halfway between the quick and easy "man-in-the-street" interview and the not-so-quick and not-so-inexpensive use of sample surveys is another information-gathering technique that can be used profitably by reporters. It's called the focus group.

The idea is to draw a small sample of people from whatever population you're interested in—voters in a city, students in a high school, automobile plant workers, doctors, whatever. You then assemble them in small groups where your questions encourage them to discuss in considerable detail whatever subject you as a reporter are interested in. Here's how to go about it:

1. Think carefully about what questions you want answered. Compile a loose guide that addresses these questions in an orderly fashion. This should be used as a map or checklist by the moderator of the group, but, unlike sample surveys, the moderator should allow the focus-group participants to deviate from the prepared list of questions as long as they stay on the subject. Remember that the purpose of the focus group is to explore a topic as fully as possible and to alert you to aspects of the topic of which you may be unaware. All the questions should be open-ended, requiring some discussion, not just yes/no answers.

2. Use a telephone book to draw a sample of a few dozen people from your target group and recruit some to be interviewed. Some focus groups give participants a small stipend ($10 or $20), or a gift (a free dinner or bottle of wine). Others find that people are so pleased that somebody is interested in their opinions that they'll do it for free.

3. Set up the groups so you'll have no more than 8 or 10 people per session. Larger groups do not allow everybody a chance to talk. Try to make the groups relatively homogeneous on key variables, such as age, sex, and race. If you're going to discuss race relations, you'll get more honest opinions if you set up whites and blacks in separate groups. Younger people tend to be more forthcoming if they're not mixed in with people their parents' age.

4. Use follow-up letters and phone calls to encourage people to keep their original commitments to participate and to remind them of the date and time.

5. Arrange for a comfortable room with a table and chairs. Also arrange for somebody other than the interviewer to unobtrusively

run the tape recorder. Refreshments, such as coffee and sodas, help set people at ease.

6. Encourage people to introduce themselves, then to speak freely as the interviewer casually guides them through the topics selected. Sessions often last from 90 minutes to two hours, depending on the number of participants and how willing they are to speak up.

7. Transcribe the session later and analyze it. Sometimes the comments can lead you to story ideas or to topics you'll want to follow up in later sample surveys. It can also work in reverse—you may have already taken a survey and the focus groups can give you colorful quotes and anecdotes to illustrate what you found.

8. Assemble at least three groups on each topic to gain an understanding of how people in general feel about that topic. Sometimes the conversation of a group is influenced by one or two individuals with strong opinions. Exposure to several groups will eliminate much of the idiosyncrasy of any particular group.

By proceeding systematically, you have done a better job at assembling the people you interview than has the haphazard man-in-the-street reporter. Because only a small group of people participate in a focus group, or set of focus groups, you can't validly generalize from their views, but such groups do give you the voices of real, live people commenting on issues and situations in the community. Focus groups help you to identify topics when you are not sure exactly what you will find or exactly which words people will use to describe an issue or situation. Furthermore, because a focus group is an intensive situation, it allows you to ferret out the complexity and nuances of opinions that exist "out there." You gain insight into how people's minds work and what things are important to them, as opposed to the things that you assume are important. In short, focus groups are a valuable reporting tool.

Another factor in the erroneous prediction of the outcome was the fact that the *Digest* relied on voluntary response in its poll. The magazine mailed out 10 million sample ballots, got 2.3 million back, and believed them. "As everyone ought to know, such samples are practically always biased," said statistician Maurice Bryson.

> The respondents represent only that subset of the population with a relatively intense interest in the subject at hand, and as such constitute in no sense a random sample. In the 1936 election, it seems clear that the majority of anti-Roosevelt voters felt more strongly about the election than did the pro-Roosevelt majority.

The result, based on whatever combination of sampling and response bias, was that the *Digest*'s "electorate" wasn't constructed in such a way that it was likely to reflect the makeup of the actual United States electorate in that year. In short, the *Digest*'s straw poll shared the problems that we also have seen with citizen interviews.

Congressional Questionnaires

Professional pollsters these days wouldn't dream of building a sample the way the *Digest* did, but there is one group of would-be pollsters that does it year in and year out—members of the United States Congress. You can hardly escape the ubiquitous congressional questionnaire, mailed to "Postal Patron" at each address in a congressional district. If the mailing goes to every address in the district, it does escape one of the *Literary Digest*'s problems. Because rich and poor alike get a questionnaire in the mail, there is not the class bias in distributing the questionnaires that occurred in the 1930s by mailing them only to people who subscribed to a literary magazine or had a telephone. However, beyond this point the procedure falls apart. The recipient may have the questionnaire in hand, but in order to be "counted" in this public opinion poll of consitutents, he or she must: Sit down and answer the questions; tear out the questionnaire; and mail it in.

Box 7-3
A National Survey from U.S. Senator Phil Gramm

Here is an excerpt from a survey questionnaire mailed out by a group of Republican members of the U.S. Senate—about the time the Soviet Union fragmented into different republics—consisting of 8 of the 33 questions asked about 15 different issues. For each of the 6 issues listed below, these are all of the questions asked about that issue. For each question, the possible answers to the survey were: strongly agree, moderately agree, moderately disagree, strongly disagree, undecided. Can you predict the pattern of response for any of these questions?

Crime

A. Generally, do you believe our legal system is more concerned with criminals' "rights" than victims' rights?

B. Should the Federal Court System be more aggressive in its efforts to stop violent crime?

Environment

C. Are you generally satisfied with the progress being made to protect the environment in the U.S.?

Soviet Union

D. Should we use our tax dollars to bail out the Soviets' failed economy?

E. Are you completely convinced that the Soviet Union no longer poses a serious military threat to the U.S.?

Balanced Budget Amendment

F. Are you in favor of a Constitutional Amendment that requires Congress to balance the federal budget?

Gun Control

G. Should more attention be paid to controlling criminals who use guns rather than controlling guns themselves?

Foreign Trade

H. Should the United States abandon its open trade policy even if it costs Americans jobs and harms consumers?

Common sense will tell you that these requirements largely restrict the responses to the most politically interested and active segment of the constituency. Considerable research indicates that these respondents are likely to be older, wealthier, and better educated. They also are more likely to vote, which after all, may be what any member of Congress really is worried about.

The problem with this kind of polling increases when a member of Congress tabulates the results from the returned questionnaires and sends a news release to the newspapers and TV stations back home. These news releases, frequently reporting alleged public opinion on controversial and emotional topics, often slight such key methodological information as the response rate.

The *Boston Globe* once reported that a poll by antibusing Congresswoman Louise Day Hicks showed that 80 percent of those in her district agreed with her. Well down in the story, the *Globe* did point out that 200,000 questionnaires were mailed, but that only 23,000 were returned. That is less than a 12 percent rate of response. During a time of intense national feeling about the Vietnam War, a 1966 *New York Times* article was headlined "54% in Ohio Poll Assert U.S. Role in War Is Mistake." In fact, it wasn't a poll of Ohio, but of only one congressional district in Ohio. In that district, the congressman sent out 130,000 questionnaires and received 4,059 responses (a return of less than 4 percent). The 54 percent antiwar sentiment was based on that response. Neither the *Globe* nor the *Times* reports surveys like that today, but many other news media still do. They shouldn't!

Question Bias

Beyond problems with the rate of response, there is an even more common failing of polling, especially in surveys sponsored by groups with a strong interest in the outcome. That failing is question bias. Consider some of these examples.

> *Do you think Congress should allow clean air laws to be weakened?*

You can easily guess how most survey respondents would answer. Who favors dirty air? About 14 percent of those responding, as it turned out when that question was actually posed in a public opinion survey. But suppose the question had been biased in the opposite direction:

> *Some people feel our air pollution laws are so restrictive that they force factories to close down unnecessarily and throw people out of work. Do you think Congress should make the laws less restrictive in order to help speed economic recovery and reduce unemployment?*

There is an alternative that avoids the extremes of these last two questions. Consider this more neutral question from a CBS-*New York Times* poll:

> *Would you favor or oppose keeping air pollution laws as tough as they are now, even if some factories might have to close?*

Presented with this question, 61 percent favored keeping the laws "as tough as they are now," 29 percent favored weakening the laws, and 10 percent had no opinion. By presenting the question in a balanced fashion, the CBS-*New York Times* poll located a significant minority (29 percent) who felt pollution laws were too tight and were hurting the economy. That's a very different finding from the first question, which found only half as many (14 percent) who thought that the current laws were too tight.

Box 7-4

Question Wording

Even the most subtle changes in wording can result in major shifts in the results of a survey. Consider this example of a question where slightly different wording for one of the response categories produced vast differences in the outcome.

Suppose the budgets of your state and local government have to be curtailed. Which activity would you limit most severely?

When the list of answers included the term "aid to the needy," less than 10 percent of the respondents singled it out for curtailment. When the same question substituted "public welfare programs" in the list of answers, almost four times as many respondents (39%) selected that category for curtailment.

Here's another example of problematic question wording from a congressional poll:

Do you think Congress should prevent the IRS from withholding 10 percent of interest and dividend payments for income taxes?

First of all, the question suggests that the Internal Revenue Service came up with the withholding idea on its own and that Congress could ride to the taxpayers' rescue. In fact, it was Congress that passed the legislation requiring withholding in the first place, and there was a clear purpose for the requirement. What if this were the question instead?

Congress has passed a law requiring the IRS to withhold 10 percent of interest and dividend payments for income taxes, much as taxes are now withheld from a worker's paycheck. Some people feel this would help catch tax evaders who now avoid paying taxes on their interest and dividends. Others oppose the withholding, saying it would reduce the interest people receive and would be more trouble than it is worth. How do you feel?

Again, the responses to this version are likely to be considerably different from the responses to the previous version.

Finally, just to show you that members of Congress are not necessarily the worst offenders in writing biased questions, consider this one from a questionnaire mailed out by the Moral Majority:

Do you believe smut peddlers should be protected by the courts and the Congress, so they can openly sell pornographic materials to your children?

There are better ways to ask questions about First Amendment rights and social problems.

When you are reporting results from polls and surveys, it is important that you devote just as much attention to question design as you do to sample design. Although pollsters work diligently to shave a percentage point or two off statistical errors in designing a sample, badly worded questions yield results that are even farther off the mark.

Public Opinion Polls

There is a wide divergence of opinion on the wisdom of public opinion polls in a democracy. Political scientists Richard Scammon and Ben Wattenberg said that "accurate and speedy public opinion polling has probably done more to advance the responsiveness of the democratic process than any invention since the secret ballot and the direct primary."

On the other hand, journalist-philosopher Walter Lippmann warned "that whether a plurality of the people sampled in the [Gallup] poll think one way has no bearing upon whether it is sound public policy." Pioneer pollster Elmo Roper said, "It would be a sad day indeed for this country if our statesmen were to follow slavishly the voice of the majority as if it were the voice of God." However, Roper noted that opinion polls can help political leaders and news media understand the nature of opinion and see where they have failed to provide enough information for informed opinion formation.

Winston Churchill condemned the use of polls to "take one's temperature. . . . There is only one duty, only one safe course, and that is to try to be right." But today politicians seek out polls, usually believe them, and frequently follow them. Polls have taken the place of political bosses, according to Democratic political pollster William Hamilton:

> You don't think somebody in 1920 was not running around to find out what Tammany Hall thought, what this guy in Albany that controlled the upstate vote felt? The candidates are making the same decisions they have always made. They are now using different instruments or different sources of information.

Politicians may use polls wisely—to understand opinion so they can know how to bring it around to believing what is "right" in their view. Or politicians may abuse polls—by using survey results to shape their own views to fit what is popular with their constituents.

But polls are going to be used. Is it wrong for the news media to give the public the same information that is already in the hands of political leaders and their campaign strategists?

Publication of the findings from a well-conducted poll allows everyone, not just the political pros, to have a better idea of how opinion is lining up on the issues of the day. This should be one of the major goals of any news organization—to show its audience how the world is working. Political pundits always have provided their readers with assessments of how a campaign is going. Before the advent of survey research, they did it by doing their own sort of primitive "polling." They interviewed leaders from different political camps, perhaps talked to a few "average citizens," then made a pronouncement on how things were. In reality, these were pronouncements of how things *seemed to be*, reports based in large measure on very self-serving statements from persons with a vested interest in the outcome of the election. The difference with political polling is that the information comes directly from the voters and is collected in a systematic, broad-based manner.

Political Polls

Political surveys, especially the increasingly popular horse-race polls that forecast upcoming elections, are the most publicized use of survey research. Just about every newspaper and TV news program that reports any polling at all uses election-year horse-race surveys.

The survey question "Who would you vote for?" elicits answers that add very little to the audience's knowledge of the world that they wouldn't find out eventually anyway. Sooner or later, there will be an election and we will all know who won. To be truly informative, polls must go beyond the horse-race questions and explore in some detail what is going on among the electorate. The great—and all too frequently, unrealized—advantage of survey research is that it allows you to see things through voters' eyes, without the filters of your own preconceptions or the spin of the political professionals. Some questions to which a well-designed political poll can elicit answers include:

What issues are most important to the voters? The issues advanced by the candidates in their campaign appearances and in their advertising, as well as the issues receiving news coverage on

TV and in the newspaper, often are very different from the issues that top the public agenda.

What is the match between voters' issue concerns and their choice of a candidate? Sometimes, we assume that because Voter X favors Candidate A, Voter X must agree with the candidate most of the time. However, many research projects from coast to coast have shown that this is not necessarily so. People are perfectly capable of holding positions on prominent issues directly contradictory to the stances of the candidates they support. Sometimes a match on one especially salient issue is sufficient to gain a vote. Sometimes it is not even issues at all that determine how a voter casts his or her ballot.

How are the candidates perceived? Are people voting for a candidate because they think he or she is honest, or an efficient and competent administrator, or a warm human being who cares about their problems, or something else? What do voters prize in the candidates they vote for?

These were the kinds of questions asked by a statewide Florida survey during a gubernatorial campaign. For instance, the survey asked voters which man "is most qualified to be governor," which "has the best understanding of business," which "has the best background in government," and which "has made the better impression in his TV ads." Overall, the survey examined perceptions of the two candidates on 12 different personal dimensions.

The candidate who ultimately won the election led on seven of the items—those dealing with experience in government, overall leadership, and familiarity with the problems of ordinary people. However, the losing candidate was not without strong points as well, being judged most knowledgeable about business, best able to expand Florida's economic base, and most likely to limit taxes and spending. Measuring the two opponents on all of these yardsticks enabled the sponsoring Florida newspapers to give their readers a much more thorough picture of the race than simply reporting the "horse-race" standings. Additional analysis from these kinds of survey questions can even identify the groups among which these candidate images are particularly weak or strong.

Surveys also can identify another key group of voters: those who remain undecided as election day approaches. Who are the undecideds? What kinds of people haven't made up their minds yet, and which candidate seems likely to profit when we compare the candidates' images among these undecided voters?

Some pollsters simply throw out the undecideds and recalculate the decided vote so that it totals 100 percent. The assumption behind this action is that the undecideds are distributed through the population in the same proportions as the decideds. This is nearly always an erroneous assumption. Don't let pollsters get away with it, and don't do it in your own surveys, either. A high undecided vote can signal instability in a political race or in public opinion about an issue, or it can mean ignorance or apathy. Failure to express a preference also can mean that people are unwilling to state their intention to an interviewer. The Gallup Organization has found that "undecideds" can be cut by one-third or more in an in-person survey by using a secret-ballot technique in which voters fill out a slip and place it in the interviewer's ballot box or in a sealed envelope instead of just telling the interviewer their preference. You can't use this technique, of course, in a telephone survey, but the point to keep in mind is that the undecideds mean something— so don't just discard them. They are worthy of consider able scrutiny and may be the subject of your best news story of all.

Research and reporting that goes beyond the horse-race performs a service for your audience that they cannot get anywhere else. As Douglas McKnight of San Francisco's KGO-TV said, "A vote is a simple declarative sentence. . . . polls can get the rest of the paragraph."

Invariably, there are people who will say that it's not the business of the news media to get involved in political polling, that journalists can alter the course of an election simply by publishing or broadcasting the results of a poll. Ethical questions clearly are involved, although the empirical record is far from clear on exactly what impact is made—if any—by public release of poll data.

Some critics say that reporting polls fosters a bandwagon effect that causes voters to leap to the side of the candidate who is ahead. However, research over the years has failed to demonstrate that this happens with any regularity. You can argue at least as persuasively for the existence of an underdog effect. In this situation, just the opposite occurs. The candidate trailing in a pre-election poll may draw a sympathy vote, or the trailing candidate's workers may apply a little extra effort in the closing days to put the campaign over the top, while the candidate supposedly in the lead sits back, relaxes—and loses.

The Turnout Factor

Political polling is not without risk. Eventually, an election will be held, one candidate will win it, and somebody will compare the outcome of the election to the numbers in the last published poll. Such

Box 7-5

The *Boston Globe*'s Polling Policy

The better a poll happens to be—the more sensitive its instrumentation, the greater its accuracy and prestige—the more profound is its impact on the political races that the poll would monitor. Over the years, the *Globe*'s poll has been a good one and its impact has been pronounced—so pronounced that the poll has long been a source of practical concern for politicians and of ethical concern for the *Globe*.

The problem has not been the poll's accuracy, which has been consistently high; the problem, purely and simply, is the poll's effect: what it does to the political process it seeks to measure; the misconceptions it fosters about the *Globe*'s proper role.

Those twin concerns have led to soul searching within this institution and a decision, effective now, to suspend the traditional practice of measuring the candidates' relative standings prior to election day for publication.

The business of the newspaper is to observe society and to measure and record change as faithfully as possible. Polling can prove an invaluable tool in doing that. Polls, after all, can be and often are the pure stuff of news. They are scientific and objective and by their impersonal nature as credible as mathematics.

But poll results translate into more than just news stories. They can and they do alter the political reality at the precise moment they seek to reflect it.

The candidate caught well behind at the moment the pollster takes his measure finds himself trapped in that position. Sources of funding dry up.

Polls, for all the scientific safeguards, are not infallible. And while *Globe* surveys in the past have almost always proved accurate within the four-point margin of error, some projections have been wide of the mark, and some may have innocently influenced the election outcome.

Voters, assured by a poll they trust that a candidate they favor is certain of victory, may not bother to vote or may vote for someone else on the assumption that their vote will not influence the results. . . .

For these reasons the *Globe* will concentrate not on projecting outcomes but on isolating and explaining issues, while getting closer to the underlying attitudes that shape the public's choice of candidates.

Getting at those concerns is one way to make certain that candidates are addressing what is on the public's mind. It also affords a way to keep in touch with public sentiment without unseemly prying into what many voters hold as an intensely private matter—their preference for specific candidates.

Reprinted courtesy of The *Boston Globe*.

comparisons can build public confidence in opinion research, or these comparisons can plant seeds of doubt about the whole process.

When smart, honest journalists publish a poll, they tell their audience at the outset that they aren't claiming to make a prediction about how the election will turn out. For instance, the *Honolulu Advertiser* has used language such as this with its polling stories:

> Polls aren't perfect, but a carefully done poll can give a good idea of public opinion at the time it is taken. . . . No poll is a prediction of what will occur on election day. It is simply a reflection of voter attitudes at the time the poll was taken.

Nonetheless, most pollsters find it irresistible after an election to compare the outcome to their pre-election polls. Critics also are going to point out any significant discrepancy between the final poll and the actual election outcome. If there is a big gap, you, too, should wonder if anything went wrong because wide swings in opinion are unusual, even in the final days of a hard-fought campaign. By then, nearly everybody has made a decision and major switches don't seem to be common, although they do happen.

Of course, as we just mentioned above, there is another major factor besides voter switching and last-minute decisions that can throw a rather large monkey wrench into things—turnout. Only about half of the eligible population in the United States actually votes in a given election. What are some of the things that a pollster does to keep his or her sample of citizens as close as possible to the actual electorate who will cast ballots?

First, limit the poll interviews to registered voters. One way is to draw the sample from a list of registered voters. This may be hard to do or prohibitively expensive because the voter lists usually lack telephone numbers and, to conduct a telephone poll, the pollster needs a phone number for each name on the list. Thus, another common way to select a sample is to use a preliminary screening question—to ask people if they are registered. If they say no, the interviewer terminates the interview with a quick thank you.

Second, ask questions about respondent's level of interest or awareness of a campaign. In its election-year polls Gallup asks respondents how much thought they have given to the coming elections, whether they have ever voted in their precinct, how much interest they have in politics, how often they have voted in the past, and whether they plan to vote this year or not. People who score "high" on such questions are, according to a secret Gallup formula, assigned more weight in predicting election outcomes. Of course, it might be embarrassing to admit to an interviewer that you aren't following the campaign, couldn't care less who won, and wouldn't vote if they paid you. Because of the "social desirability" bias inherent in such questions, pollsters have tried to devise questions that make it as easy as possible for a respondent to admit to such "uncivic" behavior. Following are some samples:

Some people are registered to vote. Others either don't like to vote or haven't had a chance to register. Are you registered so that you could vote this year if you wanted to?

In asking people about elections, we often find that many people can't vote because they aren't registered or were sick or just didn't have the time. How about you, do you think you will vote in the election this November?

As you can see, this last question suggests that it is quite legitimate not to vote, that lots of people don't vote, that not voting isn't equivalent to social leprosy, and that you can safely admit to the interviewer that you don't plan to vote in November.

Making a correction for turnout is almost always necessary to bring your poll results in line with reality. In one election, the *Honolulu Advertiser*'s final poll of 1,197 voters in a hard-fought Democratic primary for governor came out this way:

> Frank Fasi 29%
> George Ariyoshi 28%
> Tom Gill 27%

There certainly is no clear picture of the election in this raw data. However, this poll also included three questions aimed at identifying the most likely voters:

Would you say you have been fairly interested in the campaign or not very interested?

Would you say that you personally care a good deal about who wins the election for governor or that you don't care very much?

Do you expect to vote . . . or do you think something might keep you from voting?

Results from these three questions made it apparent that the most likely voters on all three measures differed from the overall poll sample. For instance, among the 882 voters polled who said they planned to vote in the Democratic primary (74 percent of the sample), the race stacked up this way:

> George Ariyoshi 31%
> Tom Gill 30%
> Frank Fasi 29%

Among these most likely voters, Ariyoshi—not Fasi—was the leader, although still well within the poll's margin of error. This enabled the *Advertiser* to point out a week before election day that "the level of voter turnout may well be the determining factor in the Democratic contest for governor" and that Ariyoshi "seems to have the strongest support in precisely those groups most likely to turn out to vote." In the end, the turnout was 70 percent and the election outcome was as follows:

> George Ariyoshi . . . 35%
> Frank Fasi 30%
> Tom Gill 29%

It is particularly ironic that journalism's fascination with polling is so strongly wedded to the use of pre-election polls for horse-race coverage. To predict the winner of an election in advance from polling data, it is necessary to identify the likely voters. It is not an easy task, and there is considerable disagreement among professional pollsters about what kinds of questions best identify this segment of the public. Other aspects of an election deserve more attention.

Exit Polls

One facet of media polling that has been criticized in recent years is the exit poll popularized by the television networks' election-night coverage. To conduct an exit poll, interviewers are stationed on election day at a sample of precincts that have been selected to represent the city, county, or state whose voters are of interest. These interviewers ask a sample of voters—for example, every third or fifth or tenth person leaving the polls—about their actual vote and the reasons behind it. The results are tabulated throughout the day and used in two ways: (1) to forecast the vote outcome, sometimes even before the polls are closed; (2) to explain the trend in the vote in terms of which demographic groups are supporting each candidate and in terms of the issues and other reasons cited by voters as important in their ballot choice.

Use of exit polls to predict the outcome of an election a few hours before the actual count is announced has been attacked by critics who argue that this discourages people from voting. One version of the argument is that persons who had intended to vote for the loser are

A voter answers questions after casting her ballot in the 1996 presidential primary.

discouraged and stay home. Another version is that persons who had intended to vote for the winner see no need to vote and stay home. In both cases, goes the argument, the projected outcome for a top of the ballot race reduces the vote for other offices lower down on the ballot and might well affect their outcome. Despite the lack of empirical evidence to support these arguments, most TV news organizations now shy away from the use of exit-poll data to project the outcome before the polls close. However, the data often is used to project the outcome during the interval between the closing of the polls and the announcement of the vote count some hours later.

The most valuable aspect of the exit poll, however, is its data on the reasons that voters give for their choice of candidates. This is the only source of such data. Unlike the outcome of the election, which becomes available in a matter of time anyway, there is no other place to find out the reasons behind the vote or to find out the distribution of votes among various groups of voters.

Even public opinion polls conducted shortly after the election suffer two disadvantages compared to the exit poll. Over time, even very short periods of time, people forget many of the elements that influ

Reprinted with special permission of King Features Syndicate.

enced their vote. The best time to find out what influenced a decision at the polls is immediately after that decision has been made. However, the greatest advantage of the exit poll is that the interviewers are talking with *genuine* voters. All other polls on elections, both pre-election and post-election interviews, have to spend considerable time and effort to identify the pool of actual voters in the larger population sampled.

Nonpolitical Polls

Just because the election polls get the bulk of attention and criticism doesn't mean they are the only kind—or even the best kind—of survey research that news media can do. Surveys measuring opinions and attitudes about issues that never appear on any ballot but are of considerable public concern can, in the long run, be more useful. Sooner or later you find out who wins an election, but in the absence of good survey research, you may never get accurate readings on attitudes about abortion, the death penalty, or balancing the budget.

Box 7-6
A Lottery Survey

A survey of who plays the Texas Lottery rebuts the longstanding criticism that the game of chance disproportionately preys on poor people, state officials said Tuesday.

The study, mandated by lawmakers in 1991 and funded by the state, found few ethnic, age, income or educational differences between Texans who buy lottery tickets and Texans who don't.

But the survey was criticized by a lottery opponent, who said it did not identify the "heavy" lottery players and glossed over the argument that lower-income players use money needed for food, rent and other essentials to buy lottery tickets.

The poll of 1,500 adults found that about two of every three Texans have bought a lottery ticket and that more men (68 percent) than women (59 percent) play.

Perhaps more important, however, is what the survey did not find: It disputed the conception that minority and lower-income Texans are more likely to buy lottery tickets, which cost $1.

The survey determined that similar percentages of blacks, Hispanics, non-Hispanic whites and Asian Americans play the lottery and that middle-income Texans are more likely than low- or high-income people to play.

Excerpted from David Elliot, "Survey: Lottery Doesn't Lure Poor,"
Austin American-Statesman, March 10, 1993.
Reprinted by permission of the *Austin American-Statesman.*

Here are some examples of newsworthy topics that probably would not have surfaced in routine election coverage but that news media examined using survey research:

- Minnesotans complain a lot about public education, but they still say schools these days are at least as good as the ones they attended. Many even say today's schools are better.
- The Iowa Poll shows a landslide conviction in the state that [credit cards] are bad for the economy because people buy things with them that they can't afford.
- The people of Los Angeles are preoccupied with crime—much more so than people in the rest of the country. They have an inordinate fear of it that cuts across socioeconomic boundaries. And they count it as the city's number-one problem. Ironically, relatively few have been touched by it.

- No amount of prodding by the Greater Richmond Transit Co. can pull many of its nonriders from their cars, a *Times-Dispatch* opinion poll has shown.
- Hawaii's public school teachers think they're doing a pretty good job. They give the public schools a B- grade . . . . The state's high school students don't think quite so highly of their education. They give it a C+. . . . Least pleased are the parents, who give Hawaii public education just above the average grade of C.
- New York State voters consider themselves overtaxed, but appear unwilling to reduce taxes sharply if such cuts would reduce the level of services provided by state government, according to a *New York Times* poll.

Each of the above poll questions explores a topic that is of considerable public concern. These are imminently newsworthy topics, yet there is little chance that they will surface in routine election coverage or even in election polls. To repeat, polling on these kinds of questions provides news coverage that is seldom available anywhere else.

Most of these topics are enduring concerns of the public that can be reported in many news stories over time. A series of polls repeating the same basic question can monitor shifts in public opinion, and follow-up questions about perceived causes and proposed solutions can monitor the maturation of public opinion. Informed, well-thought-out views on public issues do not instantly spring into existence. Individual views and public consensus evolve over time, and good journalism can report this evolution through public opinion polling. Tables and graphics help to make masses of numbers more understandable to your audience. Use the tables and graphics for the specific numbers from surveys, the story for the analysis and explanation. Don't crowd number after number through your story text (see box 7-7 for an example of how the *Wilkes-Barre Times Leader* displayed one number-filled set of findings to help their readers grasp them).

When to Publish a Poll

For news stories based on surveys—whether conducted by political candidates, commercial researchers, or the mass media—news organizations should use a "truth-in-polling" disclosure procedure to ensure that everyone, both the organization and its audience, knows how the pollster came to his or her conclusions. Did a political candidate pay for the poll that shows him or her ahead by 15 percent?

Did his or her own supporters make the phone calls, or were sample ballots passed out at one of his or her own campaign rallies? It obviously makes a difference. Polls, like people and the weather, are sometimes good and sometimes bad.

Box 7-7

"What Are the Most Important Issues Local Government Must Deal With?"

Most Important Issue	*Last Year*	*This Year*
Unemployment/jobs	37%	29%
Water problems	0%	10%
High taxes/inequitable taxes	16%	8%
Bad roads/potholes	3%	5%
Attracting new industries	1%	4%
Crime/personal security	4%	3%
Quality of children's education	4%	3%
Hunger/poverty/welfare	2%	3%
Better government response to problems	0%	2%
General economic condition	6%	1%
Youth drinking/drugs	3%	1%
Lack of recreational facilities for youth	0%	1%
Senior citizens' problems	2%	1%
School strikes	2%	1%
Cost of living	1%	1%
rash/garbage problems	0%	1%
Urban renewal/rebuilding	0%	1%
Lack of adequate housing	0%	1%
Repealing commissioners' pay raise	0%	1%
Snow removal	0%	1%
Health care/health-care costs	1%	0%
Other government services	3%	1%
All other responses	4%	1%
Can't think of any local issues	0%	7%
(587 interviewed)		

Courtesy *Wilkes-Barre Times Leader*

Box 7-8

Poll Information

When you publish findings of a survey, you owe it to your audience to give them full information on how and when it was conducted, plus details of the margin of sampling error. Here's how the *Wilkes-Barre Times Leader* in Pennsylvania handles such information in print:

Survey area: The 11th U.S. Congressional District, including all of Luzerne, Columbia, Montour, and Sullivan Counties, plus parts of Carbon, Monroe, and Northumberland Counties.

Survey population: Registered Democrats who said they will certainly/ probably vote in the April 10th Democratic Primary.

Number of interviews: 425, including 277 in the Wyoming Valley, drawn in proportion to turnout for the 1982 Democratic Congressional Primary.

Interviewing method: Telephone interviews from households selected using a scientific random probability sampling.

Conducted by: Nine interviewers thoroughly trained and briefed for this project.

Dates conducted: Evenings from Monday, March 26 through Friday, March 30.

Planned and supervised by: Dr. Gary R. Kromer, the *Times Leader*'s Director of Research, a veteran of more than 100 public opinion polls, including over 20 political polls.

Margin of error: Sampling error for 425 interviews is 4.8 percent at the 95 percent confidence level. In other words, were this survey to be conducted in the same manner 100 times, the results of 95 of them would be as reported here, plus or minus 4.8 percent. Other procedures, such as call-backs, were employed to minimize nonsampling error.

Courtesy *Wilkes-Barre Times Leader*

Some polls are "bad" and should be ignored because the people who conducted them simply didn't know how to conduct accurate survey research. In the worst case scenario, a poll is "bad" because the sponsor has consciously slanted the poll to produce a desired result. Only if the pollster provides complete information about how a poll was conducted can a reporter or editor or voter decide whether the announced results are credible. With full disclosure, you can weed out most of the bad polls. If a pollster doesn't use sound techniques or is unwilling to reveal, in full, the details of his or her methods, you should decline to print or broadcast the results of that poll.

Here are some guidelines that you can use in determining whether to publish or broadcast poll results. These guidelines will help ensure that your audience has a better chance of not being misled. These guidelines will get you started, and the next chapter will provide additional background on the art and science of good polling.

- Who was interviewed? Is the poll supposed to be representative of all adults in the United States, in one state, or in one city or congressional district? Does the poll represent all adults, just those who are registered voters or, perhaps, just those who say they "intend to vote" in the next election?
- How big was the poll's sample and how was it obtained? Were households identified from comprehensive census or planning-agency maps, from names drawn from a phone book, from a registered voter list, or from the city directory? Or did the interviewer stand in a shopping mall and question every eighth passerby?
- Who paid for the poll? What interest do they have in its outcome? Did they find what they wanted to find because of the way the poll was organized?
- Who did the actual interviewing? Employees of a full-time, professional company? Part-time help from students working on a class project? Political campaign volunteers?
- How were the respondents contacted? By telephone? By door-to-door personal interview? By mailed questionnaires?
- Exactly when was the interviewing done? Did any major news events occur just before or during the time of the interviewing that might have influenced the way people answered the questions?
- What was the exact wording of all the questions? Could the wording have influenced the way people responded?
- Were any special statistical procedures used to "weight" interviews, or to allocate undecideds? If so, what is the rationale for these special procedures?

How many persons actually answered each question? Be suspicious of any reported poll result that adds up to 100 percent but includes no undecideds or don't knows. It's hard to think of a question that won't get a refusal or don't know from somebody, and the pollster ought to tell you how many there are. A large number of nonrespondents also tells you something important, sometimes about the question and other times about the topic.

Is the pollster claiming more precision for the results than is legitimate? Polls aren't really accurate enough to justify reporting percentages down to decimal points. Since most polls have a margin of error of three to five percentage points, the reporting of results down to a tenth of a percentage point is pseudo-precision.

A Final Caution

Even when a poll measures up on all the points in the guidelines, don't embrace poll results to the exclusion of other information. Polls are very good at detecting the direction and general distribution of opinion, but not so good at measuring the intensity of opinion. A reporter who senses a lack of commitment in people's opinions should add that information to his or her reporting. Polls are a precision tool for gathering information, but they are just one of the tools for finding out about your community. A glance at the table of contents of this book will reinforce that point.

References

Adams, R. C. *Social Survey Methods for Mass Media Research*. Hillsdale, NJ: Lawrence Erlbaum Associates, 1989.

Babbie, Earl. *The Practice of Social Research*, 6th ed. Belmont, CA: Wadsworth Publishing, 1992.

Barton, Allen J. "Asking the Embarrassing Question." *Public Opinion Quarterly*, 20, no. 1 (Spring 1958): 67.

Gawiser, S. R. and G. Evans Witt. *Twenty Questions A Journalist Should Ask About Poll Results*. New York: National Council on Public Polls. Undated.

Lavrakas, P. J. and Jack Holley, eds. *Polling and Presidential Election Coverage*. Newbury Park, CA: Sage Publications, 1991.

Merritt, Davis. *Public Journalism and Public Life: Why Telling the News Is Not Enough*. Hillsdale, NJ: Lawrence Erlbaum Associates, 1995.

Payne, Stanley. *The Art of Asking Questions*. Princeton: Princeton University Press, 1951.

Schuman, Howard, and Stanley Presser. *Questions and Answers in Attitude Surveys: Experiments on Question Form, Wording and Context*. New York: Academic Press, 1981.

Watt, J. H. and S. A. van den Berg. *Research Methods for Communication Science*. Boston: Allyn and Bacon, 1995.

Yankelovich, Daniel. *Coming to Public Judgment: Making Democracy Work in a Complex World*. Syracuse: Syracuse University Press, 1991.

Chapter Eight

GOOD AND BAD SURVEYS

One often hears that there are "lies, damned lies, and statistics."
It is a foolish saying.

—Columnist James J. Kilpatrick

In a public opinion poll, the 95 percent "confidence level" is determined by this formula:

$$\pm 1.96 \sqrt{\frac{.25}{n}}$$

and n simply means the actual number of people you talked to.

Does this formula make you nervous? Unfortunately, many people in journalism do become pale and shaky when confronted by numbers. But don't panic—that's the last formula you'll see in this chapter. Nevertheless, there is no escaping the fact that a considerable amount of mathematics underlies the practice of sampling in survey research and polling. The math details the theory on which sampling practice is based. Without this theory, there is no way to tell how much confidence you should have in a news story that you base on a particular set of numbers that originated in a selected sample of people, documents, or anything else.

There is no rule that says journalists who use numbers need to pass Statistics 898 with flying colors or to know how to compute a chi-square statistic on a calculator. In fact, most reporters will never conduct a public opinion survey or draw a sample on their own. That job is usually left to the professional researchers. As a journalist, however, you will frequently be faced with the task of evaluating the work of pollsters. It will be your job to decide how much faith to put in the results and how to report them, if you decide to report them at all. A large proportion of the polls that are made available to journalists should be filed in the wastepaper basket, not in the daily news report. This chapter will explain, briefly, the theory that underlies all polls, and some of the details of the actual research methodology that will help you ask the right questions in deciding which polls to report. These guidelines also will help you get the most out of the legitimate polls that come your way.

You do need to know that sampling theory provides a sound mathematical basis that allows Gallup and dozens of other pollsters time and again to assess what the country thinks by interviewing no more than 1,500 randomly selected Americans. Despite the mathematics involved, the outlines of this theory follow common sense.

The Basics of Taking a Sample

In order to understand sampling theory, begin with the premise that you want to know something about the world—how many faulty widgets are produced by a particular factory, the number of red gumdrops in a candy machine, how many arrested drunk drivers lose their licenses, the split between supporters of Democratic and Republican candidates in an election, or the proportion of people in the United States who are unemployed.

One obvious way of finding any of this information is to count every item. That is called taking a *census*. Once every decade the United States Census Bureau attempts to do just that—to count every person in the United States. To conduct the decennial census, the federal government must open hundreds of offices around the country, hire hundreds of thousands of temporary employees, and spend more than a billion dollars. This is not a lot of money for the federal government to spend these days, but it is far more money than any newsroom will ever have to spend covering a story. Most often, a census is impossible or, at least, very impractical. Even the people at the United States Census Bureau do not claim to have counted every person in the United States during the 1990 census. They admit to an undercount of several percent for the total population, and the undercount is far greater among minority groups.

Box 8-1

The Art Poll

Polls can be done on any subject and any aspect of people's lives. Polls don't always have to be about politics or political issues. Back in 1994 *The Nation* reported a national survey about how Americans feel about art.

The poll began with simple questions, such as a person's favorite color. Blue is by far America's favorite color, and it is especially popular with people in their 40s (49 percent), who are conservative (47 percent), male (45 percent), and don't go to museums at all (50 percent). The appeal of blue decreases with education, while the appeal of red increases with education.

In terms of artistic activity for leisure or recreation, Hispanics paint, draw, or do graphic arts the most: 44 percent compared to 26 percent of blacks and 23 percent of whites.

There is considerable consensus in people's reactions to art. Large majorities agreed that "a work of art can be beautiful even if it doesn't look like anything you see in the real world" (82 percent) and that "art should be relaxing to look at, not all jumbled up and confusing" (77 percent).

Artists with a wide range of style have made a favorable impression on the American public. Receiving substantial favorable or very favorable ratings were Pablo Picasso (65 percent), Normal Rockwell (81 percent), Claude Monet (57 percent), and Rembrandt (78 percent). Largely unknown to many Americans are Jackson Pollock (49 percent), Georgia O'Keeffe (39 percent), and Salvador Dali (31 percent).

Andy Warhol received the most widely divergent ratings in the survey. While 33 percent had a favorable or very favorable impression, another 33 percent had an unfavorable or very unfavorable impression, and 18 percent had never heard of him. The remaining 16 percent did not answer the survey question.

What do you do with results like this? *The Nation* commissioned a cover for its March 14, 1994, issue that was based on Komar & Melamid's interpretation of American majority opinion.

In many ways, a *sample* can be better than a census. Data gathered by sampling can be, and generally are, more accurate than data gathered by taking a census because it is possible to invest more time, effort, and money in each unit in a sample survey. Interviewing only a sample of some of the population rather than everyone in the population permits more effort on callbacks—the follow-up attempts to obtain an interview when nobody was home the first time or the interview was refused on first contact. This opportunity for more callbacks increases the possibility of including those hard-to-contact persons who frequently slip through the net of a census and its effort at total enumeration. Furthermore, it is possible to use fewer, and therefore more capable and highly trained personnel for the interviews, which improves the quality of information gathered from each person.

Three factors—time, money, and practicality—often require that researchers and journalists focus on a typical slice of reality to count, measure, or analyze. Generalizations are made from that sample to the larger population that is of interest. The process of obtaining this typical slice of a particular population is based on a fairly simple idea called sampling. What sampling and probability theory say, in essence, is that if you take a typical piece of a large pie and taste it, the result is likely to be representative of the entire pie. When a cook wonders if his or her soup has enough salt, it isn't necessary to eat it all to find out. Just stir it and taste a spoonful—a sample.

If you have a jar filled with 200,000 marbles and want to know how many are black and how many are white, you could find out exactly by counting them all. But if you just need a very close approximation, you could sample the marbles by mixing them well, picking out, say, 500, and counting that sample. The proportion of black and white marbles in this sample would come very close to representing the actual mix. In fact, there are statistical formulas to tell you precisely how often it is that you are within 1 percent or 5 percent of the exact total.

If probability theory didn't work, there would be no gambling casinos. Odds and payoffs on throws of the dice or spins of the wheel or turns of the card are figured on the basis of statistical probability. Probability theory admits there is no way of knowing whether the next coin flip will be heads or tails. However, it does say you can be fairly certain that out of 500 flips of a fair coin, you'll get about 250 heads. If you and a friend both throw a fair set of dice 1,000 times, it is likely you will both have about the same number of 7s—and, furthermore, the number of 7s can be predicted rather accurately.

Public opinion polling applies the same sort of rules to human populations. Let's say that the United States actually is made up of 50 percent Republican voters and 50 percent Democratic voters, but you don't know that in advance. In order to find out, you decide to survey a sample of voters in order to estimate the proportion of Republicans and Democrats. Because people aren't as predictable as chicken soup, you wouldn't want to take just one or even a few spoonfuls of opinion. But let's say you draw your sample of voters carefully so that every voter in the United States has an equal chance to be contacted. Then you interview several hundred voters.

When are you justified in making generalizations about 100 million American voters based on what you find in your sample of several hundred? You are only justified if, first of all, you picked the sample in one of the tested, generally accepted ways that ensures your sample is typical of American voters. But, even if you use a sound sampling method, will your estimate come out right on the nose as 50 percent Democrats and 50 percent Republicans? Probably not. (There's even a statistical formula that will tell you how likely an exact 50–50 split is.) The odds are very heavy, however, that you'll get a 51–49 or 52–48 count one way or the other, and this would lead you to conclude that, at the time the poll was taken, the split was nearly even.

No reputable pollster claims perfect accuracy. That's why journalists need to explain in every story about a poll that a margin of error exists. (There is a formula for calculating that, too.) For instance, you would say there is only a slight chance that the outcome varies by more than about five percentage points from what you'd get if you had enough time, money, and interviewers to ask every voter the same questions you asked your sample of 500.

Bias and Sampling

A systematic tendency to exclude some kinds of people from a sample—poor people, minorities, or farmers, for example—is called bias. If bias is present in a sampling procedure, you lose the ability to generalize from the sample to the population. Furthermore, when a sample selection procedure has a bias built into it, you can't overcome it by taking bigger and bigger samples. That only produces large-scale bias. For a sample to be valid, it must be selected to allow everybody an equal chance of being represented in the sample. That is very important to remember!

A second source of bias comes from nonresponse. The people who cannot be reached or who decline to take part in a poll are likely to be different from the people successfully interviewed. You can be sure they are different in one way: they were not home when they were called or they turned down the interviewer. The same principle applies to any sample of documents—for example, court records. If you cannot obtain part of the court files, you cannot know if the ones you didn't sample are different from the ones you did sample.

Any time you introduce an element of human choice into the selection of a sample, you bring into play yet another source of bias. For instance, if you tell an interviewer to choose 20 men and 20 women to interview (this is called quota sampling) the interviewer (subconsciously) will be apt to pick people who are easier to access, who look like they will be cooperative and easy to talk to—but, obviously, who may not be typical of anything in particular. Most often, given the choice, people tend to interview others who are like themselves because they feel comfortable doing it. That makes for comfortable interviewers but bad samples.

To avoid this kind of bias, a survey should use some variation of random sampling, in which the choice of whom to interview is dictated by random numbers and chance, not by any person. This can be done by assigning each person in a population a number, then picking numbers at random. Or, most typically for national public opinion surveys, it is done by picking geographic areas at random, then working down randomly, stage by stage, from county to town to precinct or census tract to block until a particular household and a particular resident in it are chosen—again, purely by a numerical formula that allows the interviewer no choice. Selection of those to be interviewed is made purely by chance factors, by using a modern computerized version of coin flips or dice throws. Chance is impartial. It has no bias for rich or poor, black or white, Republican or Democrat. In a true random sample every member of the population has an equal chance of being drawn.

Types of Surveys

Four types of surveys are commonly used these days, each with its advantages and disadvantages.

Voluntary Response

Clip out this coupon in your Thursday *Daily Bugle* and tell us whether you favor or oppose a new nuclear power plant for West Flats.

> To voice your opinion about violence on television, call Channel 99 before 10 o'clock tonight. Call 555–1111 if you think there is too much violence on TV. Call 555–2222 if you think there is not too much violence on TV.

These are the cheapest ways to run a poll: there are no interviewers to pay, no questionnaires to print, no mailing expenses. Also, there are no meaningful results. If you get a valid sample from surveys like these, it can be chalked up to pure luck.

When columnist Ann Landers asked her readers, "If you had it to do over again, would you have children?", 70 percent of those who responded answered "No." Some readers fretted about what this attitude might mean for the future of America, so the Long Island newspaper *Newsday* put the question to a representative nationwide sample of 1,373 parents. Of these, 91 percent said "Yes, I would have kids if I could do it over again."

What happened? Apparently, the people who had "had it up to here" with their kids were the ones most motivated to write to Ann Landers and complain. In any event, the avalanche of letters to Landers apparently came nowhere close to approximating the mood of American parents.

Undaunted, Landers went back into the survey business again with the now-infamous question about whether women "would be content to be held close and treated tenderly and forget about 'The Act.'" Of her 90,000 responses, 72 percent voted for cuddling. The Landers column got a lot of news coverage and chuckles. However, it turns out that we need not fear for the future of the human race. More scientific surveys found sex to be a lot more popular among American women in general than among Landers's 90,000 respondents.

Another name for voluntary-response samples such as the ones by Landers is self-selected sample. Whenever you give people the opportunity to include or exclude themselves, the sample is no longer random. Instead, it is made up of the people most motivated on whatever issue is involved. You get the zealots on either end of the spectrum— the people who are staunchly for or against the issue in question. As one man pointed out to a *Washington Post* reporter: "When people don't have a problem, they won't write or complain to Ann Landers."

A common failing of the news media is to generalize too much from people who self-select themselves into a news story by showing up at a public hearing. The fact that 19 out of 20 witnesses at the council hearing oppose construction of the new high school doesn't mean that the community as a whole is 95 percent opposed to it. Although it is possible, of course, that these numbers represent the true breakdown of opinion, it is more likely that the antischoolers are just more vehement and better organized.

Mail

A mail survey can be a full census, as when a member of Congress sends a questionnaire to each resident of his or her district, or it can be a survey of a smaller sample of any population. Although this method is a little more expensive than a self-selected sample, because it requires printing questionnaires and paying postage, you avoid having to hire, train, supervise, and pay interviewers. However, response rates for mail surveys often run as low as 10 to 25 percent, meaning you again have a self-selected sample problem, and the people who choose to respond may be very atypical.

Besides the problem of bias due to the differences between respondents and nonrespondents, a mail surveyor also has the problem of losing control of the interview once the questionnaire is mailed out. Who in the household is actually filling out the answers? Has the respondent really understood the questions? Will the respondent answer each question, skipping none?

Mail surveys can be successfully used in some cases, but boosting the response rate to a respectable level comparable to what telephone or in-person surveys obtain is challenging. You must plan for at least a second wave of mailings, and perhaps more, to encourage respondents who didn't respond the first time or failed to get the first letter. These follow-up waves must be handled with care. If you tell people their responses will be confidential, how do you figure out who has not responded and contact them again without identifying those who have responded? This can be done with an envelope code. At any rate, you should be aware that mail surveys always involve more than a single trip to the post office to send out the letters, followed by an avalanche of immediate, thorough replies.

There are exceptions. If a newspaper mails questionnaires to elected officials or candidates and promises (threatens?) to print the replies or to publicize the lack of them, the response rate may not be bad. Politicians are motivated by a desire to avoid bad publicity. The *Honolulu Advertiser* once mailed issue-related questionnaires to 148 candidates for the Hawaii legislature and got back 80 percent of them—an excellent response rate.

If you do settle on a mail survey, there are a number of ways to improve the response rate:

- Keep the questionnaire short—as few as three to five questions, if possible.
- Make questionnaires visually pleasing, simple in format.
- Make instructions clear and concise.
- Use large type to help those with poor vision.
- Sweeten the pot a little. One researcher doubled his response rate by including a quarter with the mailing. Of course, inflation has upped the ante since then. Try offering a trial newspaper subscription or a small gift certificate.
- Time mailings to arrive in the home just before a weekend, when respondents might have more time complete them.

In the end, consider this advice from sociologist Delbert C. Miller:

> Every researcher who chooses the mail questionnaire should consider himself as a seller in a highly competitive environment in which the majority of respondents will probably not complete and return his questionnaire.

Telephone

This is perhaps the most common type of survey. It costs more than voluntary response or mail surveys but has a better chance of reaching a sample that gives you results you can believe. About 95 percent of the households in the United States now have phones, so you don't run into the same problem the editors of the *Literary Digest* had in 1936, in the middle of the Depression.

Pollsters like to use a room with many phones, so the interviewers can be supervised while they make their calls. It is much more difficult for an interviewer to "fake" an interview when a supervisor is watching in the same room or perhaps even listening in on an extension. Quality control is easiest in this situation.

Some phone-sampling methods disenfranchise people with unlisted phone numbers. Typically, at least 10 to 20 percent of the residential phone numbers in most urbanized areas of the country are unlisted, with the figure surpassing 25 percent or more in large cities such as New York and Chicago. In all areas, the number of unlisted phones is climbing, not dropping.

Unlisted numbers won't be included in your sample if you just pick numbers from the phone book. One alternative is to start with the phone book and apply some easy mathematical correction. For example, add 2 to the last digit of each number in your sample from the phone directory. This procedure will yield a lot of nonworking numbers and therefore will take longer, but this method also ensures that unlisted numbers will be called in proportion to their share of existing telephones. Software for random-digit dialing used by professional survey firms does much of this chore automatically. It will even eliminate phone number ranges not used by the local phone company and many, if not all, nonresidential numbers. There also is software that can make provision for eliminating the phone numbers of persons who have been called in the past and threatened a lawsuit if they were called again.

Box 8-2
How to Draw a Survey Sample from the Phone Book

1. Determine the sample size. For this example, the goal is a completed set of 250 interviews. The text of this chapter discusses the factors involved in determining the size of a sample.

2. Oversample. You can't expect to complete 250 calls with just 250 phone numbers. Design the sample to produce about twice as many phone numbers as you need, because there will be many not-at-homes, refusals, or disconnected numbers. In this example, our goal will be about 500 phone numbers.

3. Go to the phone book and determine how many white pages with residential listings are in the directory. In the current Austin, Texas, phone book, for example, there are 687 residence pages. If you select one name from two of every three pages, the result will be a sample of 448 phone numbers, close enough to the target of 500. To keep the selection of pages entirely random, select a number between 1 and 3 as the page to be skipped as you work through the phone directory. Placing my finger at random on a phone book page, I hit the number 1. So for this sample, we will skip page 1, draw one number from each of the next two pages, skip another page, draw one number from each of the next two pages, and so forth. After we have proceeded through the entire phone directory in this fashion, the result will be 448 names from 448 different pages.

4. Randomly determine the location of the name from each page. In the Austin directory the pages have four columns of names each. Again, select a number at random from the phone directory, this time between the numbers 1 and 4. Let's say we pick out a 2, so we'll use the second column on each page. Now measure the

depth of each page with a ruler. In our example, there are 10 and one-quarter inches of names in each column. Once again select a number at random from the phone directory, this time 0 through 10. If you pick 6, for example, that means that the name selected on each page will be the one closest to the 6-inch mark in the second column.

5. At this point, two-thirds of the pages in the phone directory have been designated as sample pages; and the designated location on the page is the name in the second column that is on the line closest to the 6-inch mark. In the end, you will have 448 randomly selected phone numbers.

6. The 448 numbers will all be listed telephones, whereas a number of the people in any area have unlisted numbers. Most surveys try to reach them, too, on the assumption that those who have their numbers listed may be very different from those who don't. To include unlisted numbers in the sample, begin with your 448 listed numbers and apply some numerical correction—add two to the last digit of each number, for instance. Again, a number was selected at random, in this case a number between 0 and 9. Instead of 555–3846, you get 555–3848. This allows you to reach unlisted numbers as well. Of course, if you do this it also will mean that the phone interviewers will reach a large number of nonworking numbers and will need considerably more than 448 numbers to wind up with 250 completed phone calls. Perhaps as many as 1,000 or 1,500 numbers will be required—two or three per phone book page.

In-Person Interviews

In this kind of survey, interviewers are sent to each predetermined address in the sample to ring the bell and conduct the interview. As you might guess, this is the most expensive method. It takes interviewers more time to travel around an area even if, as is common, clusters of three or five or ten interviews are planned on a single block or a single street to reduce travel time. Traditionally, this has been the method of choice for the best surveys. Response rate usually is higher because potential respondents find it more difficult to turn away an interviewer on their front step than they do to throw away a mailed questionnaire or to hang up on a stranger calling on the telephone.

By the 1980s, however, there was considerable debate among pollsters and survey researchers over telephone versus in-person interviews. Door-to-door interviewing has suffered because of a fear of crime (people now are less willing to open their doors to a stranger) and because of the increasing numbers of people in apartments or condominiums with tight security where it is impossible for interviewers to get past the lobby. Those factors, coupled with the loss of control inherent in having the interviewers out of sight and hearing of their supervisors, have resulted in a major shift to telephone interviewing.

Also, if nobody is home the first time you try in a telephone poll, you can easily call back in an hour or the next night. With door-to-door surveys, it costs time and money to visit someone's home a second or third time for callbacks, and callbacks must be a part of any sample design to assure its randomness. Contacting only those people who happen to be home when you first call can produce highly questionable results. People who are frequently at home differ from those who are not. What kinds of persons are you most likely to find at home on your first contact?

One advantage of in-person interviews is that they do offer an opportunity to present visual or written information to the respondent. Respondents can be asked to react to pictures or lists or graphic formats. They can be handed a written copy of a complex answer scale, allowing you to ask more complicated questions than are possible over the telephone. In pre-election political surveys, pollsters get fewer "undecideds" on a question asking "Who would you vote for?" if they give each respondent a "sample ballot," a card, or a sheet of paper to fill out and then place in a sealed envelope or ballot box. For some reason, fewer people object to revealing their vote intentions in this way, even though eventually the interviewer will go back to the car, open the envelope, and match up the "sample ballot" with the rest of the questionnaire.

Randomness of the Sample

The way in which the sample is constructed is a crucial part of survey design. The goal, of course, is to be able to generalize from a small sample of 250 or 500 or 1,500 to the larger population in which you are interested—whether it is all the adults in America or all the voters in your city or all the twelfth-graders in the local public school system. The fact that you can generalize at all from a poll is demonstrated by the preceding brief description of the statistical theory of sampling. However, all the statistical formulas depend on the key assumption that you have, at the beginning, chosen a random sample.

There are many ways to construct a sample that approximates randomness. A key requirement for all of them is that every person in the population (Americans, local voters, twelfth-graders) has an equal chance—or at least a known chance—of being selected for the survey sample. Although it is almost impossible to achieve perfect randomness when you are sampling people, certain techniques will help get closer to it. For instance, as mentioned previously with a sample from a telephone book, some percentage of people with phones have unlisted numbers and will be missed unless the pollster corrects for it as described in box 8-2.

Neither telephone nor personal interviewers can limit their contacts to normal weekday working hours because they will get too many retirees, housewives, and unemployed people and too few full-time workers. They must work evenings and weekends. Also, you can't cluster your interviews in one small geographical section of the city or take all your names from a few pages of the phone book and then claim that your poll is able to generalize to the citywide population. The interviews must be spread around.

What about door-to-door polls? How can a pollster assemble a list of all the doors on which he or she might possibly knock, so that a decision can be made about exactly which doors to approach? Sources might include city property tax listings, city zoning maps, or public utility lists of houses that have electric service. Any source that gives a reasonably up-to-date listing of the universe to be examined may be used as a sampling frame.

Size of the Sample

Once a sampling frame is assembled in this way, how many people should be questioned in the survey? There is no fixed answer to this question. The size of the sample will be dictated by the amount of money and time available to do the survey and by how much precision is needed in the final results.

A pollster willing to accept results likely to be within 5 percentage points of the "true" value in the overall population can draw a sample of about 400 of that population. If the pollster insists on being closer, he or she must talk to more people. Gallup, Harris, and the other national polls generally use samples of about 1,500 persons. With a sample that large they can be fairly certain that the results are within 2.5 percentage points of reality—based on sample size alone.

For polls of a city or a state, a more common sample size is 400 to 600 persons (or voters if it's an election-related survey). As box 8-3 shows, a sample of 400 yields a margin of error of about five percentage points. A sample of 600 reduces the margin to four points. It gets tougher to lower the margin after that. You have to go beyond 1,000 to get down to a three-point margin of error.

Sampling error merely refers to the variability inherent in the fact that in a poll you have a slice of reality (a sample) instead of the whole reality (a census of a population). For instance, if you flip a "fair" coin an infinite number of times, you'll get half heads and half tails. If you flip it only 10 times, you may well get a 6–4 or 7–3 split, or even, on occasion, 10 heads and no tails. There are statistical formulas that tell you, with a sample of a certain size, that your answer is almost certain to be within X percentage points of the true value you would get in that infinite series of flips. The same holds true when sampling people. A sample almost surely will be off by a little by the mere fact that it is a sample. Although it is unlikely that any sample will hit the exact value in the population right on the nose, the formula for sampling error allows you to say, in effect, "I may not be right on the target, but I know that 95 percent of the time a sample this big will give me an answer within X percent of the true population value."

The formulas for random sampling tell you how much error you might expect in a sample of given size just from the problems inherent in sampling itself. There are other sources of error besides the sample itself, however, and these can be even more troubling because there are no statistical formulas for estimating the size of their effect. The most common source of error is from nonresponse—people who fall within the sample but cannot be interviewed (they don't answer their phone or aren't home when an interviewer calls) or refuse to participate. That is why it is important to know the nonresponse or refusal rate when you evaluate the results of any survey. If the refusal rate exceeds 35 percent of those contacted, you should be cautious in your use of that data. Other sources of nonsampling error include everything else that can possibly go wrong, other than the sample itself—for example, interviewers can skip a question by mistake or

Box 8-3
Sampling Error at the 95 Percent Level of Confidence for Samples of Various Sizes

Here's how to interpret the figures in the table below: Let's say you have a sample of 400, which is not atypical for a citywide or statewide poll. The table lists the sample error as 4.9 percent "at the 95 percent level of confidence." What does that really mean? It means that if you have a random sample of 400 persons, you can be 95 percent sure that the figures in your poll are not "off" from the true figures in the whole population by more than 4.9 percentage points.

Sample Size	Sampling Error*
50	13.9%
100	9.8%
150	8.0%
200	6.9%
250	6.2%
300	5.6%
350	5.2%
400	4.9%
450	4.6%
500	4.4%
550	4.2%
600	4.0%
650	3.8%
700	3.7%
750	3.6%
800	3.5%
850	3.4%
900	3.3%
1,000	3.2%
1,500	3.1%
2,000	2.5%
2,500	2.2%
3,000	1.8%

*Assumes simple random sampling

How would you explain the sampling error to your readers? What follows is some suggested language to put at the bottom of a poll story. For a broadcast news story, a condensed version should convey some of the same key facts:

Because the results of this poll are based on a sample, they may differ slightly from the results we would get from a complete census—that is, if we contacted all the adults in the state and asked them the same questions. The extent of possible error in a sample survey can be estimated by statistical formulas. In a sample of 400 persons, one can say with 95 percent certainty that the results are within plus or minus 5 percentage points [you can safely round the 4.9 off to 5 in this case] of what they would be if the entire population had been polled. Any survey also can have "nonsampling" error caused by such factors as people who decline to participate in the poll or who cannot be reached.

record an answer in the wrong column; interviewers can be biased; answers can be punched into a computer incorrectly. Minimizing all these sources of error requires careful planning and double- and triple-checking of the responses.

How much do nonsampling error (e.g., nonresponse) and variations in sample design (e.g., clusters) add to the margin of error? Unfortunately, there is no formula for calculating this. One way of making an instant check on the bias introduced by nonresponse or other factors is to compare your sample with known information about the population. If half the city's registered voters are female, half the sample (or very close to it) should be female. If 15 percent of the residents are of Hispanic origin, about 15 percent of your sample should be, too. If a poll is far too high or too low on demographic factors such as age, income, or education, you as a journalist need to know this beforehand. One way to correct for such imbalances in a sample is by weighting the responses to bring the sample back in line with the population. Thus, if a poll has too few women in the sample, the responses of those you do have can be adjusted statistically to count more than do the responses from men.

Most reporters don't get involved in the mechanics of weighting. It is normally done by computer. However, you should be aware that weighting is sometimes needed, and you should always ask whether it was done and how far "off" the sample was prior to weighting. Too big a difference between sample and population should cause you to question the poll's procedures.

Who Does the Polling?

If a newspaper or TV station wants to do its own public opinion survey, who will do the work? Here are the choices, in descending order of cost and ease:

1. ***Contract the work out to a professional survey firm.*** These firms are experienced in drawing samples, drafting questionnaires, coding data once they are obtained, churning out tables from a computer, and analyzing what it all means. They also keep stables of regular interviewers who are trained in proper techniques and who, because of their experience, are better than raw recruits. Professional survey firms double-check the work of interviewers afterward to assure high quality. This is called verification.

   Costs will vary from city to city and from survey to survey because of such factors as size of sample, geographic breadth of the population (polling in a city costs less than statewide polling, which in turn costs less than a national sample), type of survey (telephone costs less than door-to-door; cluster sampling in which you do three to five door-to-door interviews on one block costs less than simple random sampling with a single interview at each sampling point), and turnaround time (news media generally want the results fast, which may mean overtime for the survey firm).

   Before a firm is hired, a news organization should talk to other clients of the firm to see if they have been satisfied. Costs are high, so negotiate the price. Generally, news media can get a lower price than private polling clients because the survey firm will get publicity when the newspaper or TV station reports the results of a poll, and this invariably brings the pollsters more business. After you hire somebody, sit in on interviewer training and actually listen to a few phone interviews. Any reputable firm should allow this.

2. An alternative to hiring a professional research firm is to **use the resources of a nearby college or university.** Professors with background in survey research techniques often do consulting work on the side or are eager for a project to use in a research class. Doing a survey in connection with a class means you may get student interviewers at low or no cost. (However, pay them if you can.) Also, time on university computers costs less than time on a private computer.

    When the *Honolulu Advertiser* did a comprehensive study of Honolulu's criminal justice system, a University of Hawaii professor provided invaluable assistance in designing the research as well as paving the way for analyzing all the data from court and police documents on the university computer. The newspaper obtained stories for less cost, and in return, the professor received information for use in his own research and writing. The project probably would not have been attempted without this assurance of help from the campus.

3. Another alternative is to **use in-house resources.** Many of the larger news organizations have their own survey operations for marketing, advertising, or audience research. The newsroom may be able to piggyback on these efforts, adding several questions for publication or broadcast. These research operations sometimes have their own interviewers and computer capability. Other times they hire part-time interviewers and contract out the data processing. In any event, these people will be experienced at drawing samples, monitoring interviewers' work, and processing the data at the end.

4. Finally, there is **do-it-yourself.** This is cheaper, but a great deal of time, energy, and expertise is required to do it right. Dozens of details are involved: drafting questionnaires and printing them, drawing a sample, hiring and training interviewers (or arranging for the services of classified phone-room personnel or news clerks), supervising or validating their work, getting the data coded when you are through (often there will be personnel in other departments of a

newspaper or TV station that can be used for this), and analyzing the results. Newsrooms or classified advertising rooms do have banks of phones that can be used. You have access to phone books, city directories, and "reverse" phone directories (arranged by phone number) from which to draw samples. Most newspapers have in-house computers that can do simple data processing, perhaps even the software for graphic presentation of your results.

Box 8-4
Letting Others Help You

Reporters doing local polls can take advantage of the expertise of professional pollsters and avoid having to think up foolproof questions. How? Piggyback on previous work by national polls.

Drawing on these sources allows a local newspaper or TV station to use tested questions and, perhaps even more important, to make valid comparisons of how the people in its city/state/region compare on a question with the opinions of a national sample who have been asked exactly the same question.

Here are some places to get information about national polls:

1. Each issue of *Public Opinion Quarterly*, a research journal published for the American Association for Public Opinion Research, contains a section called "The Polls." Each of these sections usually focuses on a single topic and describes a wide variety of actual questions asked and the results obtained. The topics vary widely. *Public Opinion Quarterly* is available in most libraries.

2. Also available in many libraries is the *Gallup Index*, an annual volume that reports all the questions asked by the Gallup Poll during the year along with the results obtained.

3. Data from another major national poll, the Harris Survey is kept on file at the Louis Harris Political Data Center, Institute for Research in Social Science, University of North Carolina, Chapel Hill, North Carolina 27599–3355. But you don't even need that zip code number. Access to the Harris material, plus much more, is possible on-line. There are more than 65,000 Harris items and over a 100,000 items overall. Included are *USA Today* polls, the General Social Survey from 1972 to present, and a number of state and regional polls. Data from many polls are available on the World Wide Web.

4. Also available on-line are over 200,000 questions in the archives of the Public Opinion Location Library (POLL) run by the Roper Center at the University of Connecticut. All data are from national samples, including Gallup, Roper, NORC and the television networks. The Roper Center also publishes *The Public Perspective*, which contains a major section in each issue reporting timely poll questions and results. Contact the Roper Center at P.O. Box 440, Storrs, Connecticut 06268. FAX (203) 486–6308/ TEL (203) 484–4440.

5. The American Public Opinion Index, an annual compilation of questions and answers from a wide variety of national, state, and local opinion polls, is now available on CD-ROM. The disc contains both the data from over 100,000 poll items and a retrieval system for locating items. Contact ORS Publishing, 4948 St. Elmo Avenue, Suite 207, Bethesda, MD 20814.

You can do it yourself, but don't underestimate the problems and the amount of time that will be required.

Questionnaire Drafting

When you decide to conduct an opinion survey, somebody must prepare a questionnaire. Some practical tips:

- •Don't make it too long. About 10–15 minutes' worth in a telephone interview and perhaps twice that in an in-person setting can be handled without difficulty. Beyond that, unless it's a fascinating topic, respondents get tired or bored, which leads to answers that aren't well considered or may cause the respondent to quit before all your questions are asked.

- •Look for time-tested questions that you can adapt to your situation or use verbatim. Using the same question previously used in a timely national survey allows you to compare the attitudes of people in your geographical area to those of the nation as a whole.

- •Avoid biased and emotion-producing words. For example, a pollster should suggest that either alternative of a forced choice is acceptable. The "some people feel this way . . . while others feel that way" design of a question is one good way to do this.

- Keep question language simple and direct, using words that have unambiguous meaning. The word "fair," for example, may mean either "equitable" or "not very good." The phrase "put up" may mean to nominate a candidate, to stay for the night, to endure an insult, or preserve fruits. A favorite example of Tom Copeland, research director of Copley Newspapers, is "When did you last see your doctor?" Reply: "I saw him Wednesday over on the golf course."

- Avoid long questions where possible and keep each to a single point. Avoid double-barreled questions, such as: "Do you think the Republican majority in Congress is or is not doing a good job, and are you or are you not married?" It's hard enough to answer one question at a time.

- Consider the respondent's ego and try to cushion it. Ask, "Do you happen to know the name of the governor?" rather than "Can you tell me who the governor is?" The first version minimizes embarrassment.

- Try to make both sides of a pro-con question clear to the person being interviewed. Ask, "Do you favor or oppose" instead of just "Do you favor . . . ?" The latter wording tends to get more "Yes, I favor . . ." responses. Simply adding "or not" at the end can make it clear that the question has at least two possible and equally legitimate answers.

- Write a low-key introduction that allows your interviewers to identify the nature of the project (without giving any details that might bias later answers), the sponsor (again, where there is no danger that the sponsor's identity might introduce bias), an assurance of confidentiality, and a promise that the interviewer isn't a salesperson in disguise. One example:

  Hello, I'm _____ from XYZ Research, a local opinion polling company. We're conducting a survey for The Daily Times to find out how parents feel about the local school system. I'm not selling anything. Your phone number was selected at random and all your responses will be kept confidential and added to those of hundreds of others to find out how people feel about the schools.

- It is also necessary to have some procedure at the top of the questionnaire for determining exactly whom in a given home to interview. Remember that the goal is to interview a representative sample of people. That means a sample balanced among men and women, young people and old people, and so forth.

- Try to ask some interesting questions first, to encourage respondents to continue with the interview. When you change topics, make the transition smooth by letting the respondent know you are switching gears: "Here's a different topic," or "This subject interests a lot of people."

- Place potentially embarrassing questions—such as those about behavior or attitudes toward sex, drugs, and gambling, or information about personal income—at the end, where they won't cause an early termination of the interview. By then, the interviewer will have established rapport with the respondent, who is apt at this point to be more cooperative. Even if a respondent does quit, you already will have answers to nearly all the questions.

- Watch the question order to minimize chances that an earlier question will bias response to a later one. You wouldn't, for instance, ask people, "Do you think Governor Windbag is guilty or not guilty of fraud?" and then follow up with a question about which candidate for governor the respondent prefers. This is why it's important for you to ask for copies of the entire questionnaire when you are offered polling results for a possible news story. You need to know both the wording and the order of the questions to make sure the survey was fair.

- Before you put together your final questionnaire, go over the questions one by one and ask yourself exactly what you plan to do with the information. What, really, will it tell you? How will you make use of it in a news story? There are many questions that fall into the "wouldn't it be nice to know . . ." category, but when you sit down and think about it you are not sure how to make use of the information even if you get it. Throw out all these questions. They add cost without adding value.

- Consult with the data-processing people on designing the layout of the questionnaire so that it will be easier to punch the results into the computer. Of course, if you are lucky you will have access to a CATI system (computer assisted telephone interviewing) in which the questionnaire is on a computer screen in front of the interviewer, and the answers are recorded in the computer by the interviewer at the moment they are given over the phone by the respondent.

- Run a pretest of your questionnaire once it is drafted. This step can uncover holes or problems in the wording that the drafters overlooked. One legend at the University of Michigan Survey Research Center tells about a pretest of a questionnaire that included the question "What did you do right before you entered the service?" Replied one respondent: "Lady, you should ask me what I did *wrong* before I entered the service." The word "right" was changed to "just."

In drafting or selecting questions the major choice to make is between open-ended and closed-end questions.

Open-Ended Questions

An open-ended question simply means the respondent is free to define his or her own terms for answering it. Examples:

What do you think is the most important problem facing this country today?

In your opinion, what are the major causes of the violence that sometimes occurs in our public schools here?

The open-ended question is most useful when you aren't sure what the answer categories may be and don't want to impose your own set of limits and structures on the responses. If you ask whether crime, inflation, or unemployment is the most important problem in America, you ignore the possibility that people might really think something entirely different is most important. An open-ended question lets people say whatever is on their minds, instead of responding to multiple-choice answers of the pollster's choosing.

The disadvantages of open-ended questions are the difficulties in recording them and sorting out the answers afterwards. First, the interviewer must get the response down at the time the respondent gives it. Often the best you can hope for is that the interviewer is able to record the key words or phrases of the answer. There is no doubt some precision is lost at this stage. Second, someone on the research staff has to discern a pattern and develop a scheme for sorting the answers into categories. This can take considerable time and can result in arbitrary decisions. Then, coders go through the answers one by one to actually do the sorting—placing each answer in a category. This introduces a possible source of error and bias because there is never 100 percent agreement among the people who do the coding. A response that one coder might put in an "economic problems" category might be viewed by another coder as an "inflation" answer. Furthermore, the coding may vary from what the respondent really had in mind.

The time and effort to do all this translates into higher costs for a survey, but there are times when an open-ended question approach is the only fair way to get at a set of attitudes and beliefs.

Closed-End Questions

More common in survey research are closed-end questions, in which all the answer categories are defined in advance.

Do you approve or disapprove of the job being done by President Clinton?

Do you think parents who send their children to private schools should get a tax break for the tuition they pay, or do you think they should not get a tax break?

If the election for governor were held today, would you vote for Ann Richards or George Bush?

The answer categories are easily understood by respondent and interviewer alike. The coding of these answers also is easy. Time and cost are minimal.

The disadvantages are that this sort of forced-choice question sometimes incorrectly categorizes a respondent. What if somebody approves of the president's foreign policy, but not his domestic economic plan? What if you think that low-income parents should get a tax break for private school tuition, but not upper-income people?

Closed-end questions must be worded so the answer categories are exhaustive (covering all possible answers) and mutually exclusive (each answer falls in one and only one category). Often, human opinions on complex issues just don't work that way. That is why, on a particularly complex issue, it is best not to rely on a single question—especially a single closed-end question—as the sole indicator of opinion. It is not unusual for any serious survey of a complex topic to ask respondents a half dozen or more questions. A marketing firm once came up with 18 different questions about cottage cheese. How many questions would you need for a thorough poll on what local residents think about their city council?

Interviewer Training

If you decide to oversee a survey yourself and are going to hire your own interviewers or use staff members for the interviewing, they must be trained first. This is particularly crucial if journalists themselves are doing any survey interviewing. The style of journalists' typical interviewing can spell disaster for a public opinion survey. Journalists are used to making small talk with the people they interview, sometimes arguing with them, letting an interview flow in whatever direction the subject reasonably takes it. All of these things destroy the controlled setting of the survey interview.

Here are some tips for conducting survey interviews:

- Be neutral and noncommittal. The sponsor of a poll doesn't want the interviewer's opinions, he or she wants the respondent's. Make sure the interviewer understands there are no "right" or "wrong" answers to questions. The interviewer's view on any subject should not become known during the interview. Take what is given and write it down. Charles Backstrom and Gerald Hursh give this advice to interviewers in their book, *Survey Research*:

    > Merely soak up information like a sponge without giving any of it back. Your job is to record that information, regardless of whether you think it good, bad, indifferent, boring, or exciting. Don't, by word or reaction, indicate surprise, pleasure, or disapproval at any answer. Even a slight intake of breath will cue a respondent that you have reacted.

    This advice is especially important when an interviewer is instructed to probe for additional detail in an answer. A probe can help to fill out an incomplete, vague, or irrelevant answer, but the probe should not direct the respondent in one direction or another. Say something neutral, such as "Uh huh, I see," that may encourage further discussion. Other options include: "What do you mean?" "Why is that?" "Anything else?"

- Tone of voice is crucial. Do not let the respondent feel that you, the interviewer, are endorsing or arguing with anything said.

- All questions must be asked exactly as worded on the questionnaire. Any rephrasing may change the meaning and impact of the entire question and make it worthless.

- Ask all questions. Don't skip any unless the questionnaire instructs you to.

- Don't change the order of questions.

- Don't explain the questions or try to define their terms. If a respondent asks what a particular question means, the interviewer should say: "I really can't say, just consider whatever it means to you." The interviewer may repeat the question again, exactly as worded—if necessary.

- Be familiar with the questionnaire. In some questionnaires, there may be some questions or sections asked only if the respondent answers in a particular fashion to a previous question. For instance, the poll might ask whether the respondent favors capital punishment for some serious crimes. For those who answer "Yes," the poll might want to pin down the issue further by asking about specific crimes—murder of a police officer, murder for hire, rape, and so forth—and whether the respondent favors the death penalty for each. For respondents who answer "No" to the first question, the interviewer would skip over the follow-ups and go onto the next topic. One of the great advantages of the CATI systems mentioned earlier is that the computer can be programmed to move on to the correct question on the basis of the answer punched in.

- Stick to the answer categories given. If a particular question is looking for a choice of "excellent, good, fair, or poor" and the respondent says, "O.K.," the interviewer must not assume it means "fair." Ask for a choice from the categories listed.

- Use role playing for training. Have one interviewer go through the questionnaire with a second (perhaps more experienced) one playing the respondent and trying to gum up the works so everyone can learn ways out of rough spots.

- Make clear to each interviewer that a percentage of his or her work will be checked after completion and before payment is made. Then do it. Call up a sample of the people interviewed (many questionnaires conclude by having the interviewer determine the respondent's name and phone number, if not already known, "in case my office needs to verify that I have talked to you"). When you check back, thank the alleged respondent for cooperating and say that you want to double-check a couple of things from the interview. Then re-ask a question or two of the type where the answer isn't apt to change much (age or years of education) to see if the answers match what the interviewer recorded. The first clue that something is wrong will be if the person answering the phone says "There's no Charlie here" or if Charlie says he never was interviewed. If a cheater is discovered among the interviewers, discard all of that person's completed questionnaires and replace them with more interviews. Generally, it doesn't happen often, if interviewers have been forewarned that results will be spot-checked as they come in.

A Final Note

Because they go beyond the traditional interview with a single news source, surveys enable journalists to interview representative samples of their community on key topics of the day. This chapter and the preceding one offer detailed guidelines for expanding the scope of your reporting through carefully constructed questionnaires and fairly drawn samples. The guidance in these two chapters is useful for evaluating the ever-increasing volume of survey research offered by news sources as well as for initiating surveys under the full control of the newsroom.

References

Adams, R. C. *Social Survey Methods for Mass Media Research.* Hillsdale, NJ: Lawrence Erlbaum Associates, 1989.

Backstrom, Charles and Gerald Hursh. *Survey Research.* Evanston, IL: Northwestern University Press, 1963.

Rubin, Rebecca, Philip Palmgreen and Howard Sypher, eds. *Communication Research Measures. A Sourcebook.* New York: Guilford, 1994.

Watt, J. H. and S. A. van den Berg. *Research Methods for Communication Science.* Boston: Allyn and Bacon, 1995.

Chapter Nine

USING THE SELF-ADMINISTERED SURVEY

A poll is only as good as the questions it asks.

—Charles W. Roll, Jr. and Albert H. Cantril
Polls: Their Use and Misuse in Politics

Do not overlook the self-administered questionnaire when planning a story—or series—requiring hard data. Scientific survey methods enable the reporter to place within a much larger context the anecdotal data collected through personal interviews. Surveys can help show how individual cases fit into an overall pattern. Self-administered surveys, a subset of these sampling techniques, are just what their name implies: questionnaires filled out by the survey participants themselves. The questionnaires can be hand-delivered or mailed to the participants.

Self-administered surveys offer at least three obvious advantages over methods involving one-on-one data collection: They provide the participant with a greater degree of anonymity on sensitive issues; they can be conducted by a small staff (or even by one reporter); and they are usually less demanding of the journalist's time.

This chapter was compiled by Jon Hill.

A Close-Up Look

This chapter provides a close-up look at how the self-administered survey can form the basis of journalism that addresses important issues while at the same time appeal to readers. In 1995, University of North Carolina at Chapel Hill journalism classes used the self-administered survey to explore the issue of binge drinking, a common problem on college campuses across the country. An eight-page questionnaire (consisting of a one-page cover letter and seven pages of questions) was developed based on a 1993 Harvard School of Public Health study of drinking behavior on 140 campuses. This question-naire (figure 9.3 at the end of the chapter) is an excellent example of how questions can be phrased in a self-administered survey. The instructions provided in the cover letter are very clear—not misleading or vague; the survey's comprehensive questions seek information regarding the participant's background, experience, and feelings; the questions are unambiguous, brief, and allow the participant to choose from a viable range of answers which are listed below each question.

Four hundred fifty-one UNC undergraduates answered questions about their alcohol use. Philip Meyer, Knight professor of journalism, supervised student writers in medical-writing and specialized-report-ing classes as they collected and analyzed the data, conducted per-sonal interviews, and wrote several articles that were published in the *UNC Daily Tar Heel*. The package of stories, which began on page 1 and covered an entire page inside, was illustrated with photographs and highly informative graphics.

Karen Kemp's front-page story opening the news package pre-sented an overview of the issue and highlighted several of the survey's findings. It ran with a box detailing how the survey was conducted. Below is a portion of that article:

"UNC: A Hard-Drinking School?"
Karen Kemp

The results are in: UNC is not the beer-drinking capital of the world.

Heavy drinking among undergraduates was pegged at barely above the average for college students nationally in a new survey just completed by the School of Journalism and Mass Communication. Forty-eight percent of UNC undergrads—compared to 44 percent nationwide—are "binge" drinkers, according to a technical definition set by the Harvard School of Public Health in its national study.

UNC falls near the top of what the Harvard researchers called "medium-binge" schools. Colleges whose heavy drinking rates were 50 percent or greater were classified as "high-binge" schools. At the hardest-drinking school, 70 percent of undergraduates were binge drinkers.

Matt Sullivan, coordinator of alcohol and substance-abuse programs at UNC Student Health Service, said it was good to know UNC is not much worse than average, but not good enough. "Binge drinking is a very serious issue. . . . No, we aren't as bad off as some, but the numbers are alarming. Students who binge drink put themselves at risk."

Both the Harvard and UNC studies showed that the minimum-age drinking law isn't working. At UNC, 71 percent of undergraduates under the legal drinking age reported having had at least one drink in the previous month. For those of legal age, the rate was only slightly greater at 79 percent. In the Harvard study, 17,592 students on 140 U.S. campuses were surveyed in the spring of 1993. The UNC project replicated portions of the Harvard study by collecting self-administered questionnaires from 451 undergraduates.

Binge drinking was defined by the Harvard team as having five or more drinks in a row for men and four or more for women within the two weeks prior to the survey. Students who drank that much three or more times were classified as "frequent bingers"—19 percent in the national study and 18 percent at UNC.

UNC students who meet the Harvard definition of "binging" don't consider it abnormal. Ninety-two percent of the so-called bingers and even 80 percent of the "frequent bingers" classified their drinking as infrequent to moderate.

Frequent bingers at UNC were five times as likely as the non-binge drinkers to have been hurt or injured in the past year due to their own drinking or drug use. They were four times as likely to "have done something I later regretted." Auto accidents, unplanned and unsafe sex, physical and sexual assaults, and drinking-related social and psychological problems are among the consequences associated with this level of drinking.

Ken McGee is living the nightmare of what it can mean to take those risks. His daughter, UNC freshman Jamie McGee, toppled off a rooftop ladder and died April 27 after an 11-hour stretch of semester-end partying. Now, "a gifted person, a beautiful child," is gone, McGee said. "It can happen when you get caught up in the scene." . . .

The journalism school project took pains to deal with an important secondary debate on the subject: Exactly what constitutes binge drinking? Kelly Pattison spelled out the differences of opinion:

"Critics Challenge 'Binge' Definition"
Kelly Pattison

Does downing four or five drinks in a row really make you a binge drinker?

No, it doesn't, according to most students who drink at that rate. Some textbooks on alcoholism back them up.

Yes, it does, according to the definition of "binge drinking" used by some health authorities, including the Harvard School of Public Health and UNC's Student Health Service.

A School of Journalism and Mass Communication survey classifies almost half of the university's undergraduate students as binge drinkers by the Harvard definition. But 82 percent of these so-called binge drinkers claim to be only light-to-moderate drinkers, and only 12 percent have ever thought they had a drinking or drug problem.

A male student was counted as a binge drinker in the survey if he consumed five or more drinks in a row at least once in the two weeks preceding the survey. Fifty-four percent of Carolina men in the survey met this standard, For a female, the test is four or more drinks in a row; 45 percent of women surveyed qualify. The test is different for men and women because women's bodies metabolize alcohol slower than men's bodies.

The word "binge" presents a problem for substance-abuse counselor Andy Orr of The Recovery Partnership program. He said he thinks it is counterproductive to negatively label people as "alcoholics" or "binge drinkers."

The term "binge drinking" also has been used historically in textbooks about alcoholism to denote a pattern of drinking or staying drunk for 24 hours or more. . . .

    Dr. Henry Wechsler, the primary researcher in the Harvard study, explained that the standard of "five or more drinks in a row" was never intended to be based on comparisons of blood-alcohol levels. "We're looking for a style of drinking," said Wechsler, not "whether or not someone is drunk." . . .

The UNC reporters didn't rely on numbers alone to tell their story; they also tried to put a human face on the drinking issue. Statistics from a survey offer a reliable picture of the extent of a problem in a community and of public attitudes toward an issue, but they are less capable of conveying to the reader the personal impact of an problem. Stephanie Greer highlighted one young woman's story as an example of the potential effect of binge drinking on an individual college student.

What Exactly Is a Binge Drinker?

According to the UNC survey, a male student was considered a binge drinker if he consumed five or more drinks in a row at least once in the two weeks before the survey. For a female, the test was four or more drinks in a row.

A drink is defined as:

A four-ounce glass of wine   A 12-ounce can or bottle of beer or wine cooler   A shot of liquor straight or in a mixed drink

Figure 9.1
This graphic appeared with the news package on binge drinking in the Dec. 4, 1995. Courtesy *UNC Daily Tar Heel.*

"Woman Recounts Drunk Rape Ordeal"
Stephanie Greer

It wasn't the way she planned to lose her virginity.

The night started like any other in college, drinking and partying, but it ended on her front lawn, she naked, confused, crying, bleeding, a used condom left on the ground. She doesn't remember it very well, but she knows it wasn't what she wanted.

For Jane, a senior at UNC who characterizes herself as a heavy drinker, it followed the usual script. There was a party and then another party and then a bar and then another party, until she lost count of how much she had to drink and didn't really care. "I was drinking throughout the night, and I don't remember a lot of the night," she said.

She does know she met a group of male acquaintances and went with them to a party. She lost her car keys and wound up kissing a guy she knew. He offered to take her home. The scenario continued from there.

"We're on the lawn, and he somehow got my clothes off—I don't remember that, probably because it happened so quick, and I was so out of it, completely impaired," she said. "I was on my period, and so I was like, 'No, we can't do this, I'm on my period' . . . and I don't know how this happened, but he took my tampon out for me, so he had to have known something about what he was doing, The problem was that I didn't know what he was doing. I don't remember how all this happened, but I know that's how it must have happened because that's how I ended up.

"I do remember him . . . this was the horrible part, I don't know why this was happening, but I do remember him saying, 'You're going to charge me with date rape, aren't you?' and I was like, 'What are you talking about? Why would I want to do that?' . . .

"I treated it like, 'Hey, I had sex, lost the old virginity,'" she said. "I was being very positive about it. That was the way I was dealing with it, sort of laughing it off. . . . And in the few days that ensued, I was getting more depressed about it, thinking about it more and worrying about it more. This part of me that I didn't want to lose until it was going to mean something was gone."

Jane's experience sounds horrifyingly common to local health professionals who work with rape victims. They said one of the biggest problems about rape was so few victims actually reported the assaults (Jane didn't). "We see about 20 cases a semester, and that's just the tip of the iceberg," said Peggy Norton, a family nurse practitioner in the Women's Health division of UNC Student Health Service. . . .

What Binge Drinkers Do To Themselves

Percentage of surveyed students that in the last year have:	Non-binge drinkers	Bingers	Frequent bingers
Had a hangover	48	91	91
Got nauseated or vomited	35	81	86
Missed a class	21	60	79
Done something they later regretted	18	57	79
Had a memory loss	17	53	76
Driven under the influence	16	55	63
Performed poorly on a test or project	11	30	39
Got into an argument or a fight	8	47	65
Been hurt or injured	6	20	29
Been in trouble with police or campus authorities	4	26	37
Been taken advantage of sexually	4	13	21
Thought they had a drinking or drug problem	3	13	23
Damaged property	3	12	24

What Binge Drinkers Do To Others

Because of students' drinking, other students have:

BINGING LEVEL ON CAMPUSES	Low	UNC	HIGH
Had their studying or sleep interrupted	42	43	68
Had to "babysit" another drunken student	31	44	54
Been insulted or humilitated	21	23	34
Experienced an unwanted sexual advance*	15	16	26
Had a serious argument or quarrel	13	15	20
Been pushed, hit or assaulted	7	6	13
Had their property damaged	6	11	15
Had unwanted sexual intercourse*	2	1	2

*Based on women only

Figure 9.2

This chart presented additional information from the self-administered survey upon which the reporting classes' project was based.Courtesy *UNC Daily Tar Heel*.

The self-administered survey enabled the reporters to make comparisons between groups of students. But the project didn't stop there; it went on to reveal some of the dynamics of the issue by seeking out the views of people directly involved with those student groups. Steve Baragona wrote about Greek organizations, which have had a reputation for serious partying.

"Fraternities Drink at Higher Rate"
Steve Baragona

Greeks are more likely than independents to be binge drinkers, according to the survey conducted by the UNC School of Journalism and Mass Communication, The binging rate for fraternity and sorority members is 71 percent, compared to 41 percent for other undergraduates.

For frequent binging—with "frequent" defined as three or more times in the two-week period before the survey—the Greek rate was more than double: 33 percent compared to 13 percent for everybody else.

As high as that seems, recent risk management programs have mellowed fraternity parties, said Ron Binder, director of Greek Affairs.

Initial efforts began before Binder arrived in the summer of 1994. In 1991, fraternities were prohibited from buying alcohol with chapter funds. The sorority walkout rule was also instated around this time: If members of a sorority arrived at a fraternity party and found alcohol being served, they were to walk out or share responsibility for it.

"The sorority walkout rule really ended kegs," said Brooks Battle, president of Phi Delta Theta.

When Binder arrived, he focused attention on the problem of risk management.

The presidents and chapter advisers of all the fraternities were informed of their legal responsibilities if someone who had been drinking at one of their parties was injured, injured another person or damaged property. . . .

Many students use alcohol because of its relaxing effects and see it as easy entertainment in a town lacking social options. "It helps you lose your inhibitions and come down from a long week," said senior Gina Pagani.

"It's instant fun," said senior Jeff King. "You always know something's going to happen." . . .

Achieving Successful Results

This UNC news package demonstrates the value of self-administered surveys in a carefully designed investigation that incorporates several ways of obtaining information. Participants were given a high degree of anonymity as they completed the questionnaires, encouraging them to reveal personal information about controversial behavior. A relatively small number of reporters collected the information from a sizable sample (more than 70 percent of the students initially contacted responded) in a limited time span. Combining the results of the survey with information from other sources—in particular, through interviews with people involved with the issue—the reporting classes presented an examination of the problem that was thorough and authoritative while maintaining the sense of immediacy and poignancy found in a good feature story.

The self-administered survey, like other survey methods, is only as good as the standards by which it is conducted. Accepted standards are discussed in this book as well as in texts such as Philip Meyer's *The New Precision Journalism* and Earl Babbie's *The Practice of Social Research*. A second area to pay close attention to is interpretation. Take care to generalize the results of a survey only to people and groups of whom the survey participants are representative. For instance, the UNC survey offers a reliable picture of UNC undergraduate drinking behavior in the mid-1990s, but it cannot be construed to precisely reflect the behavior of undergraduates in the 1970s, of 20-year-olds around the world, of all Americans, or even of graduate students currently enrolled at the university.

Finally, strive to collect a high rate of completed questionnaires by making it easy for the participants to return their paperwork and by following up on initial mailings with reminders. Meyer emphasizes that achieving a high completion rate is more important than amassing a large sample—an example of the old saying that if something is worth doing, it is worth doing well.

References

Babbie, Earl. *The Practice of Social Research*, 7th ed. Belmont, CA: Wadsworth, 1995.

Meyer, Philip. *The New Precision Journalism*. Bloomington: Indiana University Press, 1991.

Roll, Charles W. Jr. and Albert H. Cantril. *Polls: Their Use and Misuse in Politics*. New York: Basic Books, 1972.

Campus Alcohol Study

UNC-CH School of Journalism and Mass Communication

Dear Student:

Thank you for agreeing to take part in our survey. Please complete it as soon as possible and return it in the postage-paid return envelope.

Notice that it has a serial number. It is there so that we'll know you have responded and we can cross your name off the follow-up list. It will not be used to identify you in any other way. As soon as we receive your response, Nancy Pawlow (my secretary) or I will tear off the number so that it can never be linked to your answers. No other person will have access to your identifying number. (If you want, you can tear it off yourself.)

Your participation is voluntary. You do not need to answer any question that makes you uncomfortable.

Thank you for your help. Please take part and let your views be represented. If you lose the envelope, please return the completed questionnaire to:

Questions? Call me at my office (962-4085) or at home (933-0605) or by e-mail:

philip_meyer@unc.edu

If at any time during this study you feel your rights have been violated, you may contact:

Academic Affairs Institutional Review Board
Frances Campbell, Chair
CB 4100, 300 Bynum Hall
(919) 966-5625

Nancy Pawlow
Room 204-A
CB 3365 Howell Hall
Campus

Sincerely,

Philip Meyer
Professor

Figure 9.3
Self-Administered Survey

continued

A1.   How old are you?   __ __

A2.   Are you male or female?
      1. Male
      2. Female

A3.   What is your current year in school?
      1. Freshman (1st year)
      2. Sophomore (2nd year)
      3. Junior (3rd year)
      4. Senior (4th year)
      5. 5th year or beyond

A4.   Did you transfer to Carolina from another college?
      1. No, did not transfer
      2. Yes, during this current school year
      3. Yes, before this school year

A5.   Are you a member of a fraternity or sorority?
      1. Yes   2. No

A6.   Where do you currently live? (Choose one answer)
      1. Single-sex residence hall or dormitory
      2. Co-ed residence hall or dormitory
      3. Fraternity or sorority
      4. Other university housing
      5. Co-op or university-affiliated group house
      6. Off-campus house or apartment

A7.   What is your major field of study?
      (Choose one answer)
      1. Biological Sciences (zoology, physiology, etc.)
      2. Business (accounting, marketing, personnel, etc.)
      3. Education (elementary, special, physical, etc.)
      4. Humanities and Fine Arts (music, religion, English, etc.)
      5. Physical Sciences, Mathematics (chemistry, etc.)
      6. Social Sciences (psychology, economics, etc.)
      7. Other academic field
      8. Undecided about which major field

A8.   How important is it for you to participate in the following activities at college? (Choose one answer in each row)

	Very Important	Important	Somewhat Important	Not at All Important
a. Athletics	1	2	3	4
b. Arts	1	2	3	4
c. Academic work	1	2	3	4
d. Drinking	1	2	3	4
e. Religion	1	2	3	4
f. Fraternity or sorority life	1	2	3	4
g. Political activism	1	2	3	4
h. Parties	1	2	3	4
i. Community service	1	2	3	4

A9.   In the past 30 days, how often have you gone to...   (Choose one answer in each row)

	Not at All	Once	Two or More Times	Not Applicable
a. gatherings of faculty with students	1	2	3	4
b. student gatherings in dorm rooms	1	2	3	4
c. dormitory social events or parties	1	2	3	4
d. fraternity or sorority events or parties	1	2	3	4
e. on-campus dances, concerts, etc.	1	2	3	4
f. keg parties on-campus	1	2	3	4
g. intercollegiate sports events	1	2	3	4
h. on-campus pub	1	2	3	4
i. parties at off-campus housing	1	2	3	4
j. parties or events at other campuses	1	2	3	4
k. off-campus bars or clubs	1	2	3	4

continued

SECTION B: ALCOHOL POLICIES AND PROGRAMS

B1. Based on what you have heard or experienced, to what extent is each of the following a problem for students at Carolina (Choose one in each row)

	Not a Problem	A Minor Problem	A Moderate Problem	A Major Problem
a. Physical assaults	1	2	3	4
b. Drug abuse	1	2	3	4
c. Racial tension or conflict	1	2	3	4
d. Suicide	1	2	3	4
e. Sexual assault or date rape	1	2	3	4
f. Heavy alcohol use	1	2	3	4

B2. Based on what you have heard or experienced, approximately what proportion of the following do you think are _heavy or problem drinkers_ at this school? (Choose one answer in each row)

	0%	1-9%	10-19%	20-29%	30-39%	40-49%	50-59%	60-69%	70-79%	80-89%	90-100%
a. All students	0	1	2	3	4	5	6	7	8	9	10
b. Your friends	0	1	2	3	4	5	6	7	8	9	10

B3. Which of the following do you think should be Carolina's approach to student drinking? (Choose one answer)
1. The current alcohol policy
2. A policy which imposes greater restrictions on alcohol use
3. A policy which imposes fewer restrictions on alcohol use
4. Don't know current policy

B4. Since the beginning of the school year, has our school provided the following types of information to you? (Choose one answer in each row)

	Yes	No
a. The college rules for drinking	1	2
b. The penalties for breaking the rules	1	2
c. Where you can get help for alcohol-related problems	1	2
d. How to recognize when someone has a drinking problem	1	2
e. The long-term health effects of heavy drinking	1	2
f. The dangers of alcohol overdose	1	2

B5. To what extent do you support or oppose the following possible school policies or procedures? (Choose one answer in each row)

	Strongly Support	Support	Oppose	Strongly Oppose
a. Prohibit kegs on campus	1	2	3	4
b. Offer alcohol-free dorms	1	2	3	4
c. Require non-alcoholic beverages be available when alcohol is served at campus events	1	2	3	4
d. Ban advertisements of alcohol availability at campus events and parties	1	2	3	4
e. Let students drink regardless of age	1	2	3	4
f. Provide more alcohol-free recreational and cultural opportunities such as movies, dances, sports, lectures	1	2	3	4
g. Enforce the alcohol rules more strictly	1	2	3	4
h. Make the alcohol rules clearer	1	2	3	4
i. Crack down on drinking at sororities and fraternities	1	2	3	4
j. Hold hosts responsible for problems arising from alcohol use	1	2	3	4
k. Have no policies or procedures which attempt to control alcohol use	1	2	3	4

continued

B6. What should be the legal drinking age? (Choose one answer)

    1. Under 18   2. 18   3. 19   4. 20   5. 21   6. 22 or over

SECTION C: PERSONAL ALCOHOL USE

> The following questions ask about how much you drink. A "drink" means any of the following:
> A 12-ounce can (or bottle) of beer
> A 4-ounce glass of wine
> A 12-ounce bottle (or can) of wine cooler
> A shot of liquor straight or in a mixed drink

C1. Do any of the following reasons prohibit or restrict your drinking?
(Choose one answer in each row)

	Yes	No
a. Medical or health conditions	1	2
b. Religious reasons	1	2

C2. Think back over the <u>last two weeks</u>. How many times have you had five or more drinks in a row?

    1. None ⟶ SKIP TO QUESTION C4   4. 3 to 5 times
    2. Once   5. 6 to 9 times
    3. Twice   6. 10 or more times

C3. Who were you with the <u>last time</u> you drank <u>five or more drinks</u> in a row?
(Choose one answer in each row)

	Yes	No
a. I was alone	1	2
b. With a date or partner	1	2
c. In a small group (2-10 people)	1	2
d. With a larger group (more than 10 people)	1	2

C4. During the <u>last two weeks</u>, how many times have you had four drinks in a row (but no more than that)?

    1. None   4. 3 to 5 times
    2. Once   5. 6 to 9 times
    3. Twice   6. 10 or more times

C5. During the <u>last two weeks</u>, how many times have you had three drinks in a row (but no more than that)?

    1. None   4. 3 to 5 times
    2. Once   5. 6 to 9 times
    3. Twice   6. 10 or more times

C6. When did you last have a drink (that is, more than just a few sips)? (Exclude use in religious ceremonies)

    1. I have never had a drink ⟶ SKIP TO QUESTION C13
    2. Not in the past year ⟶ SKIP TO QUESTION C11
    3. More than 30 days ago, but less than a year ago
    4. More than a week ago, but less than 30 days ago
    5. Within the last week

> Answer questions C7 through C10 if you have had a drink <u>within the past year</u> or <u>within the past 30 days</u>

C7. Are there places in or near Chapel Hill where you or your friends usually can get alcohol without showing an ID?
(Choose one answer in each row)

	Yes	No	Don't Know
a. At a local bar or club	1	2	3
b. At a local liquor or grocery store	1	2	3

continued

C8. Do you keep any of the following in your dorm or apartment? (Choose one answer in each row)

	Yes	No	Don't Know
a. Beer	1	2	3
b. Wine	1	2	3
c. Wine coolers	1	2	3
d. Liquor	1	2	3

C9. What type of alcohol do you drink most often? (Choose one answer)
1. Beer
2. "Low alcohol" beer
3. Wine coolers
4. Wine
5. Liquor (or mixed drinks)
6. No "usual" drink

C10. How important are each of the following reasons for you to drink alcohol?
(Choose one answer in each row)

	Very Important	Important	Somewhat Important	Not at All Important
a. To get away from my problems and troubles	1	2	3	4
b. To relax or relieve tension	1	2	3	4
c. To get drunk	1	2	3	4
d. To have a good time with my friends	1	2	3	4
e. Because of boredom	1	2	3	4
f. To celebrate	1	2	3	4
g. To help me get my work done	1	2	3	4
h. Because I like the taste	1	2	3	4
i. As a reward for working hard	1	2	3	4
j. To fit in with my friends	1	2	3	4
k. To feel more comfortable when I'm with the opposite sex	1	2	3	4

Answer questions C11 and C12 if you have ever had a drink of alcohol (more than just a few sips)

C11. Have you ever...

	Yes	No
a. felt the need to cut down on your drinking	1	2
b. become annoyed at criticism of your drinking	1	2
c. felt guilty about your drinking	1	2
d. needed a drink first thing in the morning to get going	1	2
e. thought you had a drinking problem	1	2
f. thought you had a drug problem	1	2

C12. How would you best describe yourself in terms of your current use of alcohol?
1. Abstainer
2. Abstainer - former problem drinker in recovery
3. Infrequent drinker
4. Light drinker
5. Moderate drinker
6. Heavy drinker
7. Problem drinker

continued

C13. How important are each of the following reasons for you not to drink alcohol? (Choose one answer in each row)

	Very Important	Important	Somewhat Important	Not at All Important
a. Drinking is against my religion.	1	2	3	4
b. Drinking is against my values.	1	2	3	4
c. My family has had alcohol problems.	1	2	3	4
d. I am not old enough to drink legally.	1	2	3	4
e. It costs too much money.	1	2	3	4
f. I don't like the taste.	1	2	3	4
g. My friends don't drink.	1	2	3	4
h. I don't want to disappoint someone I care about.	1	2	3	4
i. It is bad for my health.	1	2	3	4
j. It interferes with my studying.	1	2	3	4
k. It interferes with my athletic activities.	1	2	3	4
l. I don't want to lose control.	1	2	3	4
m. I've had problems with alcohol.	1	2	3	4
n. It's fattening.	1	2	3	4

SECTION D: STUDENT ALCOHOL USE

D1. In your opinion, how much do you think is appropriate for a college student to drink in each of the following situations?
(Choose one answer in each row)

	No alcohol at all	Only 1-2 drinks	Enough to get high but not drunk	Enough to get drunk
a. At a party	1	2	3	4
b. In an off-campus bar	1	2	3	4
c. In an on-campus pub	1	2	3	4
d. Before driving a car	1	2	3	4
e. On a date	1	2	3	4
f. With friends	1	2	3	4
g. Alone	1	2	3	4
h. Before noon	1	2	3	4
i. On a week night	1	2	3	4

D2. Indicate your agreement or disagreement with the following advice for a new student at your school.
(Choose one answer in each row)

	Strongly Agree	Agree	Disagree	Strongly Disagree
a. Students here admire non-drinkers	1	2	3	4
b. It's important to show how much you can drink and hold your liquor	1	2	3	4
c. You can't make it socially at this school without drinking	1	2	3	4
d. Drinking is an important part of the college experience	1	2	3	4
e. School rules about drinking are almost never enforced	1	2	3	4

continued

D3. Since the beginning of the school year, how often have you experienced any of the following because of other students' drinking? (Choose one answer in each row)

	Not at all	Once	Twice or More
a. Been insulted or humiliated	1	2	3
b. Had a serious argument or quarrel	1	2	3
c. Been pushed, hit or assaulted	1	2	3
d. Had your property damaged	1	2	3
e. Had to "baby-sit" or take care of another student who drank too much	1	2	3
f. Had your studying or sleep interrupted	1	2	3
g. Experienced an unwanted sexual advance	1	2	3
h. Unwanted sexual intercourse	1	2	3

D4. Please indicate how often you have experienced the following due to your drinking or drug use during the last year? (Choose one for each line)

	Never	Once	Twice	3-5 times	6-9 times	10 or more times
a. Had a hangover	1	2	3	4	5	6
b. Performed poorly on a test or important project	1	2	3	4	5	6
c. Been in trouble with police, residence hall, or other college authorities	1	2	3	4	5	6
d. Damaged property, pulled fire alarm, etc.	1	2	3	4	5	6
e. Got into an argument or fight	1	2	3	4	5	6
f. Got nauseated or vomited	1	2	3	4	5	6
g. Driven a car while under the influence	1	2	3	4	5	6
h. Missed a class	1	2	3	4	5	6
i. Been criticized by someone I know	1	2	3	4	5	6
j. Thought I might have a drinking or other drug problem	1	2	3	4	5	6
k. Had a memory loss	1	2	3	4	5	6
l. Done something I later regretted	1	2	3	4	5	6
m. Been arrested for DWI/DUI	1	2	3	4	5	6
n. Have been taken advantage of sexually	1	2	3	4	5	6
o. Having taken advantage of another sexually	1	2	3	4	5	6
p. Tried unsuccessfully to stop using	1	2	3	4	5	6
q. Seriously thought about suicide	1	2	3	4	5	6
r. Seriously tried to commit suicide	1	2	3	4	5	6
s. Been hurt or injured	1	2	3	4	5	6

SECTION E: OTHER PERSONAL BEHAVIORS

E1. In the past 30 days, how many times did you... (Choose one answer from each row)

	Not at all	Once	Twice or More
a. get involved in an automobile accident while you were the driver	1	2	3
b. drive after drinking alcohol	1	2	3
c. drive after having 5 or more drinks	1	2	3
d. ride with a driver who was high or drunk	1	2	3
e. serve as a designated driver	1	2	3
f. ride with a designated driver	1	2	3

E2. How many drinks do you think you can consume within a one-hour period and still drive safely? _____

continued

E3. How often, if ever, have you used any of the drugs listed below. Do not include anything you used under a doctor's orders. (Choose one answer in each row)

	Never used	Used, but NOT in past 12 months	Used, but NOT in past 30 days	Used in past 30 days
a. Marijuana (or hashish)	1	2	3	4
b. Crack cocaine	1	2	3	4
c. Other forms of cocaine	1	2	3	4
d. Barbiturates (prescription-type sleeping pills like Quaaludes, downs, yellow jackets)	1	2	3	4
e. Amphetamines (prescription-type stimulants like speed, uppers, ups)	1	2	3	4
f. Tranquilizers (prescription-type drugs like valium, librium)	1	2	3	4
g. Heroin	1	2	3	4
h. Hallucinogenics like mushrooms, mescaline, PCP, LSD or Ecstacy	1	2	3	4

SECTION F: STUDENT ACTIVITIES

F1. In general, how happy are you these days?
1. Very happy
2. Somewhat happy
3. Somewhat unhappy
4. Very unhappy

F2. How may close student friends do you have?
1. None
2. One
3. Two
4. Three
5. Four
6. Five or more

F3. Is there a member of the faculty or administration with whom you could discuss a problem?
1. Yes   2. No

F4. Which of the following best describes your grade point average so far this year?
01. A
02. A-
03. B+
04. B
05. B-
06. C+
07. C
08. C-
09. D
10. No grade or don't know

SECTION G: BACKGROUND INFORMATION

G1. Are you of Spanish or Hispanic origin?
1. Yes
2. No

G2. Which of these racial or ethnic groups describes you best? (Choose one answer)
1. White
2. Black/African American
3. Asian/Pacific Islander
4. Native American/Indian/Native Alaskan
5. Other: _____

G3. In what religion were you raised?
(Choose one answer)
1. None
2. Catholic
3. Jewish
4. Moslem
5. Protestant
6. Other: _____

G4. During your last year in high school, how often did you drink alcohol (beer, wine, liquor) during a typical month? (Choose one answer)
1. Never
2. 1-2 occasions
3. 3-5 occasions
4. 6-9 occasions
5. 10-19 occasions
6. 20-39 occasions
7. 40 or more occasions

G5. How did your family feel about drinking alcohol when you were growing up?
1. My family did not approve of drinking.
2. They accepted light drinking but disapproved of heavy drinking.
3. They accepted heavy drinking.
4. There was no agreement about drinking in the family.

PART IV

DOCUMENTS AND ELECTRONIC RECORDS

Chapter Ten

DOCUMENTS

... It is one thing to say that the utterer of what may or may not
be an "official lie" is a liar; it is another to hunt down in the
record and to publish what was said so that the reader can see
the words that were spoken ...

—George Bain
"The World According to I.F. Stone"

Documents trail behind the important events of our personal and
collective lives. For each of us there is a birth certificate. For some
there are marriage certificates. For each of us there will be a death
certificate. All these documents, when collected, show the types of
people we are, the states of our health, the ages and types of people
we marry, and the conditions of our deaths, which sometimes hint at
the kind of life we lived. Consider how many documents we carry
around—driver's license, credit cards, club membership cards,
check-cashing cards, various types of identification—all documents
that, considered together, contain a composite view of us. The social
system, like an individual, also contains many documents that record
our collective activities.

As a journalist you will have many opportunities to monitor community life by examining documents and databases or, if necessary
for your story, by devising your own content analysis of selected public documents. Many stories are based entirely on quotes from a single interview. However, unless you are interviewing a rape victim or
the president, these stories probably are too thin to justify publica-

tion. During the early 1970s Watergate period, *Washington Post* reporters Bob Woodward and Carl Bernstein sought at least two sources for each story about the operation of the special committee appointed to help President Richard Nixon with his re-election. Woodward and Bernstein were forced to use people because the police documents soon ran out, showing how closely related paper and people can be as sources for journalists. Documents often are the start of investigations.

Documents reflect routine activities. Documents are put together close to the time of events and therefore are likely to be more accurate, if sometimes dull and incomplete, than human memories of events. Human memory is fallible, and details erode from our minds over time. Documents remain the same; their perspective does not change, even if a lot of time has passed since the event was documented.

Documents tip you off. For example, you might see that a prominent official was arrested for driving while intoxicated. Further searching might reveal that this public official has a previous record for this offense, and the problem—if it turns out to be a problem—might actually be influencing his or her work as an official. Or, you might be reviewing the annual report for the community fire department and notice that there were a lot of fires in small apartment buildings last year. Something clicks in your mind. You check property records and discover that the apartments are owned by the same corporation, and still other records show the amount of insurance on the buildings. Additional fire department records show that arson was suspected in several of the fires in the buildings owned by the corporation. In other words, you see the outlines of a possible pattern— a spiderweb is visible but not the spider. You are ready to begin interviews with firefighters, police, insurance companies, and eventually perhaps the corporate owners of the building. In such a way, reports link information from documents to setting up interviews.

But it could also happen the other way. Interviews can lead you to appropriate documents. You might be working your beat and learn from a secretary that the boss was away for the morning on business at a land sale. You think about the number of times that this agency head has been gone from the office—quite a few, it seems to you. So you become curious about land sales and go to the county office of deeds to determine just how much property the agency head has purchased, if any. You discover from these documents that the agency head has purchased several houses and lots in the southeastern area of town, and the tax stamps attached to the property provide a rough estimate of just how much they cost.

You might wonder how he or she is financing the purchases—the agency head is not known to be a rich person—and why one area is favored for purchase. Then you remember some discussion around city hall months ago about the possibility of a shopping center being put in the same dilapidated part of town. You have a hunch. You detect a pattern. You begin to suspect that the agency head may be using special knowledge to pursue special profit. In such a way, interviews or information from other sources can lead to documents.

Documents as Primary Records

You cannot be present to witness most of the exciting things about which you will write. Tornadoes do not announce when they will arrive, and certainly no one involved in an automobile accident knew it was going to happen. Those stories come from seeing events afterward, interviewing people, and reviewing records. Of course, you know ahead of time about many events such as sports, speeches, press conferences, and meetings.

All public agencies and nearly all organizations record daily, monthly, or annual activities. By law, public agencies are required to record information and make much, if not most, of it available to the public. Citizens can look at these records, and reporters, as citizens, have this same right. Reporters who cover beats need to identify the key documentary records on their beats and monitor them, using interviews to obtain additional information or talking to people to elicit tips or perspective about important events that might be buried in the documents.

Documents Galore

There are many different kinds of documents. Nearly everyone is familiar with the U.S. Census, which surveys all Americans every 10 years. In recent years the Census Bureau has used some sampling techniques with a short version of the longer questionnaire. The purpose is to provide regular information about Americans, such as where they live, how much money they make, their sex, and their racial background.

Many news media use census information as a document. Also, many census data are available on the World Wide Web. The information published in census books is used to determine population sizes and character. The Census Bureau makes information available in a form that news media computers can access and use to develop stories that fit particular localities. The Census Bureau also does several different types of surveys between the regular 10-year censuses.

Box 10-1
Using the Census

Census Bureau products provide reporters with a wealth of information that can be mined for stories on a variety of issues. Much of the information is grouped into categories. The overall population data are available on computer tapes, and the subgroups are available in print, compact laser disk, microfiche, or on line. Data are presented for each state and, in many cases, for much smaller areas, such as counties and communities of 1,000 or more inhabitants. Census Bureau brochures not only describe the data files and how to obtain them but also cite interesting examples of how the material has been put to use by businesses, neighborhoods, even newspapers. Among the files are:

General population characteristics: detailed statistics on age, sex, race, Hispanic origin, marital status, and household relationship characteristics.

Social and economic characteristics: data focusing on population subjects such as income, education, and occupation.

Detailed housing characteristics: data on housing subjects such as year structure built, number of bedrooms, plumbing and kitchen facilities, telephone, vehicles available, source of water, sewage disposal, and shelter costs.

U.S. merchandise trade: Selected domestic and foreign exports, general imports, and imports for consumption.

Consolidated federal funds report: Grants, salaries and wages, procurement contracts, direct payments to individuals, government loans and insurance, total direct spending for defense and nondefense functions, and other programs.

Excerpted from Census Bureau documents

A reporter checks census records at the public library.
Courtesy Harold Washington Library, Chicago.

Information is also gathered by many other federal government agencies—the Federal Bureau of Investigation gathers data about crime; the Department of Agriculture, about food production, crop growing and many other topics; the Department of Commerce, about world trade; and the Environmental Protection Agency, about topics relating to where we live and our health. There are hundreds, even thousands, of examples. Most states have departments that deal with and gather information on traffic safety, education, courts, police, sheriffs, state patrol operations, commerce, agriculture, taxes, and many other topics.

Local governments record information about many aspects of community life. Police record statistics on traffic accidents, crimes, and investigations. The department responsible for traffic control gathers information on traffic patterns, location of stop lights, need for street repairs, and many other kinds of statistics. The fire department keeps records on all emergency calls, both real and false. The same department investigates the cause of all fires, and most make ongoing inspections. County offices maintain all kinds of records on property, such as the amount that it is valued for tax purposes and a record of who has owned it over the years. One can follow the trail of a parcel of property over time.

Local, state, and federal agencies routinely prepare annual reports. These are excellent starting points to follow developments, especially if you look back over reports for the past four to five years. You can see if there has been an increase or decrease in a particular type of crime by comparing annual reports of police or sheriffs' departments. You can see if the community is more or less fire prone by comparing the reports of fire departments. You can study the extent of property sales by examining property records (using a sampling). While annual reports usually provide a good source for a story when they are released, they provide a more important source if you read them carefully for trends that you may be able to support with other documents. Some of this can be done by computer.

You can also develop hunches from a single document and see if that document is illustrative of a trend by examining several similar documents. For example, pretend you are a police reporter and you are examining the report of an auto mishap, such as that shown in figures 10.1A and 10.1B.

A close study of figures 10.1A and 10.1B can generate many story ideas, such as whether a particular road's reputation for dangerous conditions is deserved. To investigate, collect accident reports over time and look at the "Location" section (near the top of figure 10.1A) and the "Estimated Damage" and "Injury Class" (farther down). Compare this information to data for similar roads elsewhere in the area. Is a certain category of drivers—say, elderly people or teenagers—more likely to be charged in serious accidents? Look at the date of birth ("DOB") under sections marked "Vehicle 1" and "Vehicle 2," check again for injuries and damages farther down the page, and note the charges at the bottom of figure 10.1B.

Does a particular officer charge some drivers—for instance, women or black people—disproportionately more often in accidents? Look at the "Race/Sex" box in the bottom section of figure 10.1A and the charges and filing officer's name on 10.1B. How about medical treatment? Is emergency care taking too long to reach the accident scene? Look at the time of the accident, listed at the top of 10.1A, and the time the ambulance arrived, listed at the bottom of the page, and compare this difference to response times posted by other emergency services or in other cities.

If you study any type of regular police document you will see the potential for many stories. In such a way a single document can suggest a starting point for a more comprehensive story that uses many of the same documents. The growth of databases and use of computers, which enable reporters to spot trends, make this type of story much easier to do today than in the past.

Some Typical Records

Vital Statistics

Births, marriages, divorces, name changes, and deaths all have to be recorded. The record may be filed with a county clerk or health department (births or deaths), a family court (divorces), a secretary of state or courthouse (name changes). Somewhere, the government keeps track of the rites of passage that mark all our lives.

Generally, such events are public record at the time they occur. Some newspapers still carry agate-type summaries of all recent births, deaths, and marriage license applications. However, concern over rights of privacy in recent years has caused some jurisdictions to deny access to such information. For instance, although you can obtain a copy of your own birth certificate or marriage license, in some places a reporter cannot.

However, *don't assume* you can't get such information. Don't take the first "no" for an answer. When seeking vital statistics, as with any other arguably public record, operate on the premise that you have a right to it. You may be cut off at the pass by some midlevel civil servant afraid of erring on the side of openness, but pressure on a higher-up by you (or the news media lawyer) often can free the originally denied material.

Divorce Records

A divorce file is perhaps the best example of a useful lode of facts in the vital statistics category. When a couple civorces, often there is a

THIS REPORT IS FOR THE USE OF THE DIVISION OF MOTOR VEHICLES. THE DATA IS COLLECTED FOR STATISTICAL ANALYSIS AND SUBSEQUENT HIGHWAY SAFETY PROGRAMMING. DETERMINATIONS OF "FAULT" ARE THE RESPONSIBILITY OF INSURERS OR OF THE STATE'S COURTS.

No. of Units Involved

☐ Supplemental Report

Date	Day of Week	County	Time	Local Use / Patrol Area	Date Received by DMV
MONTH DAY YEAR			(24 Hour Clock)		

L
O
C
A
T
I
O
N

Collision occurred ☐ In ☐ Near

Municipality   ☐ outside municipality

on ___ Highway Number, or Highway, Street. I if ramp or service road, indicate on line) ___ or ___ Miles ___ ☐ N ☐ S ☐ E ☐ W

(R.R.Crossing #) ___ Miles (0 ft.-intersection) ___ ft. ☐ N ☐ S ☐ E ☐ W

at or from ___ toward ___ ☐ N ☐ S ☐ E ☐ W

Use Highway Number, Street Name or Adjacent County or State Line

☐ VEHICLE 1   ☐ HIT & RUN

Driver 1 ___
First ___ Middle ___ Last

Address ___

City ___ State ___ Zip ___

Same Address on Driver's License? ☐ Yes ☐ No   Driver's Phone No. W( ) ___ H( ) ___

D.L.# ___ State ___ DOB ___ month/day/year

Vision Physical
1. Obstruction ___ 2. Condition ___ 3. Intoxication ___ Restrictions ___

Owner ___

Address ___

City ___ State ___ Zip ___

VIN ___

Plate # ___ State ___ Year ___

Veh. Year ___ Veh. Make ___ Veh. Type Code ___

Commercial Vehicle ___ ☐ Yes ☐ No   Trailer Type Code ___
Air Bag Deployed ___ ☐ Yes ☐ No   1st Trailer No. of Axles ___
Passenger ___ ☐ Yes ☐ No   Width ___ inches
Vehicle Drivable ___ ☐ Yes ☐ No   Length ___ feet
Post Crash Fire ___ ☐ Yes ☐ No   2nd Trailer No. of Axles ___
Rollover ___ ☐ Yes ☐ No   Width ___ inches
Hazardous Cargo ___ ☐ Yes ☐ No   Length ___ feet

☐ VEHICLE 2   ☐ PEDESTRIAN   ☐ HIT & RUN   ☐ OTHER

Driver 2 ___
First ___ Middle ___ Last

Address ___

City ___ State ___ Zip ___

Same Address on Driver's License? ☐ Yes ☐ No   Driver's Phone No. W( ) ___ H( ) ___

D.L.# ___ State ___ DOB ___ month/day/year

Vision Physical
1. Obstruction ___ 2. Condition ___ 3. Intoxication ___ Restrictions ___

Owner ___

Address ___

City ___ State ___ Zip ___

VIN ___

Plate # ___ State ___ Year ___

Veh. Year ___ Veh. Make ___ Veh. Type Code ___

Commercial Vehicle ___ ☐ Yes ☐ No   Trailer Type Code ___
Air Bag Deployed ___ ☐ Yes ☐ No   1st Trailer No. of Axles ___
Passenger ___ ☐ Yes ☐ No   Width ___ inches
Vehicle Drivable ___ ☐ Yes ☐ No   Length ___ feet
Post Crash Fire ___ ☐ Yes ☐ No   2nd Trailer No. of Axles ___
Rollover ___ ☐ Yes ☐ No   Width ___ inches
Hazardous Cargo ___ ☐ Yes ☐ No   Length ___ feet

N.C. COLLISION REPORT FORM — Send To: N. C. Division of Motor Vehicles Raleigh, N. C. 27697-0001

Spilled .... ☐ Yes ☐ No   TAD
Crossed Median .... ☐ Yes ☐ No   Est. Damage $
Removed to
By _____ Authority _____

Spilled .... ☐ Yes ☐ No   TAD
Crossed Median .... ☐ Yes ☐ No   Est. Damage $
Removed to
By _____ Authority _____

Other Property Damaged _____   Estimated Damage $ Owner Name _____
Address _____

OCCUPANT SECTION INSTRUCTIONS: Give Injury Class, Belt/Helmet Usage, Race/Sex and Age of all occupants in the space corresponding to the seat occupied (see codes at top). Names and addresses are necessary for all occupants.

Seat	4. In. Class	5. Belt /Hel.	Race /Sex	Age	Names and Addresses First Name	Last Name	Seat	4. In. Class	5. Belt /Hel.	Race /Sex	Age	Names and Addresses First Name	Last Name
Left Front					DRIVER 1		Left Front					DRIVER 2, PEDESTRIAN, OTHER	
Center Front							Center Front						
Right Front							Right Front						
Left Rear							Left Rear						
Center Rear							Center Rear						
Right Rear							Right Rear						

Total Number Occupants   Total Number Injured

Ambulance Requested ☐ Yes ☐ No   If yes, Ambulance Arrived At _____ _____ (24 Hour Clock)   Serviced by _____

Injured Taken To _____ (Treatment Facility and City or Town)   NAME OF EMS

Total Number Occupants   Total Number Injured

MARKS >   < ADDED BY (Initial)

Figure 10.1A

A North Carolina accident form. Courtesy Burlington Police Department

POINTS OF INITIAL CONTACT (Write in Codes)

VEH. 1	VEH. 2

Passenger Cars/Small Trucks

Motorcycle, Bicycle or Moped (See Front)

Tractor-Trailers

UNDERNEATH: 0. No Contact 22. Front 23. Center 24. Rear 25. Rollover 25. Unknown

CIDENT SEQUENCE	Veh. 1	Veh. 2 or Ped.		Veh. 1	Veh. 2 or Ped.
6. Veh. Maneuver/Ped. Action					
7. First Harmful Event			Speed Limit (for each vehicle)		
7. Most Harmful Event			Estimated Original Traveling Speed		
8. Object Struck			Estimated Speed at Impact		
9. Distance to Object Struck			Tire Impressions Before Impact (ft.)		
10. Vehicle Defects			Distance Traveled After Impact (ft.)		

ROADWAY INFORMATION (See Front)

11. Locality	
12. Development Type	
13. Road Feature	
14. Road Character	
15. Road Class	
16. Number of Lanes	
17. Road Configuration	
18. Road Surface	
19. Road Defects	
20. Road Condition	
21. Light Condition	
22. Weather	
23. Traffic Control	
Operating ☐ Yes ☐ No	
Visible ☐ Yes ☐ No	

INDICATE NORTH

Vehicle 1 was Traveling ☐ N ☐ S ☐ E ☐ W ☐ on

DESCRIBE WHAT HAPPENED:

Vehicle 2 was Traveling ☐ N ☐ S ☐ E ☐ W ☐ on

RESERVED FOR CITY OR OTHER USE

CIRCUMSTANCES CONTRIBUTING TO THE COLLISION (Check as many as apply)

DRIVER					DRIVER	
1	2				1	2
☐	☐	1. None		19. Safe movement violation	☐	☐
☐	☐	2. Alcohol use		20. Following too closely	☐	☐
☐	☐	3. Drug use		21. Improper backing	☐	☐
☐	☐	4. Yield		22. Improper parking	☐	☐
☐	☐	5. Stop sign		23. Unable to determine	☐	☐
☐	☐	6. Traffic signal		24. Left of center	☐	☐
☐	☐	7. Exceeding speed limit		25. Right turn on red	☐	☐
☐	☐	8. Exceeding safe speed		26. Other	☐	☐
☐	☐	9. Failure to reduce speed				
☐	☐	10. Pass stopped school bus				
☐	☐	11. Passing on hill				
☐	☐	12. Passing on curve				
☐	☐	13. Other improper passing				
☐	☐	14. Improper lane change				
☐	☐	15. Use of improper lane				
☐	☐	16. Improper turn				
☐	☐	17. Improper or no signal				
☐	☐	18. Improper vehicle equipment				

RESERVED FOR STATE USE

	Driver 1	Driver 2
24. Direction		
25. Violation		
26. Misc. Action		
27. Charges		
28. Investigating Agency		

WIT- Name _____ Address _____ Phone No. ( )

NESSES: Name _____ Address _____ Phone No. ( )

ARRESTS: Name _____ Charge(s) _____

Name _____ Charge(s) _____

Sign Here _____ _____ _____ _____

Officer's Rank and Name   Number   Department   Date of Report

Figure 10.1B

The reverse of a North Carolina accident form

property dispute. To resolve the dispute, the judge needs comprehensive information on the couple's assets: income earned, stocks owned, real estate in husband's or wife's name (or both), cash balances in the bank. Names and ages of children are often in the record, something that can be of use years later if you are trying to cross-check names of a public official's relatives for a story on nepotism (birth certificates are another good source for nepotism stories, because they tell the mother's maiden name and can help you track in-laws on her side of the family). As mentioned previously, one major obstacle may be privacy rights. Some states keep most divorce proceedings hidden behind a veil of secrecy in a family court where only the principals have access to the facts. Confidentiality is also an issue when a birth occurred out of wedlock. Statistics indicate that nearly one-quarter of the nation's unmarried women are having children, and some jurisdictions treat these birth certificates with more secrecy.

Tax Information

It is difficult or impossible to obtain state or federal income tax records. This information is withheld on grounds of privacy. However, there are exceptions. The Internal Revenue Service does have procedures for making available certain tax information of nonprofit entities and other charitable groups. Your local IRS office can explain the procedures to you.

Property taxes are another matter. Just about everywhere you can find in public records detailed information on every taxable parcel of real property: who owns it; who used to own it; the amount for which it is assessed; to whom the tax bill is sent. There are ways to keep some of this information concealed—such as by holding property in the name of corporations, partnerships, or blind trusts—but generally, property tax records are among the most valuable repositories of public information for the journalist.

Voting Lists

These records are public. Voting lists have names and addresses. Sometimes they show party affiliations, social security numbers, telephone numbers (even unlisted ones), birth dates, or even arcane bits of data like the voter's mother's maiden name (obtained at the time of registration so that, if challenged at the polling place, the voter can verify his or her identity). If voting registers are available from past years, you can use them to trace a person's previous address (at least where they said they lived) at given times in the past. Or you can demonstrate that some civic-minded candidate for public office never even bothered to vote until he or she decided to run.

You also can compare voting lists with other public records to find inconsistencies. Let's say Sam Sleazy is registered to vote in the 19th District. Sam also owns a house in the 23rd District, and the property tax records on that house show that Sam is getting a $10,000 homestead exemption on that house because he claims it is his personal residence. Either Sam is voting illegally or he is claiming the exemption illegally. You have a story.

Reverse Telephone Book

Most television stations and newspapers have phone directories that list phone numbers in numerical order and tell you who has each number. These books also organize phone number information by street and house number. Thus, if you want to identify the neighbors of someone who lives at 336 West Siwash Avenue, this cross-indexed telephone directory will tell you the phone numbers and names of the people at 334 and 338 (assuming the phone numbers are not unlisted).

Building Department Records

As mentioned at the start of the chapter, you need a permit to build something or to make modifications above a certain value to buildings. There may be as many as 15 or more required inspections. City inspectors are supposed to check construction in progress to make sure that electrical, plumbing, and other building codes are being followed. Inspectors also go through completed buildings to make sure changes have not been made that take the building out of compliance with the codes. Building or fire inspectors also check for compliance with fire codes. A building found in violation is issued a notice of violation and may be fined or brought into court. Permits, inspections, and violation records normally are on file at your municipal building department.

City Directories

Private firms publish city directories for most midsized and large cities in the United States. These can be found in newsrooms. In addition to the basic information you can find in the phone book, city directories often give name of spouse, place of employment, officers of a corporation, and type of business. Occasionally a phone number unlisted by the phone company will creep into the city directory because directory information is compiled independently. Because people move every five years on average, some data in directories are outdated.

Corporate Records

Laws vary, but every state has some procedure for organizing a corporation. In some states, the annual statements that corporations are required to file contain updated lists of officers and stockholders, and even financial information on how much business the corporation did during the year according to broad categories of commerce.

Normally, with a small, privately-held local company, you can track down information about its original owners and officers, capitalization, and stockholders. However, original incorporation papers for a small company may be misleading. In most cases, an attorney will have done the incorporating and the attorney's name or the names of legal secretaries in the attorney's law office may show up in various official positions on the incorporation papers. You need to be aware of which names have to do with who really owns the company. Make sure you do not put outdated or incorrect information into a news story.

Sometimes you must track through records in more than one state to get a true picture of the activities of a corporation. An out-of-state corporation may file minimal records in your state capital but have a full record in the state where it has its headquarters. Delaware is a useful place to look for corporate records. Many corporations incorporate in Delaware because the fees are less expensive and it takes about an hour to charter a corporation there.

Publicly traded corporations comply with the rules of the Securities and Exchange Commission (SEC). SEC data are available on the World Wide Web. Reports filed with the SEC contain information about major stockholders, the increases and decreases in their holdings, and the buying and selling of stock by corporate officers, directors, and other "insiders." This information gives a reporter insight into what is going on inside a big firm.

Courthouse Records

When a person is charged with a crime, the system starts building a paper trail. The file eventually may contain information on the crime itself, the testimony of witnesses, details of an indictment, recommendations by probation officers, sentencing, and any appeals. Probation reports can also be useful. A probation officer's presentence report often contains details about the person's background that a judge can use in determining the proper sentence. In many jurisdictions this report remains confidential for privacy reasons.

Crimes are not the only incidents that are litigated in court. Thousands of civil suits are filed daily when people can't settle disputes over such matters as property or money. Just as with a criminal charge, the filing of a civil suit starts an official file in some court clerk's office. The plaintiff lays out the case in simple terms. The defendant files an answering brief. Both sides begin the discovery process of obtaining records and interviewing witnesses. Transcripts of the trial appear. Appeal briefs summarize the facts in support of the case for each side. By the time a civil case works its way through all steps, a great deal of material has been entered into the record.

Except in extraordinary circumstances, all the material relating to a civil lawsuit is public record. Even better, the fact that something you report comes from a court record usually gives it *qualified privilege*. This means that generally, in most states, if you make a fair and accurate report of the contents of a court file, you cannot successfully be sued afterward for libel. This is why some reporters get excited when they come upon a particularly interesting and useful fact in a courthouse file.

Civil lawsuits over money frequently expose to public view a broad look at the participants' financial status—income statements, outstanding loans, or business connections. The contents of a lengthy civil suit are often the best place for you as a reporter to get a good grasp of the financial and business connections of anyone about whom you are curious.

Two special categories of civil court records are worth mentioning: probate records and bankruptcy records. When a person dies, the distribution of the estate goes through a legal process in court known as probate. As *Honolulu Advertiser* investigative reporter James Dooley observes, "It's a little crass to say, but when people die suddenly, often secrets that they have labored all their lives to keep secret get stuck in the probate files." Probate files are public record. They can be helpful even if you are investigating living persons. Often, their parents or other relatives have died and left them something in a will. Details on this property can be found in the courthouse's probate file on the deceased.

Going bankrupt is a little like dying in one regard—all your financial affairs get spread out in public view. When people file for bankruptcy (the bankruptcy laws are federal laws and the filings are in federal court), they generally must outline in detail their assets and liabilities. This information is available even about people and corporations who are just one step short of bankruptcy; the federal bankruptcy law has a provision (known as Section 11) that allows people to get under the wing of the bankruptcy court while they try to get their affairs in order to reorganize their overwhelming debts so they eventually can pay them. This, too, requires a public filing that is full of financial information.

Charities

Many states require charities to file at least some rudimentary financial information. From these records you can get names of officers and often full details on budgets, including how much of the donated funds are spent on administration and fund raising.

Three other useful sources of information about specific charities are: the National Charities Information Bureau (NCIB), 19 Union Square West, Dept. 326, New York, NY 10003; the Philanthropic Advisory Service (PAS) of the Council of Better Business Bureaus, 4200 Wilson Blvd., Suite 800, Arlington, VA 22203; and the American Institute of Philanthropy (AIP), 4579 Laclede Ave., Suite E17, St. Louis, MO 63108. NCIB and PAS compile reports primarily based on information that the charities themselves volunteer, and they note which charities refuse to cooperate. AIP evaluates charities solely on the basis of financial information, including tax forms, available audit reports and state documents. Each of the monitoring groups has a set of standards by which it evaluates charities and their fund-raising activities. The Council of Better Business Bureaus frequently publishes lists of charities that fail to disclose pertinent information or that generate many "inquiries."

Licensing Records

State and local governments license and regulate all manner of professions from doctors and dentists and lawyers to masseurs and barbers and escort agency operators. David Anderson and Peter Benjaminson, in *Investigative Reporting*, note that in New York City, "a person must have a license to hold a block party, be an able seaman, embalm, exterminate, grade hay and straw, smoke on piers . . . store rubber cement, make sausages, transplant hard shell clams, and open a deli." Licenses are also needed for seaplane bases.

Although you are not apt to run across many unlicensed seaplane bases to expose during your journalistic career, it should be obvious that there are a variety of files filled with licensing information. Applicants sometimes file personal background information to get licensed, and that material is often public record for the journalist to peruse. Unfortunately, many jurisdictions are beginning to lock these files from public view to preserve the licensees' privacy. At a minimum, however, you can normally determine if Person X is properly licensed by State Y to do business in Profession Z. That in itself can be a story.

You may find that the Amalgamated Towing Company got a city contract to haul away overparked cars even though the company lacks a city towing license in the first place, or that Dr. John Doe, who got his medical license yanked in North Dakota after pleading guilty to Medicare fraud, is happily practicing in your state even though the law prohibits convicted criminals from having medical practice privileges.

Records of Regulatory Agencies

This century has seen the proliferation of a new kind of government agency—arms of the executive branch that function similar to courts or legislatures. Examples of these agencies at the federal level include the Federal Communications Commission (FCC), Federal Trade Commission (FTC), and National Labor Relations Board (NLRB). At the local and state level, zoning and land-use boards and public utilities commissions work in the same way. These government panels, which often have part-time members, are given wide authority to adopt regulations having force of law, to carry out licensing activities, to sit as judicial panels and settle disputes, and to set rate schedules for private companies or utilities. A regulatory agency's meetings and hearings are generally open and often instructive.

The best place to look for insight into a labor union or a labor dispute is often in the National Labor Relations Board records. The NLRB records contain filings by unions, by constituent employers, and by the NLRB's own investigative staff. For a given labor-management dispute, the NLRB file can give you the same sort of information that courthouse files provide on a civil lawsuit.

Campaign Spending Records

The laws fluctuate widely, but the federal government and most states now have some requirement that candidates for public office file reports stating where they got their campaign funds (at least the larger contributions) and how they spent them. These filings make news while a campaign is taking place as political reporters write stories about who gave how much to whom and which candidate has the most money. The reports often remain available years down the road when a reporter tries to establish a history of the political ties of someone in the news.

Scouring campaign spending reports for meaningful information can be challenging. Lists generally are not alphabetical or structured to make analysis easy. In most states, there is no need for the candidate to provide information about contributors. Thus, if you want to find out how much money came to "Governor Phoghorn" from "Wallcrack Architectural Partners, Inc.," you must look for the names of all the principals (and their spouses) to see if they made monetary contributions which might be tied to "Wallcrack." Even if you discover a connection, you probably will not feel confident that you have found everything. The task can be eased by using a computer to match up lists of, for example, campaign contributors against government contractors. The search often is worthwhile.

Grantor-Grantee Index

Most land transactions and mortgages are filed in some public place. The grantor-grantee index to property in your area may be located in a land court, at a bureau of conveyances, with a registrar of deeds, or in some other office with an obscure title. This is where you will find answers to questions such as: When did John Jones buy and sell any land or real property? What are his outstanding mortgages and from which bank and at what rate? Has any creditor placed a lien on his home that he must pay off before he sells it? What was the purchase price of a parcel of land?

In many jurisdictions, you will find the latter information in the form of tax stamps that give you at least a rough idea of monetary values. Because of the existence of two sets of property records, you can find out both who owns a particular piece of property (tax records) and what property a particular person owns (grantor-grantee index).

Property records are fairly complete and up to date, but they are not perfect. During the past ten years, mortgage rates soared and

declined, and some people resorted to different financing arrangements for property transactions. These transactions may or may not
be publicly filed. One common method is for the seller to take back a
mortgage, accept a down payment, and agree to formally transfer the
property some years later after the buyer pays the balance of the
money. In some states this is called an agreement of sale, in other
places a contract for deed. Practices vary, and the existence of such
agreements often will show up on property tax records because the
buyer assumes responsibility for tax payments right away, even
though the deed has not formally changed hands.

Some Other Records

Every government office keeps some sort of records about what it
does. What's in them? Expense account information for civil servants,
board members, and commissioners who travel at public expense;
information on who has guns registered and who is allowed to carry
a concealed weapon; results of restaurant health inspections and
inspections for water pollution, air pollution, and sewage outflow.
Depending on how useful your state's "sunshine law" is, you can get
at some, most, or all of what you want with just a simple request for
access to the particular file drawer or folder that contains what you
need.*

A final caution about public records: All such information is put on
file by people who can sometimes make mistakes or act wrongly. Double-check findings with other sources. Some public records are privileged, meaning that you are not apt to be successfully sued if you
write about them fairly and accurately. However, the fact that the
information is privileged does not absolve the journalist from double-
checking and trying to determine its accuracy. No piece of information is true just because it's in writing.

Access to Records

Accessing all the viable records, both paper and electronic, may be
more difficult than you think. In 1967 the federal government passed

---

*For a more thorough look at hundreds of types of documents, and how to get and
use them, pick up *The Reporter's Handbook: An Investigator's Guide to Documents and Techniques*, edited by John Ullmann and Steven Honeyman for
Investigative Reporters and Editors, Inc. New York: St. Martin's Press, 1983.

the Freedom of Information (FOI) Act requiring public agencies to make public records available within a reasonable amount of time. If a request is made for records—and the request should be for clearly defined records—the records should be provided within 10 working days. According to the FOI Act, the federal government is required to let you see all of its records except the following:

1. Classified defense and foreign policy information.

2. Internal personnel rules and practices of an agency.

3. Data exempted by another law. (This has been dubbed the "catchall" exemption by the FOI Service Center, which reports that federal agencies at one time or another have cited nearly 100 other laws as justification for withholding documents. The "catchall" covers such predictable areas as income-tax forms and Central Intelligence Agency and Census Bureau records. The "catchall" also has made it difficult to obtain information from the Federal Trade Commission, farm loan and parity programs, and some Postal Service information.)

4. Trade secrets.

5. Internal memos or communications—the so-called executive-privilege exemption that applies to internal working papers, preliminary drafts, and letters between bureaucrats. (The FOI Service Center says this exemption, which also includes communications between bureaucrats and the government lawyers serving them, is widely used by the government to deny public access to records.)

6. Personnel, medical, or other files that would "constitute a clearly unwarranted invasion of personal privacy."

7. Current law-enforcement investigation files.

8. Records relating to bank regulation.

9. Information about geology and geography of oil and other wells.

Government agencies sometimes find other reasons to delay answering requests. If a request for records is vague or undefined—for example, a request asking for *all* records pertaining to President Franklin Roosevelt—an agency will return it. If the agency is overburdened with requests, it will delay your request, although it will tell you so by letter within the required 10 working days. The average amount of time required to obtain records is often months, and sometimes years.

Former AP Bureau Chief Terry Anderson, imprisoned as a hostage in Lebanon for seven years, used the FOI Act after his release to seek records about the type of U.S. government efforts made over the years to free him. Although famous, and even the subject (along with fellow hostages) of a 1993 Broadway play, Anderson often ran into the same stone wall as did other reporters and individuals. Anderson wrote:

> The Freedom of Information Act was conceived in the 1950s by members of Congress desperate to gain the release of files on people who had come under attack by Senator Joseph McCarthy for supposed disloyalty. Approved finally by Congress in 1966, the act established as law the simple belief that Government records should be available to the public. The burden of proof was to be on the Government to justify keeping information classified. It hasn't worked out that way.

Still, many reporters have found the frustration of using the FOI Act well worth the wait.

The Uses of Many Documents and Databases

The paper trail may not be followed for very long because agencies are beginning to shift files from paper to computer databases. You can use individual documents to answer simple questions, such as the who, what, when, where, and how of a specific event—for example, a car accident. Individual documents tell an individual's story. However, to find the whys of general events, it is necessary to check many documents. Databases are excellent for locating, accessing, and organizing appropriate information contained in several documents.

A database is a collection of documents and other information in electronic form. From a database that summarizes information from many individual reports, you may be able to discover that a particular street location is the site of many accidents, suggesting an engineering problem or a traffic light problem, or perhaps the police are not doing their job at that location. From your database or spreadsheet, which may take time to put together, you can generate the types of perspectives that you want because you have control over what data you obtain and how you organize them.

Reporters can use databases as sources, especially to find patterns in documents. With Nexis, one of many information databases that index hundreds of newspapers and journals, reporters can look up stories on topics that already have been published. For example, a reporter, given a little time, should be able to prepare for an interview with the most brilliant scientist by using the scientist's name to retrieve already-published stories about and by the scientist. Another feature allows you to select any word at random—take "peanuts," for example—and define it or link it to another topic in such a way that the information you retrieve enables you to generate a local story. For example, "peanuts" and "agriculture" and "south" would likely show that peanuts are emerging as an important Southern cash crop. Or, "peanuts" and "politics" might show that peanuts can be a political issue that influences how politicians get things done. Or, "peanuts" and "health" might reveal that the humble peanut makes an important contribution (or not) to personal diet and health. Not all word combinations produce background stories during a search, but the point is that you can introduce your own terms and build your own background.

Reporters seek to dig up news about specific, concrete events, such as murders, new budgets, the construction of streets, or the purchase of new equipment. Specific events generate many documents and establish trails you can follow. When you are writing about specific events, you are well served by the standing questions to which reporters seek answers: who, what, when, where, and sometimes why and how. You always have to keep deadlines in mind and usually have to use a variety of sources to complete a story about specific events. Most journalism education is designed to enable reporters to handle specific events, which are, after all, what we deal with daily.

Reporters also can learn to think more generally, developing stories from documents that spell out in more detail how one incident is related to a class of events. Computers, as we shall see, are helpful in putting these stories together. When you search for patterns in the "how" of events you are better able to attempt to answer the hardest question—the "why" of events. This will require interviews and other sources. It is easier to see the results of a car accident or murder than to know how or why the event happened. Lengthy trials cannot always establish the how or why of serious crimes. Reporters can explain the how and why of specific events no better than anyone else, yet if reporters look at events collectively, through documents, they can add a perspective to public discourse that is not readily available from other sources. One event does not make a pattern, but a variety of similar events might.

For example, David Michelmore and Bob Donaldson, reporters for the *Pittsburgh Post-Gazette*, sought to learn whether the 122 industrial towns that line the region's rivers had shared in the 1993 economic recovery of the region as a whole. They used a computer to analyze large sets of publicly available data to compare the river towns to the 426 towns in the rest of the region in more than 40 categories, including household income, tax rates, kinds of jobs, and housing values. The data came from the 1980 and 1990 censuses, the State Tax Equalization Board, the state Department of Community Affairs, and the Southwestern Pennsylvania Regional Planning Commission. They found that the river towns did not compare favorably to the rest of the region, and that these towns shared with each other common elements of decline.

To illustrate another example of thinking generally, you might be interested in determining the most dangerous neighborhoods for certain kinds of crime—say, auto theft—so you can write a story that informs readers about how to take precautions when they are in those parts of town. The police station would provide records dealing with auto theft. If you look back over the records from today through a year ago, you will probably discover patterns that give you an idea of the areas in which a car is most likely to be vandalized or stolen. You can determine the time of day and day of the week that the crime is most likely to happen and the types of cars most vulnerable to theft. Nearly any record can, like this one, be divided into its parts for collective analysis. In such a way, reporters can always be searching for the patterns buried in individual documents.

Rather than starting with an idea, you might use a document, such as an annual report, to discover a topic for a story. Annual reports are designed to make certain trends clear, and usually the trends highlighted in such reports make a company or department look good. For example, you may note that the police annual report shows a decline in overall crime. Yet after looking closely at the figures, you find that, while there is a big decrease in citations for jaywalkers, the number of drug-related cases has increased, so the overall decline is nothing to celebrate. Your discovery of the trend concealed in the annual report has generated substance for a story. On the other hand, sometimes agencies highlight problems to increase support for their needs. For example, a fire department may need better equipment and design its report to elicit more funds to purchase equipment. Journalists should always be looking for nuances in annual reports.

Gathering information for a story about overall trends in crime might cause you to go back to the original arrest documents and construct your own annual report to compare with the official one. If there are differences, you will want to conduct a number of interviews to highlight the problem. Documents are one of the best sources for finding patterns, but documents do not tell you what the patterns are. You have to search for them.

Using Computers as Detectives

Reporters can use computers to search among data, add up facts, and bring facts together from different places where they are stored on documents. Of course, the data are not really moved. An electronic impulse enables you to collect and organize data without disturbing the original information.

Stories that deal with money are sometimes more accessible by computer because to examine so many records by hand would be time consuming and allow high possibilities for error. Computers are dumb machines with infinite patience for such tedious work.

During 1985 in Rhode Island, three children were run over by school buses in separate incidents. Reporters at the *Providence Journal* used computer-assisted cross-indexing to match the names of public school bus drivers with a list of all traffic tickets given out in the state over a three-year period. They found that several drivers had collected 10–20 driving violations. Next, they matched the list of drivers with the criminal court tapes to identify drivers who had been convicted of drug dealing. Elliot Jaspin, the reporter whose enterprise resulted in the story, noted:

> At this point in the story we had matched more than one million records to find school bus drivers with questionable backgrounds. Obviously we could not have done this without a computer. But the computer was more than just a quick way to find information. It made our story definitive. If, using traditional reporting techniques, we had found one or two bad drivers, the government could have shrugged the story off as one or two people who slipped through the cracks. Using the computer we were able to look at *all* the drivers, *all* the court records, and *all* the traffic violations. Given that kind of thoroughness, there was no way to refute the story.

As a result of the story, the person in charge of the state's bus safety program was replaced, all the bus drivers were rechecked, 65 drivers had their licenses revoked, and the entire licensing procedure was revamped.

The *Washington Post* decided to examine the state of bank loans in the area of the District of Columbia to see if banks favored certain racial groups who tended to have high incomes over others—in other words, did banks discriminate against blacks or other minorities who might not be considered "attractive" loan prospects. Reporters at the *Post* used computers to read the loan records of banks in the areas, comparing the areas where people were able to get loans with those areas where bank loans were not easily available or not available at all. The *Post* discovered, as have other newspapers, that area banks did favor borrowers who were white and lived in acceptable, more upscale areas. (See box 10-2 for the *Post* story.)

Box 10-2

Uncovering Discrimination

A racially biased system of home lending exists in the Washington area, with local banks and savings and loans providing mortgages to white neighborhoods at twice the rate they do to comparable black ones, a study by the *Washington Post* has found.

The computer-assisted study, which analyzed more than 130,000 deeds of homes sold in 1985 and 1991, showed that race—not income or housing characteristics—was the decisive factor in determining where local banks and thrifts made home loans in the Washington area.

Residents of black communities, with few government-regulated banks and thrifts in their neighborhoods to rely on, often turn instead to private mortgage companies. These mortgage companies pursue minority business aggressively, but critics say they often charge higher fees and interest rates for loans in black neighborhoods than they do in comparable white communities, which can cost minority borrowers additional thousands of dollars over the life of the loan.

Despite toughened federal laws that require banks and thrifts to lend money equitable in all areas, the study found that local banks and thrifts haven't increased the percentage of loans made in predominantly black neighborhoods.

The *Post*'s analysis also found that:

Although mortgage companies grant the bulk of the area's home loans, many of these businesses concentrate their lending in the black neighborhoods that banks and thrifts often ignore. But even the credit they provide does not bring lending in black neighborhoods up to the level in comparable white ones.

The pattern of inequality begins with the location of bank branches and the variety of financial services they provide. Predominantly white areas have three times as many branches per resident as do black neighborhoods, and generally receive service that is far superior to that in black areas.

Old-line Washington banks and thrifts do less business in predominantly black neighborhoods than do newly arrived financial institutions whose headquarters are hundreds of miles away.

Lending discrimination, while evident in the suburbs, is most pronounced in the District, where some areas almost never receive home mortgages from local banks and thrifts.

Nearly all the top executives of local banks and thrifts live and work within the predominantly white suburbs or in Northwest Washington and have devised bank policies that, intentionally or not, serve to discriminate against minority borrowers.

This unequal pattern of lending by banks and thrifts appears to violate what Congress intended when is passed the federal Community Reinvestment Act more than 15 years ago. This law requires banks and thrifts to meet the credit needs in all areas where they collect deposits. The Clinton administration recently has tightened enforcement of the law in an effort to push bankers to lend more in minority neighborhoods.

Because Mortgage companies don't take money from the community in the form of deposits, they are not bound by this law and can pick and choose the communities where they want to do business.

Joel Glenn Brenner and Liz Spayd, "Separate and Unequal,"
Washington Post, June 6, 1993, A1.© 1993 The *Washington Post.*
Reprinted with permission.

Content Analysis of Documents

Sometimes you cannot find what you want from an examination of individual documents, and databases may not have the information either. If you have the time, you can still mine documents by using the research method of content analysis. Content analysis is used to explore the meaning of documents. For example, during World War II, United States and Allied intelligence specialists wanted to figure out the thinking of Germany's leaders, especially Adolf Hitler, in order to guess how German forces would be used. Would German troops be used mostly in the East against the Soviet Union or in the West against the United States, Britain, France, or other allies? Analysts obtained translations of key broadcasts or other documents and examined the words with the assumption that if a particular word appeared frequently (say, "Russia"), it could be significant. Analysts also discovered it could be significant if certain words that *should* be mentioned frequently (again, say, "Russia") did not appear at all. Content analysis assumes that documents reflect thinking. Using content analysis to read the German mind, analysts were able to get a picture that reflected some of the thinking of Germany's leaders. Following World War II, the facts confirmed these results of projected invasions and other military operations. Content analysis attempts to discover what documents really say.

Before you use content analysis, first see if there is any other way to obtain the information that you need. Content analysis is a laborious way to obtain information. If data already exist in some form, then you may be able to obtain it from an existing database. If not, then you may want to use content analysis. Reporters should consider the following as the most sensible approach to documents.

Step 1: Examine one or more documents, taking notes. Do you need to go further to complete your story?

Step 2: If examining a few documents does not provide what you want, is there a database that already exists that can provide the pattern of information you need?

Step 3: If documents or a database do not provide what you want, consider conducting a content analysis.

The process might work like this: You want to know if blacks and whites and men and women are treated the same way by the courts. You have a hunch that blacks, who are more likely to depend upon less experienced, younger, court-appointed attorneys, may obtain longer sentences. You also suspect that women, who may have families or who are less likely to be habitual criminals, might be given lighter sentences than men. Social scientists would call your hunch a hypothesis.

You focus on the crime of robbery because you want to see whether the sentences differ for different people who are convicted of exactly the same crime. You are ready for Step 1, examination of documents, to see if your questions about blacks versus whites and men versus women can be answered.

You discover that a single document provides a lot of information about a single case. Several documents provide information about more cases, but not enough to establish a trend. Your question cannot be answered easily from an examination of documents.

So you move to Step 2, looking for an existing database that will answer your question. There are a number of computerized records that are maintained by the court system. These do not answer your question about race and sex. You should ask yourself: Is my story idea worth pursuing beyond this point?

If so, move to Step 3, consideration of a content analysis. You should not perform Step 3 without careful planning. A content analysis requires that you identify and establish access to a reasonable body of public records stored either on paper or on a computer (but in a computer form that does not fit your questions). You will need to decide what time period you want to examine. It is best to look at the performance of a court system for at least an entire year, so you will need access to a year's worth of records. You certainly want the most recent year, but it is possible that you will want to look at trends over several recent years.

Once records are located, you need to sample among them. Just as a public opinion poll does not ask questions of everyone in the nation to get a picture of national opinion, you usually need not examine every document. Perhaps one document in every ten will do. If so, decide how you will pick the first one, then take every 10th document following. Or use some other strategy to make sure that you have a representative sample of documents. You also need to make sure you have enough documents. The idea is to look at as few as possible, but still enough to be able to generalize to all cases represented by the documents.

You need to devise a coding sheet to record information. For example, for each case you will need to mark whether the defendant was male or female, black or white, and the type and length of each sentence. You will want to keep up with the record of individual judges, and you will think of many other types of information that you might mark down. (For example, you could note the month of the trial to see if judges give longer sentences in the winter than in the spring, when presumably the hearts of men and women judges turn more to thoughts of love).

Your coding sheet might look something like figure 10.2.

Name of Court   _____
City, District of Court   _____
Date of Trial   _____
Guilty?   _____
Length of Sentence   _____
Sex of Defendant   _____
Race of Defendant   _____
Name of Judge   _____
Race (if known) of judge   _____

Figure 10.2
A sample coding sheet

We could add more criteria. However, if you go through a sample of paper documents and consistently mark down information for each of the categories in figure 10.2, you will be able, with the help of a computer, to compare the lengths of sentences given blacks and whites, for example. One can visualize a record sheet like figure 10.3.

You could also use the coding sheet (figure 10.2) to compile other data, such as sentences given by different judges or in different seasons which could be transferred to a record sheet to showcomparisons.

If your sample were large enough, you actually could prepare a graph that illustrates the number and type of sentences given to black defendants versus white defendants to see more clearly if there is any unwitting bias. In fact, the *Richmond Times-Dispatch* did a study several years ago very much like the one we have described and found that there were differences in lengths of sentences given to whites versus blacks convicted of the same crime, armed robbery (see figure 10.4).

If the court system maintains a database, and you can program your computer to generate the same type of information that is in our content analysis example, you will save time. For instance, a court

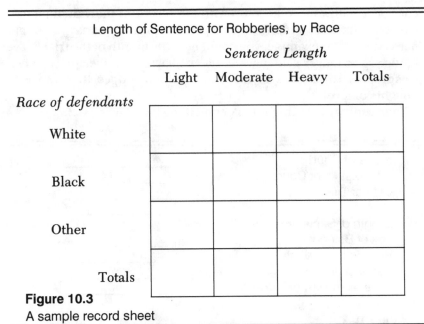

Length of Sentence for Robberies, by Race

	Sentence Length			
	Light	Moderate	Heavy	Totals
Race of defendants				
White				
Black				
Other				
Totals				

Figure 10.3
A sample record sheet

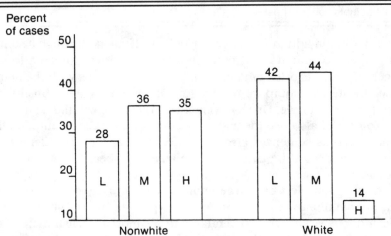

Light sentence (L): 0 to 3 years
Medium sentence (M): 4 to 8 years
Heavy sentence (H): 9 years and over

Figure 10.4
Sentence length by race in Virginia. Reprinted from "Unequal Justice,"
Richmond Times-Dispatch series, Oct. 16–21, 1983, p. 8.

system might file cases by type of crime, length of sentence, and the race and sex of defendants, as well as some other types of information. In fact, in 1995 the *Nashville Tennessean* performed a computer analysis very similar in content to the *Times-Dispatch* example. The study examined all 80,000 federal court convictions during 1992–93 and found that black defendants got prison sentences about 10 percent longer than did white defendants for similar crimes.

In the computer, records sit as still as paper documents in a file. Your challenge is figuring out how to make your computer do the work that you did by hand in the content analysis and to produce the tables you need. Of course, you need to obtain permission to access these computer records—a challenge if you go far back—and you likely will have to pay for a copy of the original data tape, normally a reasonable cost but sometimes set outrageously high to discourage use.

Officials and Documents

Leaders dislike information that does not reflect well on them or their agencies. Reporters soon learn that leaders always see what they do as good or beneficial—never as harmful or selfish, although it sometimes is. Leaders do not lie when they provide good reports on their organization's or their own performance. They believe what they say. But reporters know that while there is often agreement over facts, there is seldom agreement over interpretations and explanations of facts. Reporters have the challenging job of digging up facts and providing different perspectives on those facts.

This is not easy because news sources on beats usually are careful to provide only those facts required by law and to support those facts with favorable interpretations. If there is an increase in crime, police officials would see this as a failure of the community to hire enough police officers rather than a failure of the police to do an efficient job. Confronted with student bodies that complain about poor teaching on campuses that emphasize research, deans nearly always call for more money to hire more teachers rather than examine the performance of those already in teaching positions. Police chiefs and deans are not lying, and there may be support for their positions.

Sleeping Giants

Documents are the sleeping-giant sources of public affairs stories. A single document can reveal much about an individual, but many documents reveal a great deal about how groups of individuals work and about how the community functions. Databases allow you to search for patterns among records stored by the thousands. Content analysis allows you to generate data that no one else has and to combine and present it in original ways. Take out the documents from your wallet or purse (such as your driver's license) and lay them on the table. What do they say about you? Your name, age, address blood type, driving restrictions (need glasses?), organ donor status? What would a sample of licenses say about your community? Within documents lie many interesting patterns.

References

Anderson, David and Peter Benjaminson. *Investigative Reporting*. Bloomington: Indiana University Press, 1976.

Bain, George. "The World According to I.F. Stone," *Maclean's*, July 24, 1989: 35.

Barrett, Richard. *Using the 1990 U.S. Census for Research*. Thousand Oaks, CA: Sage, 1994.

Bernstein, Carl and Bob Woodward. *All the President's Men*. New York: Simon & Schuster, 1974.

"Blacks' Prison Terms Average 10% Longer." Durham, NC: *Herald-Sun*, Sept. 25, 1995, A3.

DeParle, Jason. "Big Rise in Births Outside Wedlock," *New York Times*, July 14, 1993, A1.

Jaspin, Elliot. "Out With the Paper Chase, In With the Data Base," Speech given to participants of "Newsroom Technology: The Next Generation," a technology studies seminar at the Gannett Center for Media Studies, March 20, 1989.

Michelmore, David L. and Bob Donaldson. "Can mill towns revive?" *Pittsburgh Post-Gazette*, Nov. 29, 1993, A1. Thanks to Jana Frederick-Collins for this example.

Chapter Eleven

USING DATABASES FOR REPORTING

Computer-assisted reporting does not replace traditional shoe-leather reporting. The computer study only forms the underpinning for the story, the foundation.

—Elliot Jaspin
The Computer Connection

In Florida in the early 1990s, a person convicted of a crime for the first time could ask the court to shield the conviction record from public view. No one would know about the "one mistake." The law from the 1970s was intended to protect young people arrested in college pranks or other similar activities, so they wouldn't lose out on promising jobs in the future.

Somewhere, though, the state judicial system lost control. Drug dealers asked for, and received, shields on their convictions. So did child abusers, and so did criminals convicted time and time again. After all, their "first offenses" were shielded from view. Subsequent convictions then became "first" ones, available to be hidden anew. Judges in charge of sentencing were basing decisions on "one-time" offenders.

How could journalists in 1991 expose the flaws of the system? How could they discover which criminals were being allowed to commit

This chapter was written by Bradley J. Hamm.

215

crimes again? When even judges did not learn the truth about criminals before them in the courtroom, how could a newspaper reveal this information to its readers? Journalists used computers, computer records, and spreadsheet formulas. What they found, what would have been barely accessible through hundreds of hours of "regular" journalism methods, led to the awarding of the Pulitzer Prize to the *St. Petersburg Times* staff for meritorious public service.

A journalist without computer skills could have written the story, but the coverage would not have been as thorough, as well-documented, and as hard-hitting. Its genius is in the specifics, the details which formed the many bricks to build the story.

Let's look at how another reporter for the *Columbus (Ohio) Dispatch* did computer analysis on his own, based on a hunch after reading stories about the killings of several prostitutes in Ohio. Reporter Michael Berens remembered that an FBI agent once told him serial killers often target prostitutes because they might not be missed for days. Berens then did a database search of Ohio newspapers to find stories about the murders of prostitutes. In addition, Berens used traditional reporting techniques, doing interviews at truck stops, visiting law enforcement offices, and making phone calls. He discovered stories from three separate sources telling about three different cases.

The connections? All three prostitutes disappeared from the same truck stop in Ohio, and in all three cases their bodies were found along Interstate 71 in Ohio. Berens then listed pieces of information about each crime by using Excel, a spreadsheet program, on his Macintosh. He compared the Ohio crimes to other killings of prostitutes in four states. He was able to link 11 homicides. After his stories were printed in the *Dispatch*, a 15-agency task force was formed to investigate the crimes.

Students and Computer-Assisted Journalism

It is important to understand how computers can be helpful for reporters. For many years the value of a computer in a newspaper office has been limited to production. Only recently have newsrooms begun to see computers as a useful, and perhaps essential, tool in news gathering. In the 1970s, newspapers used computers primarily for typesetting. Reporters punched keys much like they did with typewriters, except the computers allowed for faster editing. In the 1980s, newspapers used the small, personal computers for graphics

Computers play an important role in handling many tasks at a large city newspaper. Courtesy Chicago Tribune.

and innovations in layout. By the end of the decade, photographs were being sent by personal computers to even the small newspapers.

But personal and mainframe computers aren't just useful for creating, organizing, and typesetting stories, graphics and layouts. They can be an essential part of news gathering and information sorting for metropolitan dailies and small-town weeklies, and student newspapers, too.

While students can't mount the type of operation done by the *St. Petersburg Times*, they can take advantage of a computer's ability to connect with information sources throughout the world, do searches in a matter of seconds, and handle large amounts of statistical data which can be analyzed to provide essential facts for a news story. In many cases, the computer equipment and software programs available to most daily and nondaily newspapers are also available on the college campus. Most campuses have personal computers (IBM, Macintosh or other types), mainframe computers, modems, and spreadsheet software programs. Students have computers and modems in their residence halls. The technology needed for computer-assisted reporting is not limited to million-dollar newspaper operations; it might be in your own room or in your neighbor's.

As discussed in chapter 10, the computer is a helpful, time-saving device that can help student reporters in three main areas: gathering background material about the story, compiling and evaluating statistical information, and searching for sources to interview.

Background information is essential for strong interviews. Reporters must know as much as possible about a story. Veteran reporters have built a network of sources. Oftentimes beat reporters will cover a story or organization for months or years, and they know the history of events and can quickly identify new story angles. Student journalists often do not have this advantage. They are strong on interest but usually short on experience. They often are given a story, having little prior knowledge about the issues involved.

A computer can help students learn historical background quickly and prepare intelligent questions. First, student journalists can search newspaper "morgues" or filing systems to locate past stories about the issue, either on a national or state level. Sometimes even the student's local newspaper is on-line. Secondly, they can search databases throughout the nation which contain articles from magazines and scholarly publications. Next, they can search specialized databases which contain myriad items such as information about state, regional, and national court cases; business and medical news; and an assortment of other features hardly imaginable—but within access in a matter of seconds or minutes.

For statistical research, student journalists can make use of a number of software programs, such as Excel, for both IBM and Macintosh computers. In these programs, students can either enter data they've collected or download the statistical information from a source who can give a diskette to them. Such information sometimes can be downloaded directly from the Internet. For example, for one of the student articles included later in this chapter, a student journalist requested and received class-enrollment information from the University of North Carolina at Chapel Hill. By loading the information directly on the computer, the reporter saved hours of work.

The computer is useful in organizing and analyzing data. It can do in seconds what journalists could spend all day trying to do. From simple math problems to complex sorting requirements, mainframe and personal computers make most tasks easier and, more importantly, some tasks possible. The project by the *St. Petersburg Times*, mentioned earlier, would be almost, if not completely, unmanageable by a reporter staff. Uses of computers for analyzing data may vary from project to project.

To find sources by computer, the student journalist can take advantage of the specific interest groups already reachable via computers. When your editor gives you a story, it is difficult to compile a list of sources beyond the obvious ones—student government leaders, college administrators, and a couple of people involved on campus. Journalists often are limited to their own frames of reference, their own friends and colleagues, in trying to find sources who aren't as obvious. Computer searches broaden the network.

For example, in doing a story about AIDS on college campuses, how would you: quickly get sources for a national perspective on the crisis? or get information about AIDS from many sources? or find out what other campuses are doing about AIDS? Using a computer and a modem, the student journalist can locate several hundred outlets about AIDS for information and sources.

With computer-assisted journalism, students can be better prepared for interviews and better able to identify inconsistencies that appear in answers. The story also can be more complete.

Students Using Computer-Assisted Methods

By now, computer-assisted journalism has become so widespread that there are numerous examples of quality stories. The St. Petersburg project mentioned earlier involved a number of reporters and editors. Large newspapers can let small groups work on projects—especially on extensive projects, such as the search of hidden records. It is unlikely that student journalists can enlist such help. While no reporter does everything without help, usually you are on your own as a student journalist when looking for the facts of a story. All kinds of stories lend themselves to the use of computer research and analysis. Included here in this chapter are two examples from an introductory course.*

* The author would like to thank Ms. Barbara Semonche, librarian at the School of Journalism and Mass Communication at the University of North Carolina at Chapel Hill, for the use of student papers from the course she taught in database research in the Spring of 1993. Also, Jana Frederick-Collins, a Ph.D. student at the UNC, helped to organize the student papers.

Michael Easterly, a journalism student at The University of North Carolina at Chapel Hill, used interviewing and computer-assisted journalism methods to gather, organize, and provide context for information on the effects of changes in enrollment and state budget cuts on class sizes at the University of North Carolina at Chapel Hill. First, he gathered and analyzed data on class sizes and enrollment. Next, he searched an information database for secondary sources on the topic. Finally, he provided context for the story by interviewing both administration officials about policy and professors about their experiences in the classroom. We present below his description of his steps in pursuing the topic, followed by his story.

Gathering Data for a Story on Class Sizes at the University of North Carolina. To start my project about class sizes, I first had to limit my search to specific comparative units. I chose to compare enrollment and class size data from spring semesters of 1987 and 1993. A representative of the registrar's office initially refused my request to get 1993 enrollment records on electronic format, so I filed a Freedom Of Information (FOI) request. After that, the registrar agreed to sit down with me and rewrite an existing SAS computer program to give me access to the statistics I needed: mean (average) number of students per class and the total number of classes for each department. The program also sorted class sections within each department by class size so that I could find for each department the median and the number of class sections with more than 100 students. The registrar said he could not give me an electronic copy because programmers had not developed a procedure for it.

The 1987 enrollment records were not stored in electronic format; therefore I had to copy the original records by hand. I then entered them into Microsoft Excel, which sorted them by size and calculated departmental averages. Presented with a potentially unmanageable volume of data, I had to narrow the field of eligible classes. I chose to examine only the 12 most popular departments, and I used a list of the number of undergraduate majors to make that determination.

Next, I conducted a database search of research on class sizes in ERIC, the education database. I requested articles with both the key words "class size" and "higher education." I got quite a few citations, so I checked their descriptor fields for additional key word ideas. I then added to my search strategy the key words and phrases: college education, large group instruction, teacher effectiveness, and teacher-student relationship. Although none of the 50 records were directly related to my research, they provided some background information and ideas for interviewing. The articles also confirmed the importance of the topic and the approach I was taking to it.

After my data was in and my search of secondary sources completed, I conducted my interviews. Again using the registrar's records, I located the three largest university classes and interviewed the first of those professors I could contact. I also interviewed various department heads. Although I didn't use all of the quotes, I still found the interviews valuable because they gave me useful clues in preparing to interview the provost.

"If Two's Company, 400 Is a Crowd"
Michael Easterly

For the past 15 weeks, students have filed into a first-floor room of Hamilton Hall every Monday, Wednesday and Friday at 11 a.m. to gain an appreciation of the finer points of drama—with about 400 of their closest friends. The class they are taking, "Elements of the Theater," is supposed to add to their knowledge of theater, to stimulate their critical thinking skills and to open their eyes to the beauties of the stage. The task of shepherding all 404 to these common goals falls on one person—lecturer Susanna Rinehart. "It's a weird contradiction," said Rinehart. "You're teaching such a personal and subjective topic in a class with so many people. But I've found a way to enjoy teaching it and of breaking it down."

In the past few years, many professors at the University of North Carolina at Chapel Hill have had to make the same adjustment. Average class sizes and the number of large class sections have increased significantly due to budget cuts and to shifts in student enrollment. Compared with the spring of 1987, average class sizes in the University's 12 most popular schools and departments have increased 14.4 percent, while in those same areas the number of class sections with more than 100 students has risen 18.3 percent.

In disciplines with increasing enrollments, the changes have been more dramatic. Since 1987 the history department recorded a 31.6 percent increase in average class size, while the number of students in chemistry sections grew 65.9 percent. Meanwhile the number of sections with more than 100 students increased from 5 to 11 in history and from 8 to 13 in chemistry.

While some of these events might have occurred only from unpredictable shifts in student interest, many of the changes can be attributed to budget cuts. In 1991 and 1992, the University suffered permanent budget reductions totaling $16.9 million. During the 1990-91 academic year, fiscal constraints eliminated 40 of UNC-CH's faculty positions. "With fewer positions it makes it tougher to be responsive to changes in enrollment," said Provost Richard McCormick, the University's chief academic officer.

Over the long term, the University can reallocate faculty positions to adjust for changes in enrollment, he said. If a professor retires or departs for another job, the position he or she left open can be transferred to another department. But many of these vacant positions have been eliminated by budget cuts, which has left many departments scrambling.

In chemistry, student enrollment has increased 72 percent while budget cuts have reduced the number of its faculty members. In the spring of 1993, 1,221 more students took a class in chemistry than did in the spring of 1987. Last fall McCormick had to allocate special funds for an additional class section after demand so exceeded departmental expectations that parents began calling his office. This spring the chemistry department still found itself unable to control class sizes.

"We decided several years ago that one of our goals would be to reduce class sizes," Department Chairman Joe Templeton said. . . .

Shannon Edge, a journalism student at The University of North Carolina at Chapel Hill, used interviewing and computer-assisted journalism methods to gather, organize, and provide context for information about the problem of drunk drivers, particularly in a college community. Her description description of the steps she took in pursuing the topic is followed by her magazine-oriented story.

Gathering Data for a Story on Drunk Drivers. Living in Chapel Hill, N.C. for three years now I am fully aware of the enormous amounts of alcohol that are consumed by students weekly. Knowing the risk that some students take driving drunk, I chose to set out and learn as much as I could about DWI offenders.

I began my search by obtaining statistics from the 1992 North Carolina Crime Report concerning DWI arrests. I then used Excel to create spreadsheets and graphs for representation of the typical DWI offender. I also used the UNC Online Catalog to find books and journal articles with such relevant topics as risk factors, personality differences and car accidents related to drinking and driving.

An interview with a local police officer helped to bring the matter close to home as he talked about DWI offenders here in Chapel Hill. I also went to the N.C. Highway Safety Research Center on East Franklin Street to obtain data concerning the number of people with drivers licenses by age, race and sex. Using Donneley's Demographics I was able to find N.C.'s 1991 estimated population. With all of this background information I was able to make conclusions about drunk driving and write an article suitable for publication in a newspaper or newsletter.

"Give up the Keys, Not Your Life"
Shannon Edge

Most Americans don't know that the leading cause of death for anyone under the age of 34 years is . . . an automobile accident. More importantly they don't know that more than one-half of these accidents involve alcohol. Every year as a result of drunk driving accidents, society loses about 2 million potential years of life and functioning. The National Highway Traffic Safety Administration estimates that at the current rate an estimated 40 percent of all people can be expected to be involved in an alcohol-related automobile accident. Unfortunately many of these crashes will take the lives of innocent victims. Therefore it is necessary to analyze the characteristics of typical Driving While Impaired (DWI) offenders and determine who is most likely to be involved in a drunk driving accident. This way society can take necessary action in preventing some of life's most serious tragedies.

The typical DWI offender is statistically a white male age 25–34. This conclusion was drawn after analyzing the statistics from the North Carolina Uniform Crime Report for 1992. Whites represented approximately two-thirds of all offenders while blacks represented less than one-third. Indians and Asians together represented the remaining 5 percent of all DWI offenders. The male-female ratio was statistically significant. In 1992, a male was nearly six times more likely to be arrested for drunk driving than a female.

Also statistically significant more than one-third of DWI offenders belonged to the 25–34 year age group. From age 15 to 21 there was a steady increase in the number of DWI arrests. However, from age 21 to 24 there was a fairly consistent number of arrests until age 25 where there was a drastic jump in the number of DWI arrests. From age 34 and older there was a gradual decline in the number of arrests leveling off around age 60. The percentage of arrests by month was insignificant as every month represented 7–10 percent of the total DWI arrests for the 1992 year. 70,174 DWI arrests were reported in 1992, a 13.2 percent decrease from the 80,863 arrests in 1991. The 1991 arrests represented only 1.64 of the total number of licensed drivers in N.C. and approximately 1.21 percent of North Carolina's population for that year. . . .

You can see how these two students used new technologies and their own creativity to gather, organize, and provide context for information, and write and present reports on important issues. The detailed analysis that is possible through the use of computer databases makes for stronger news stories because the facts are much harder to deny. Says Elliot Jaspin, a journalism professor and former Pulitzer Prize winner, "It is far harder to refute a detailed computer analysis than an anecdotal story that relies on the usual cast of well-informed sources."

Some Cautions about Computer-Assisted Journalism

A computer, like any tool, is appropriate for certain cases and essential for some projects. It is not, however, a replacement for other journalistic tools. Do not use the computer just to use it; you don't use a sledge hammer to remove the cap from a drink bottle, and you should consider how and when you need statistical analysis or database research. Some other cautions for the student journalist working with computers:

- Plan a project thoroughly if you are using statistical analysis. When creating a database, don't input statistical information before you have a clear idea of how you are going to use it. While some adjustments in data entry inevitably will be made, it's very time consuming to change your approach midway. If you do make major changes, depending on the limitations of your database software, you might even have to re-enter much of the data. Also, use a practice run with your statistical program to see if your ideas work in action. Better to learn from using 100 cases in practice than to find out with 10,000 cases later.

- Get statistical advice from the experts. The long-standing computer motto of "garbage in, garbage out" has never been more appropriate. The computer won't help if your methods are incorrect.

- Check to see if a database charges for services. Many options are free. Some are relatively inexpensive. On a few, though, you can spend the equivalent of your entire college tuition if you are not careful.

- Recognize quickly that some computer sources are more credible than others. Just because the information is on computer does not mean it's right; use the same journalistic practices of verifying information that you would use with any other nonaccredited source. Avoid using computer bulletin boards open to anyone and that allow the posting, or placement, of information without regard to accuracy. These types are free-for-all exchanges and should be treated as such.

- Verify all sources (often it's best to use the computer to find sources, but not to interview them—you can get their phone number for traditional interviews). Ethically, it's important never to quote someone without his or her knowledge, especially if you gain access to personal exchanges not meant for you.

Sample Story Ideas

Following are some story ideas for your campus newspaper.

- If your college or university keeps such records, enter the maintenance ones that document vandalism, or unexpected repairs (such as for broken windows), or extra cleanup. Using a database, determine which area of campus, or which residence hall, has had the most destruction in a year. See if weekends have been particularly costly (from campus parties). Provide a total cost for vandalism and other similar, extra costs. Check to see whether anyone has been charged for the destruction, how much of the cost has been recovered, and how much came from the general budget.

- Run a crime pattern check for a period of several years. Which areas have the most crime reported? At what times of the day? Are there similar elements to the crimes that you could extract to use as security warnings for students? How many of the crimes have been solved? Are those arrested for campus crimes more likely to be students, or people from outside the college community (such as guests or area residents)?

- Likewise, on a less serious note, enter the records for parking tickets on campus and figure out which types of students (for example, seniors vs. freshmen) are most likely to be cited. In which areas are you most likely to be ticketed? At what times of the day? Get a total for the amount paid by students for parking tickets and see if there's any record of where the money is spent.

- On some campuses you can obtain information about particular scholarship winners (without their names, but with other important items that do not reveal identity). See which factors stand out. On one university campus, for example, a student editor checked the common factors of scholarship winners in a particular nonsports fund. The overwhelming majority of these scholarships were awarded to members of one sports team—and their grade-point averages were much lower than expected for scholarship recipients.

Newspaper reporters use a combination of methods to check sources. Courtesy Chicago Tribune.

The Computer, a Support

The computer provides a journalist with a powerful tool, a coworker in a sense, who can help in the search for information and sources. In addition, the computer can do statistical analysis at a far greater rate than can reporters (even if they are math experts). The time saved from letting the computer do the work can be applied to strengthening the story in other areas.

Computer-assisted reporting will become *essential* for journalists of the twenty-first century. It's not only an option for student journalists to learn computer-assisted reporting, it is important for their training and for their futures in the field. When students begin to look for professional reporting positions, experience with computers can help a candidate stand out. The newspaper won't have to train you in how to operate a computer. Instead, you can join in computer-assisted reporting with the rest of the staff.

References

Barnett, Tracy L., ed. *IRE 100 Computer-Assisted Stories, Book II.* Columbia, MO: Investigative Reporters and Editors, 1995.

Bogart, Leo. *Press and Public: Who Reads What, When, Where, and Why in American Newspapers*, 2nd ed. Hillsdale, NJ: Lawrence Erlbaum Associates, 1989, p. 345.

Berens, Michael. "Tracking a Hidden Killer on the Interstate," *NewsInc.*, April 1992, 18.

Cohn, Victor. *News & Numbers: A Guide to Reporting Statistical Claims and Controversies in Health and Related Fields.* Ames: Iowa State University Press, 1989.

Garrison, Bruce. *Computer-Assisted Reporting.* Hillsdale, NJ: Lawrence Erlbaum Associates, 1995.

Jaspin, Elliot. "Computer-Reporting Tool." In *The Computer Connection: A Report on Using the Computer to Teach Mass Communications.* Syracuse: Syracuse University, 1989.

———. "Out with the Paper Chase, in with the Data Base." Speech delivered at the Gannett Center for Media Studies, March 20, 1989.

Meyer, Phil. *The New Precision Journalism.* Bloomington: Indiana University Press, 1991.

Paul, Nora. *Computer-Assisted Research: A Guide to Tapping Online Information.* St. Petersburg, FL: Poynter Institute, 1993.

Uplink monthly newsletter. Columbia, MO: National Institute for Computer-Assisted Reporting. The newsletter is a joint effort between NICAR and IRE.

Chapter Twelve

REPORTERS, TEAMS, AND COMPUTER-ASSISTED REPORTING

The greater the power of technology, the more empowered its
individual user has become.

—John Naisbitt
Global Paradox

Digitized information and new approaches to reporting and writing
stories are reshaping U.S. newsrooms. At an increasing number of
newspapers, beat reporters regularly use computers, databases, and
online services to do even routine stories.

News organizations are only beginning to appreciate the depth and
breadth of the ocean of information—and potential stories—that
resides in the databases maintained by local and state governments
and the federal government. Indeed, some governments themselves
do not know how many databases they owe.

Here is a list of some of the state-government databases available
to reporters at the *Raleigh (N.C.) News & Observer*:

abortion	air pollution
adoption	asbestos
agriculture	bad debt
AIDS	beaches

This chapter was written by Bob Nowell.

buildings
business
cancer
child abuse and neglect
child care
child labor
consumers
correction
courts
crime
dams
deaths
domestic violence
drunks
education
elderly
encroachment
environment
escheat system
federal assistance
fire
fish
gas
generators
hazardous waste
health
highways
hospitals

injuries
jobs
lakes
land
maps
marijuana
marriages
Medicaid
migrants
military
occupational injuries
  and illnesses
oil pollution
purchasing
property tax
race
radiation surveillance
safety inspections
sales tax
septic tanks
sterilizations
taxes
traffic accidents
unemployment
unidentified persons
vehicles
water quality
wildlife

Pat Stith, the *News & Observer*'s computer-assisted reporting editor and a 1966 co-winner of a Pulitizer Prize for reporting, estimates that the state of North Carolina owns more than 10,000 databases. Then there are untold numbers of databases owned by cities, counties, and the federal government. "They're just sitting there, waiting, chock-full of never-told stories," Stith says.

The majority of these databases have become available to reporters at the *News & Observer* since 1990, when the newspaper began a computer-assisted reporting program. The paper now employs 21 database editors, or "news researchers," who spend much of their time writing computer codes and "cleaning" data so it can be used in the newsroom.

Frequently updated databases provide reporters quick information and context for spot news. For example, the *News & Observer*'s
CARnet (Computer-Assisted Reporting network) has phone and public personnel directories, economic and demographic information,
data on state and county government records, and DMV records.

A proliferation of online sources means newspapers will no longer
have to get most of their national and international news from wire
services such as the Associated Press, Reuters, or the *New York
Times* News Service. Moreover, as recent events have demonstrated,
broadcast media are no longer the only media for breaking news.

Using the Internet to Cover a Breaking Story

By using the Internet to learn emerging details of the 1994 earthquake
that devastated Northridge, California, journalism Professor Randy
Reddick of Texas Tech demonstrated how citizens or reporters can
create their own "news services." Reddick's story about newsgathering
was posted to CARR-L, a discussion group on computer-assisted
reporting. From his home computer, he used a gopher—a series of
menus that let him narrow his way down to the information he was
seeking—to connect first to a computer in a seismology laboratory at
the University of California at Berkeley, then onto a bulletin board
service (BBS) maintained by the Office of Emergency Services. From
the OES site he was able to obtain the Richter magnitude of the quake,
the epicenter and some preliminary information on damages—all less
than an hour after the quake struck California. This BBS was
constantly updated throughout the day—faster than any of its data
appeared on television—with information such as proclamations from
the governor, reports on the condition of highways and utilities,
aftershock times and magnitudes, deaths, and relief efforts. From
other bulletin boards (also called "discussion groups" or
"newsgroups"), Reddick was able to obtain firsthand accounts of the
disaster. He concluded that by using only the Internet, he could have
produced stories that were "just about as good as anything that went
out over the wire, and probably as good as 90 percent of what on-the-
scene media produced."

The 1994 bombing of the federal building in Oklahoma City also
demonstrated how people can get closer to crisis news by logging on
to a local site. Soon after the April 19 blast, amateurs, student journalists at the *Oklahoma Daily*, and online services found themselves

in the role of information providers to individuals and media organizations. For example, David Bourne, a pharmacy professor at the University of Oklahoma, posted on his World Wide Web site a list of federal agencies located in the building, the names of victims (obtained from local television), and a map of downtown. The *Daily* posted staff stories and photos on its Web site. Prodigy and America Online opened "chat rooms" devoted to the bombing; at one point America Online had 15 such dedicated rooms. Internet Oklahoma provided numbers for relief agencies and a live feed from local station KOCO-TV. Leonard Conn, president of Internet Oklahoma, said users from 43 countries read about the bombing, wrote to look for loved ones, expressed their sympathy, or said thanks for the information.

"What the public may have learned out of all of this is not to turn to the media but rather to turn to amateur pages like those in times of crisis," journalism Professor Eric Meyer told *The Quill.*

San Francisco Examiner columnist Howard Rheingold agrees. "When amateurs all over the world can transmit eyewitness reports to everyone else in the world—including pictures—via the Internet, the traditional news business will be severely challenged," he wrote. "In the old days, you had to own a press and a distribution network to get your message to a mass audience. Nowadays, a personal computer and an Internet account will do. It's no wonder that more than 100 of the biggest newspapers have launched Web sites."

Online Sources

The popularity of the Internet and online services has raised the question of whether cyberspace will replace the art of face-to-face interviewing. Dan Gillmor of the *San Jose Mercury News* responds by saying that in most instances online services are most helpful for long-term assignments; checking online sources on deadline can be very difficult unless the service is a real-time "chat line." Gillmor also contends that certain long-term topics lend themselves more to online communication than do others. For example, fans' reactions to an event such as the major-league baseball strike may be long-term and cover a wide menu of subtopics; online interviews, he argues, may be more effective than "hasty, spur-of-the-moment, reporter-on-the-street interviews at the ballpark." Postings to online bulletin boards can also quickly produce personal experiences needed to round out a story.

Gillmor also points out that the Internet and the Online World are so specialized (from Usenet newsgroups to CompuServe forums) that online sources may bring to the story a passion not found in everyday interviews. Because each segment of the online community has its own set of rules, he advises caution in using direct quotes off e-mail postings. To avoid lawsuits and copyright infringement, he suggests using the phone to clear each direct quote off a posting with the person quoted. However, deadline pressure usually does not allow time to obtain such permission.

Jon Katz, media critic for *New York* magazine, says,

> E-mail is the best thing I've ever done as a journalist. I never interacted with readers before, and now I have a rich and ongoing dialogue with them. I used to think everything I wrote was absolutely correct. Now I never think anything I write is absolutely correct, especially when the academics, lawyers, housewives, teachers and other experts online get through with me.

Katz recommends that every article in every newspaper have an e-mail tag at the end.

> It would be great for sources, corrections, story ideas and would foster the sense of people's involvement with media, something the traditional media have never done but that new media are all about.

Cruising the Internet

Every journalist is expected to keep up with trends in his or her field. To do so, the reporter may read other newspapers and industry publications, attend professional conferences, and perhaps take continuing education courses. But the best way to stay current is through professional contacts and networking. Electronic mail (e-mail) is the latest boost to networking capacity.

Indeed, Chip Rowe, an assistant editor at *Playboy* magazine, says that e-mail is all that a person needs to get started on the Internet, which he calls "the computer system of computer systems." The Internet is an estimated 35,000-plus networks, linking millions of computers and perhaps tens of millions of people in dozens of countries. It got its start in 1969 as a Defense Department project called ARPANET, which worked out a way to link researchers with data stored on distant computers. The success of ARPANET spawned the creation of other networks for scientific research and, eventually, for all sorts of purposes, including business, entertainment and the typed equivalent of talk radio.

For newcomers, navigating the Internet can be a forbidding task, Rowe concedes. But the basic skill involved is the ability to send and receive messages outside an interoffice e-mail system. For journalists who do not have Internet access through their jobs, the simplest way to get acquainted with e-mail resources may be through a commercial online service such as America Online, CompuServe, Delphi or Prodigy. These services allow a reporter to dial in with a computer modem and access a menu- or icon-driven interface. "Not only does that save you a lot of typing, but you don't have to know the inner workings of the 'Net to get started," Rowe says.

Once you have established an e-mail address, you can send messages, receive messages and reach out and grab background information. A popular and relatively easy way to introduce yourself to the types of messages that are exchanged on the Internet is to join "discussion groups" (also called "bulletin boards" or "newsgroups") that cover any number of topics. On such e-mail lists, experts, newcomers, and those in between exchange ideas, advice, and tidbits on specific topics.

With most e-mail discussion groups, everything you write is sent to every person on the list (listserv), and everything they write comes to you. Subscribing to a group is free; you must send a simple e-mail message to a computer program that keeps track of members and distributes the group's e-mail. You will receive a message confirming your membership and providing instructions on how to post messages to members of the group.

E-mail also lets you hook up with free services such as ProfNet and MediaNet that will find experts knowledgeable on virtually any topic you are researching. If you have been assigned to write an in-depth article on spina bifida, you could use ProfNet to find expert sources. ProfNet (short for "professors network") is a cooperative of public information officers from about 800 institutions in 17 countries. In addition to university faculty, ProfNet includes members of medical centers, business schools, federal research agencies, corporate research labs, and scientific and educational institutions. Experts on ProfNet can tell you whether the local version of a national issue tracks with the same phenomenon nationwide, or they can tell you what to look for when you ask professionals about their situation. The average turnaround on a query is 24 to 48 hours, and you usually get several replies. Note that ProfNet is available only to journalists, and the information obtained from ProfNet experts can only be used for news stories; no students are allowed.

Newsgroups Using the Internet

"Newsgroups" put you in touch with your colleagues around the world at the push of a button. Suppose your beat requires you to stay current on the latest trends in health care. You can subscribe to an electronic newsletter or join an electronic "bulletin board" where you will find postings relevant to your beat. For another example, suppose you want to know whether anyone out there in cyberspace has a story to share about their battle with compulsive gambling. You can take advantage of a free service offered by Stanford University (Netnews Filtering).

Box 12-1

Online on the Cheap

1. Use the resources of the public libraries, university libraries and federal depository libraries.
2. Negotiate short-term trials with different vendors.
3. Find flat-rate deals.
4. Look at the rest of your media group; see if other papers or stations have access.
5. Make friends with an eager service salesperson. He or she may do an occasional custom search.
6. Check out nonsubscribers' services that might be offered, i.e., one-time search.
7. Check out the home computer services: CompuServe, America Online, Prodigy.
8. Find out about "off-hours" services, i.e., DIALOG/knowledge index.
9. Join a freenet.
10. Use a bulletin board service.

Adapted from: Rick Tetzeli, "Is going online worth the money?" *Fortune*, June 13, 1994; Larry Krumenaker, "The dean's list of university BBSes," *Online Access*, June 1994.

Service) that will search the contents of more than 6,000 electronic bulletin boards. You supply the keywords for which you want to search, and the service sends you back a daily digest with the contents of any message containing those words. In addition, you can use e-mail to stay in touch with the spokesperson for the Environmental Protection Agency or a fellow reporter at the *San Francisco Chronicle*.

Government agencies also are using bulletin boards as a way to disseminate information electronically.

Moreover, "newsgroups" allow you to listen to conversations of people you do not know. Eavesdropping or "lurking" on the 'Net has several advantages. First, lurking is a great way for reporters to stay in touch with public opinion. For example, a newsgroup named for a fast-food restaurant chain might be filled with customer and employee complaints of which the chain's corporate managers might be unaware. Second, lurking enables a reporter to gather e-mail addresses for people at companies and organizations whom they might want to reach or write about later. Third, a reporter can use e-mail to sneak past security guards, avoid flak, and reach real employees at the company he or she covers. As Gillmor says, "The fewer people who ask 'What is this in reference to?' the better hunting for my story will be."

Mark Stencel, a *News & Observer* reporter, wanted to do a story on a major high-tech firm's plans to offer health benefits to the "spouses" of its homosexual employees. Because the company's communications staff balked at identifying employees who would be affected by the policy, Stencel posted a message to a local newsgroup used by the gay and lesbian community, saying he was researching domestic partner policies and was looking for people who were pursuing them at their companies. Within a few hours, he received an e-mail message from a source who was willing to talk anonymously about the policy at the company that Stencel was researching.

In mid-1995, about 1,500 newsgroups were accessible through Nando.net, the *News & Observer*'s online service. Topics range from Isaac Asimov books to beer to Rush Limbaugh fans to pets to Eastern religion to politics of the Raleigh-Durham-Chapel Hill Triangle area of North Carolina.

MediaNet is a journalist owned and operated research service that can help reporters quickly find sources, case studies, and information from corporations, associations, and nonprofit groups. Most of its 1,000 subscribers are public relations firms. Reporters may conceal their identity to protect their story, and they will not be put on mailing lists or otherwise harassed by public relations people.

Talking Directly with Readers

The 1990s have seen a boom in glitzy, new online editions of daily newspapers. But Rosalind Resnick, editor and publisher of the monthly newsletter *Interactive Publishing Alert*, says she is disturbed that interactivity with online readers "is on the back burner" at many of these same papers.

"Reporters and editors do not yet view interactivity as part of their jobs," she says. "Responding to reader e-mail inquiry won't win anybody a Pulitzer Prize—or even overtime pay in most cases." She notes that the majority of journalists do not know how to use modems or online services, that too few training programs are available and that many papers require reporters to pay the cost of their own online access. Thus, "many editorial staffers view interactivity as an imposition, rather than an opportunity," she concludes.

Bruce Siceloff, new media editor at the *News & Observer*, sees that opportunity as "the potential to connect readers to us and to each other at a local, personal level of service unimaginable in the printed *News & Observer* and unavailable from any competing local medium. When is our church picnic, and do we need more volunteers to bring napkins or clean up afterward? Who in my neighborhood has obtained a pistol permit this month? What do people in my community think about the White House . . . . [or] about today's restaurant review?" To realize that potential, Siceloff says, would require the participation in the new media channel of every reporter, researcher, photographer and editor—a position that *News & Observer* management has backed by providing enough online computers, the training to operate them, free Nando.net accounts, and encouragement to "get with the program," even to the extent of including computer skills on performance evaluations.

Peter Lewis, cyberspace columnist of the *New York Times*, says online reporters must prepare for the Interactive Age by "imagining that the Letters to the Editor page was suddenly unlimited and uncensored." He says he spends an hour a day reading and sending his e-mail. Beyond the time commitment, he says, is the influence that attentive online readers can have on the way stories are told. "I've been wondering about the 'chilling effect' that a barrage of 'flames' [hostile or critical commentary about a posting] can induce," he says. As reader feedback evolves from a trickle of letters and phone calls to a flood of e-mail and online-forum postings, it may even be necessary for newspapers to hire full-time editors to respond. Nevertheless, Lewis says he has found e-mail to be a "wonderful communications tool" because "there are some brilliant folks out there who can suggest good stories, offer valuable insights [and] provide factual and research support."

Interactivity also pays off for bulletin boards. James Calloway, new media manager of the *News & Observer*, reports that about half the subscribers to Nando.net's BBS are women, in contrast to the Internet's predominantly male users. "We've really pushed the interactive part of the board," he says. "That tends to appeal to more women, so that helps balance it out."

By going online, newspapers are able not only to reach out but get feedback and gauge public reaction as well. Journalistic practices, and the nature of news itself, is changing. Some have even predicted that the traditional newspaper is doomed by the interactive sharing of experiences. Publishers and editors have been wringing their hands for decades over the fact that young people have never developed the habit of reading newspapers. But Jim Tynen, adviser to the University of Pittsburgh's student paper, sees the salvation of newspapers in the demand for old-fashioned watches with hands instead of digital readouts, and for the music of Tony Bennett. Tynen says MTV-generation people like being able to see the hands move around the dial of a watch, and they regard the 68-year-old Bennett as cool because he has parlayed talent and integrity into a craft that has outlasted most musical fads of the last half-century. "Maybe if journalists are just as dedicated to excellence and honesty, newspapers might someday be considered cool, too [by young people]," Tynen says.

Information on CD-ROMs

Another valuable resource for computer-assisted reporting is information that is available on CD-ROM (Compact Disk Read Only Memory). These compact disks can be expensive, but many are available at a low cost. For example, the *Statistical Abstract of the United States*, available from the Census Bureau, has about 140 tables with data from the Census Bureau and other governmental agencies on social, political and economic aspects of American life. It is available from the Census Bureau for $150. Another useful CD is the *Federal Assistant Award Data System*, which covers all grants of all sizes made by all agencies; it includes small business grants, college aid grants, and federal money to schools and local governments. It is also available for $150 from the Census Bureau.

If a newspaper has little budget for acquiring CD-ROMs, the reporter can use them for free at federal depository libraries, large public libraries, and university libraries. A good selection of CD-ROMs

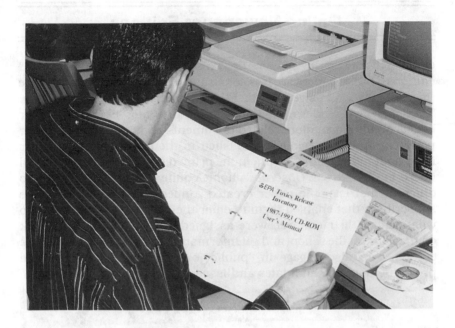

A journalism student examines a manual for accessing EPA records on CD-ROM. Courtesy Harold Washington Library, Chicago.

is available at any of the approximately 1,300 government depository libraries in the United States. For example, the University of Maryland depository library has 10 computers available, each with several CDs.

You can print or download to a disk, all for free. Penny Loeb, business reporter for *U.S. News & World Report*, says useful CDs at the Maryland library include the Environmental Protection Agency's Toxic Release Inventory; the Census; the Schools and Staffing Survey; the National Economic, Social and Environmental Data Bank; and the National Trade Data Bank. The fastest way to find a list of government depository libraries is to go online to the Government Printing Office bulletin board. The Library of Congress has a wide selection of more expensive commercial CDs, and it has a good selection of CD abstracts and indexes to magazine and journal articles. Finally, many of the larger public and university libraries also are building their collection of CDs; a phone call will tell you whether your local library has these resources.

Online Newspaper Editions

Online editions of newspapers have distinct advantages over printed editions. Online papers are less constrained by time (deadlines), space (increasingly expensive newsprint) and industrial-era distribution. They can give readers of almost any story later updates, deeper background information, related documents and data, easy access to pertinent stories previously published in the newspaper, and other information that cannot be put in the printed edition. When the school board in the *News & Observer*'s home county reassigned children to different districts, the paper created a special database for online subscribers that enabled them to enter their address and find out to what school their children were assigned; parents could then click on the name of the school and get information about the school. Online editions can also engage in "public journalism" projects, include providing data on candidates and issues in addition to traditional

The Chicago Tribune *is a prime example of an online newspaper, providing readers with many services. Courtesy* Chicago Tribune.

newspaper stories, says Bruce Siceloff, new media editor at the *News & Observer*.

Instead of an online edition, some newspapers have set up bulletin-board systems that provide articles, interactive forums, and other information not found in the printed edition. The difference between them and services tied to outside distributors is that the newspapers with BBSes must maintain the hardware, phone connections, billing, and marketing.

Box 12-2

A New Medium

Owen Youngman . . . said that the idea behind taking the newspaper and its other assets onto the Web is to anticipate how the next round of media evolution will play out.

He noted that as long as radio consisted only of people reading the stuff they found in the local newspaper, even though they did so in great voices, the new medium foundered.

"It wasn't until they realized the power of live, remote broadcasts that radio started to soar," Youngman said.

Likewise, when television came along, the early programming consisted of taking pictures of the same people who were reading their lines on radio.

It added visual stimuli to the mix, but television didn't take off until it added the unique powers of film editing, animation, titling and, of course, live remote video, that took it well beyond radio.

And thus, noted Youngman, if the widely heralded World Wide Web really is to emerge as the newest iteration of America's media landscape, it must go beyond what has gone before.

"It's not enough to just add the sounds of radio, the video clips of television and the content of newspapers to a single site on the Internet and proclaim that a new medium has been born.

"The whole," Youngman noted, "has got to become more than the sum of its parts."

So the idea behind the Tribune Web presence is to take Tribune Co.'s news-gathering and entertainment organization, which includes not only newspapers but also television, as in CLTV and WGN, and radio and marry aspects of all they produce into a new medium.

That new medium will be unique, because it gives the reader/ viewer/listener more than can be had any other way.

Let me use just one of the Web site's current offerings to make the point: the icon on the on-line sports page that points toward the world's greatest basketball player, Michael Jordan. . . . Youngman's staff has zeroed in on Jordan for a full multimedia profile that illustrates how a Web site can take its audience the same step beyond television that television took beyond radio and radio took beyond newspapers.

The Jordan file includes comprehensive biographical materials such as photos of him playing various sports as a child in North Carolina, as a college star and, of course, during a brief and unrequited flirtation with Major League Baseball.

There also are movies of him taking to the air on scoring drives and a couple of animation files showing the physics behind shooting hoops or jumping for the catwalks at the United Center....Thus, Youngman explained, much of the thinking behind this site is to lay the groundwork so that when high-speed Internet access arrives.... the *Tribune* will be ready with a tested team of New Age journalists capable of turning out the unique type of multimedia content that the Internet allows.... For a glimpse of what that brave new wired world promises, click on http://www.chicago.tribune.com . . .

* * *

Binary Beat readers can participate in the column by visiting Digital Coffee, its home on the Internet, at http.//www.chicago.tribune.com/ coffee/ or by sending e-mail to jcoates1@aol.com.

Librarians and Other "New" Team Reporters

The revolution in journalism is not confined to new technological tools. As Nora Paul, director of news research at the Poynter Institute for Media Studies, said in a 1993 speech: "For the possibilities of online research and computer-assisted reporting to be fully and successfully explored, I believe that librarians need to define and enhance their role and that librarians and reporters need to forge a whole new relationship." At the *News & Observer*, the *Miami Herald*, the *Providence Journal*, the *Minneapolis Star Tribune*, and other papers, the information-gathering role of librarians—now often called news researchers—is more important than ever.

At such newspapers, news researchers have written software programs to create databases from government data tapes or disks. Reporters at the *News & Observer* frequently use a database called "The North Carolina Government Information Center"; it contains information on state law and people in North Carolina government and allows bills to be tracked in the General Assembly. This database has also been turned into a for-profit product sold outside the newspaper. Another *News & Observer* database called "The Money Machine" allows the reporter to see who contributes to political candidates.

In another nontraditional journalistic arrangement, librarians are working with reporters and editors to evaluate data sources before stories have been assigned or defined. At the *News & Observer*, librarians at times do actual reporting on secondary research sources, often yielding them a co-byline or credit line on news stories and information graphics.

Such collaboration or "team journalism" occurs more frequently in the era of computer-assisted reporting. For example, news researchers at the *Charlotte Observer* set up a database to analyze all the divorce property-division cases scheduled for trial in Mecklenburg County in 1993, enabling reporter Nancy Stancill to describe how long the cases were taking, how they were being handled, and how they illustrated the weaknesses in the court system. Another example of CAR team reporting was the *Belleville (Illinois) News-Democrat*'s investigation of traffic tickets; the paper discovered that the all-white police force stopped a disproportionate number of black motorists to keep them out of largely white areas of town. Also in the realm of public affairs, in March 1995 the *Detroit Free Press* published a story on state employees who received whopping bonuses and wage hikes.

The *Free Press*'s David Migoya explained that a reporter went to state unions and obtained salary figures already arranged in a spreadsheet. "Quattro Pro [a spreadsheet program] has a nifty built-in equation that allowed us to tally up the cumulative amount paid out to each employee from the date of each wage hike through the present," Migoya said. "We could also sort and tally by department to see which departments were giving away the most money."

Reporting teams that include librarians sometimes produce stories that resemble social science. For example, the *Charlotte Observer*

Box 12-3
Basic Background Checks on People

Elizabeth Donovan, research manager of the *Miami Herald*'s Information Center, describes how reporters can use databases and Information Center resources to do a basic background check on a person:

First, the microfiche of Florida motor vehicle records contains the names of everyone in the state who owns a vehicle, alphabetically and only identifiable by name, town and birthdate. CompuServe also has a DMB database allowing a reporter to get the vehicle registration and license tag number, or a driver's license. A commercial database, DBT, also has these records and more.

The reporter can search the Florida Secretary of State's database to find whether the person owns corporations.

The *Herald* has a Metro-Dade computer that provides access to lists of civil court cases, criminal records, marriage licenses, occupational licenses, tax assessor's records (which include description of delinquent taxes), waste collection, building and zoning permits and parking tickets.

Other databases for background checks include:

- Bankruptcy Court has a computerized record of all bankruptcy filings that can be accessed via telephone or computer.

- District Court for the Southern District of Florida has a records system called Pacer that provides case dockets for the last two years and case indexes for the last four years.

- TRW credit reports can tell how a person's company fulfills its financial obligations. They cost from $20 to $49 each.

- The Credit Net database provides the other addresses a person has used when applying for credit. They cost $15 to $23 each. Note: Reporters cannot see credit histories.

- Real estate records are online for Dade, Broward and Palm Beach counties. The Information Center also has microfiche of most Florida counties. Data from about 18 other Florida counties and some other states are available from TRW for a fee.

- Reports on public and private companies are available on commercial databases via Dialog or Dow Jones. Some of these have biographical information on corporate officers, and they are expensive to search.

> • A CD-ROM version of a national Phonefile and people find can find
> listed phone numbers nationwide. You generally need an address
> unless the name is unusual.
>
> Reprinted by permission of Elizabeth Donovan.

used statistical methods to measure the degree of desegregation in
local schools. To track the impact of a 1992 pupil assignment plan
that leaned heavily on magnet schools, the *Observer* used such tools
as the index of dissimilarity (or "Tauber index" after its creator, Karl
Tauber of the University of Wisconsin) to determine the percentage
of students who would have to be transferred to make all schools
match the system's racial mix. The paper also used methods by Gary
Orfield of Harvard University to compare the percentage of black
students in mostly black schools nationally, by system, region, and
state, along with changes over time. The *Observer*'s analysis showed
that the Charlotte-Mecklenburg schools, although more desegregated

A reporter is videotaped for CLTV, the Chicago Tribune's *24-hour cable TV
channel. Courtesy* Chicago Tribune.

than most systems in the country, had become increasingly segregated. After a one-year moratorium on the assignment plan, another analysis showed that new magnet schools by their third year had reversed that trend.

Other team reporting projects involve multimedia. For example, the *News & Observer* and Durham television station WTVD collaborated on a 16-week series called "N.C. Discoveries," comprising feature newspaper stories, audiotext versions on the *News & Observer*'s telephone information service CityLine, electronic versions on the *News & Observer*'s online paper *The Nando Times*, and televised news stories. To participate in this effort, some print reporters were required to learn broadcast skills, such as coordinating audio and video in TV story production and asking questions that would produce answers in a form suitable for recording. The *News & Observer* hopes eventually to be able to do all stories as multimedia projects.

Are You Computer Literate?

Most journalists, like the vast majority of their readers, are not yet online—but they soon will be. Though reporters and editors regularly use computers in the newsroom, relatively few of them know how to use modems or online services. Not many newspapers and magazines spend the time and money to train them, according to *Interactive Publishing Alert*'s Rosalind Resnick.

At the *News & Observer* and most newspapers, computer literacy is technically voluntary but increasingly is a de facto condition of employment. Pat Stith contends that two important reasons dictate that reporters acquire such skills. "One, these skills enable us to publish stories that our readers want and that they can't get anywhere else," he says. "Two, all other things being equal, the reporter who knows how [to do computer-assisted reporting] and the editor who knows how will defeat reporters and editors who don't. And not just defeat them; they will tear them limb from limb." He points not only to the many Pulitzer Prizes won by computer-assisted stories at U.S. newspapers but also to local features, such as the *News & Observer* article, "How Fast Can You Go without Getting Caught?", that could not have been done without consulting the North Carolina Highway Patrol's citation database.

Box 12-4

**Computer-Assisted Reporting on the City Hall Beat:
30+ Stories You Can Do**

I. Data source: payroll records
A. Top money-makers in your city or town (including overtime)
B. Political preference in summer hiring
C. Early retirement—who wins?
D. Residency: Where do city workers live? Salary differences?
E. Public employee salary raises vs. cost of living
F. Salary extras: court time, dog allowance, clothing
G. Dead people collecting health insurance benefits
H. City payroll according to race/gender? How does it compare
to local companies? To city's population?

II. Data source: property records
A. Exempt properties: Who owns them?
B. Assessment trends: assessment vs. sales data; business vs.
residential
C. Land speculation: Who's buying where?
D. Group homes: Are they concentrated in any one area?
E. Property scams
F. Vacant property: urban wreckers, cost of demolition
G. City/town as slumlord
H. Who owns the 10 most expensive homes (according to
assessment value)?

III. Data source: political contributions, voter registration
A. Political contributors using multiple names to mask giving
B. Contributors and their city/town projects
C. Dead voters
D. Contributors by zip code, gender, interests

IV. Data source: city/town budget
A. Spending over time on big-ticket items like police/fire or
specialized services like libraries
B. Checking them on the tax rate: Is the budget really holding the
line?
C. This year/last year: Compare spending by department, among
towns per capita

V. Data source: Ask and you shall find: specialty databases that you
can ask for or create yourself

A. Gun permits/concealed weapons permits: Who has them? Why?

B. Dogs and weddings: The clerk keeps these, too.

C. Cityscape: Where are the billboards? The public telephones?

D. Lawsuits, claims: What does your town/city pay out and why?

E. Expense accounts: Public officials dine out at public expense

F. City fleet: Who drives what and how far?

G. Parking tickets: hot spots; scofflaws

H. Back taxes/water/sewer: Who owes?

I. Restaurant inspections: The dirty dozen?

VI. Data source: Finding data in city hall corners

A. Purchasing contracts: matching companies to political contributors

B. Fires: Track location of arson fires and locations of drug raids

C. Parking rates: How your city compares to others on hourly rate

D. What neighborhoods are getting community development block grant money: Compare census data on those areas

E. Inspections: Which owner leads in violations?

Compiled by Rose Ciotta, Computer-Assisted Reporting Editor, The *Buffalo News*. Reprinted by permission.

References

Agrawal, Rakesh. "Getting the Word Out." *Quill*, July-August 1995: 32–35.

Moeller, Philip. "The Digitized Newsroom." *American Journalism Review*, January-February 1995: 42–47.

Naisbitt, John. *Global Paradox*. New York: Avon, 1994.

Noack, David. "Newspapers Online: The Big Rush to Cyberspace." *Online Access*, September 1994: 42–47.

Rheingold, Howard. "Newspapers in the Web Age," San Francisco Examiner, Aug. 9, 1995.

Rowe, Chip. "A Journalist's Guide to the Internet." *American Journalism Review*, January-February 1995: 30–34.

Schlukbier, George. "Internet." *Presstime*, January 1995: S11–S15.

Toner, Mark. "Getting on Boards." *Presstime*, May 1995: 47–50.

PART V

ENTERING THE EVENT

Chapter Thirteen

PARTICIPANT OBSERVATION

Shamming insanity and keenly observing, she [Nellie Bly] lived among the maniacs as one of them, often in danger.

–Arthur Brisbane
New York Evening Journal

Neville St. Clair was a reporter for an evening newspaper in London whose editors wanted a series of stories about begging in the city. "It was only by trying begging as an amateur that I could get the facts upon which to base my articles," he recounted. St. Clair had done some acting before going into journalism, so it wasn't difficult to make himself up as a pitiable character with a scar on his face and a red wig.

St. Clair soon discovered (this was in the days before the Newspaper Guild) he was such a good beggar that he was making more on the streets than in the city room. He took a leave from his paper, and ultimately quit his reporting job to become a full-time panhandler. His suburban wife and kids never knew. In the end, however, he was unmasked by a clever detective named Sherlock Holmes.

The story is Sir Arthur Conan Doyle's "The Man with the Twisted Lip." It's one of the earliest accounts—albeit a fictional one—of a journalist using a popular social science tool, *participant observation*, in search of a story, and, perhaps, freelance opportunities too. Other examples, all nonfictional:

- Nellie Bly of the *New York World* faked insanity to look at an asylum from the inside in the 1880s. That ploy has been repeated over the decades.

- *Philadelphia Inquirer* reporter Eric Harrison spent two weeks undercover in a housing project, then went back as a reporter for nearly three months, finding "an isolated world in which a different set of rules applies . . . lawlessness is the norm, sanitation is a hopeless struggle, and something as simple as taking out the trash becomes a fearful task."

- Mike Keller of the *Honolulu Advertiser* spent five nights in Hawaii State Prison with "32 murderers, 17 rapists, and 114 other convicted felons" and wrote an eight-part series on problems behind bars. His conclusion: "It's an intriguing place to visit. But I sure as hell wouldn't want to live there. . . . Animals at Honolulu zoo are housed better."

- *Wall Street Journal* reporter Beth Nissen worked three weeks on an electronics factory assembly line to look into charges of unfair labor practices.

- Mike Goodman of the *Los Angeles Times* posed as an employee in a detention home for juveniles. After his story about abuses appeared, many top-level supervisors were out of jobs.

Seeing Everyday Life

Participant observation is a social science research method in which the observer takes part in the daily life of the people under study over some extended period of time sometimes openly in the role of researcher, often covertly in some disguised role—in order to observe what happens, listen to what is said, and to talk with the participants at length. Unlike interviewing and other techniques where the journalist is a brief visitor who stands well apart from the activities and persons under observation, participant observation involves ordinary interaction with a group and, usually, participation over a considerable period of time.

Participant observation has two major strengths as a technique for gathering information. Most importantly, this social science technique enables you to work in situations where the overt presence of a journalist could change people's behavior. Participant observation can be as simple as a newspaper's restaurant critic making reserva-

tions under a false name to conceal his or her identity from restaura-
teurs. If it's known by the owner, the maitre d', the waiter, and the
chef that a restaurant critic is in the house, the meal and service
almost certainly will be far from typical. The journalist's goal is to
describe normal times, not an artificial reality constructed for the
benefit of a reporter.

However, working without a "cover" does not mean you can't successfully use participant observation. Elliot Liebow, who is white,
based his sociological classic, *Tally's Corner*, on his direct experience
in a black area of Washington, D.C. He later wrote of his work:

> On several different counts I was an outsider, but I also was a partici-
> pant in the full sense of the word. The people I was observing knew
> that I was observing them, yet they allowed me to participate in their
> activities and take part in their lives to a degree that continues to sur-
> prise me.

Liebow's work also illustrates the second major strength of participant
observation, the opportunity to take an in-depth, comprehensive look
at complex situations, such as a neighborhood community. You can't
just line up the members of a community or organization for
interviews and hope to understand the dynamics of the situation. You
have to immerse yourself in their daily routines.

Author George Plimpton has made a career of participant observation, trying his hand at being a pro football quarterback and a professional golfer, among other things, and then writing books about the
experience. For him, he admits, it's a "gimmick"—but a useful one for
information gathering. Plimpton enjoys the process of understanding
the professionals he writes about "because I've tried to do what
they've done. They talk to me slightly differently from the way they
talk to reporters. So the point of the gimmick is to open the door to a
kind of relationship with the subject which is a little different from the
one they'd have with an ordinary interviewer."

Plimpton is known to his subjects, and the technique still works.
Mike Keller's subjects also knew who he was, during his five-day stay
in Hawaii's prison, but he wrote that the inmates "were eager to talk,
even though I had not expected it. I thought they would be resentful
of me as an outsider who didn't rightfully belong." One inmate slipped
him drugs, even though he was known to be a reporter, to show how
easy it was to obtain and conceal drugs behind bars.

Sociologist Elijah Anderson spent considerable time over a three-
year period with the habitués of Jelly's, a bar and liquor store in a
black area on the south side of Chicago. "I socialized with the peo-

ple—drinking with them, talking and listening to them, and trying to come to terms with their social world," Anderson explained. He wrote about the different social strata that he found there, the "regulars," the "wineheads" (on whom everyone looked down), and the young "hoodlums." From his research Anderson produced a 216-page book, but much of the anecdotal material used to illustrate his sociological conclusions would have made riveting reading or viewing if recast into a newspaper or television series on life in the Chicago ghetto.

Participant observation frees the journalist from relying solely on "official" versions of the truth. Public officials and other news sources too frequently posture in front of the press, putting a self-serving positive spin on the news. It's one thing for a nursing home supervisor to tell you that bedridden patients are bathed every second day. It's quite another to see for yourself as an orderly that once a week is the rule.

Political scientist Richard Fenno spent years travelling with 18 members of the House of Representatives in their home districts. His perspective on these congressmen is considerably different from that of the journalists who show up at the occasional press conference or public hearing. And in an unexpected bit of serendipity, Fenno had just completed a case study based on seven years of observation of Indiana senator Dan Quayle when he was nominated as the Republican candidate for vice president. Fenno's set of essays, *Watching Politicians*, suggests some new paths for political reporting. These paths contrast sharply with the search for scandal and negative news that, as Thomas Patterson's *Out of Order* documents, has come to dominate political reporting in recent decades. Fenno's years of patient observation outline a cycle of campaigning—which is mostly local—and governing—which occurs on Captiol Hill—and the evolution of young politicans that gets at the core of how national politics really works.

The participant observer technique adds the richness of human interaction and emotion to news. It can capture the flesh and blood of a situation, especially of sensitive situations not amenable to the usual news reporting techniques. Social scientist Leon Festinger and two colleagues affiliated with a millenium group whose leader had predicted the date for the end of the world. Their book, *When Prophecy Fails*, is a fascinating account of a deviant religious group and a good primer on how to observe the behavior and beliefs of people in sensitive situations not ordinarily open to journalists.

Human Observation

Novel approaches or perspectives, such as participant observation, often let you see things in a new light. Frequently this is your experience when you study a foreign language. For the first time you gain a real appreciation of the structure of English, a language we mostly learned piecemeal as children. An analogy with reporting methods holds. Most of us learned piecemeal the traditional methods of journalistic observation. We learned them by doing simple interviews, rewriting press releases, and scanning a variety of reports and records. Participant observation has the same relationship to traditional reporting methods as the study of a foreign language has to English. Some experience with participant observation provides useful sensitization to the observation methods of journalism and their limitations.

Participant observation uses the human as an observation instrument. This also is true of the other methods of observation discussed in this book, but the point is sometimes obscured by such intermediate tools as questionnaires, coding sheets, and copies of public records. In addition, even the most alert, sensitive, and professional journalists bring a certain amount of intellectual baggage and previous experience to any observation task. The themes, ideas, and concepts we use to organize our observations impose an order on reality that it does not inherently possess. Although two naive observers will not come up with the same set of facts, two journalists almost certainly will, because, consciously or unconsciously, they apply the news values of professional journalism to their observations. This too can structure—a tactful way of saying distort—the observations.

To grasp the variety of possibilities raised by the strategy of participant observation, consider this method of reporting as a *bridge* between the very distinct roles that are assigned to reporter and source by traditional journalistic practices. Traditional journalism is based on a well-defined link—most commonly an interview or press release—between a participant (the source) and the observer (the journalist). The technique of participant observation blends these two roles, but not in a single, fixed way.

In describing any particular application of participant observation, either of the two words in the phrase *participant observation* can be emphasized. This becomes even clearer if we reverse the phrase and call the reporter's role *observer-participant*. In some instances, the degree of participation is actually quite small, in part because the observer does not want to actively influence the process under observation. In such a situation, the reporter is an *observer* participant and the technique is participant *observation*. In other instances, the reporter is fully a participant in the activities under observation. The reporter's identity may be known to all the others around, as in George Plimpton's books; or not known to any members of the group at all, as in *When Prophecy Fails* by Leon Festinger et al. In these instances the reporter is an observer *participant* and the technique is *participant* observation.

Two sets of considerations govern which of these two roles, observer or participant, a journalist emphasizes. These considerations—ethics and efficacy—also are criteria for deciding whether to use participant observation at all. Is it ethical to deceive the people that you are covering for a news story? Is it all right if the leaders of the group know your identity and only the rank-and-file are deceived? Journalists always look askance at secrecy in government. Should their own reporting be shrouded in secrecy? The answer: It depends! This answer is, of course, a warning to think through a project carefully before making even the initial contact with a group or organization. Further reflection on these points is provided in two boxes included in this chapter, a brief description of the *Chicago Sun-Times*' famous—and equally controversial—Mirage Bar* series (box 13-1) and media critic David Shaw's discussion of undercover reporting (box 13-2).

Another ethical question is simultaneously an important methodological consideration: To what extent do you actually participate? This is a journalistic instance of the Heisenberg principle, an axiom originating in physics which states that the very act of observation can sometimes effect major changes in what is being observed. At first thought, it might seem that major participation can rarely be justified; after all, you are present as a journalist to observe the situation, not influence it. However, when the focus of a story involves a group or an organization, the known presence of a reporter can be highly inhibiting. Through participation, rapport can be established and posturing for the benefit of the media can be averted; participation can enhance the "naturalness" of what is observed. Thus, the primary advantage of

---

* Although the Mirage Bar, the subject of the article in box 13-1, has been out of business for many years, controversy over the use of deception in news reporting continues. It is, of course, a central question for participant observation. The Mirage Bar is an excellent case study for this question because the *Sun-Times* was denied a Pulitzer Prize for its series. Many of the arguments relevant to that decision in this classic case are reviewed by media critic David Shaw in this *Los Angeles Times* article reprinted in box 13-2.

participant observation is substantive, not methodological. Through immersion in the dynamics of the group, the reporter can gain understanding and a more subtle and nuanced view of a group or organization and its pattern of behavior over time. The range of opportunities extend from thinking about your own experience in the situation to engaging in confidential and intimate conversations with members of the group.

Box 13.1
The Mirage Bar

It looked like any neighborhood tavern in Chicago. The beer was cold, the bratwursts hot.

But the Mirage, 731 N. Wells St., was never quite what it seemed.

It was a tavern operated by the *Sun-Times* and the Better Government Assn.

The bartenders were reporters and investigators. The repairmen were photographers headed for a hidden loft.

All were investigating years of complaints from small businesses about the day-to-day corruption they have to endure in Chicago, the city that works if you know how to work it.

The *Sun-Times* will tell the Mirage's story—with names, dates and amounts—in the days to come.

This newspaper will detail:

Payoffs of $10 to $100 grabbed by city inspectors who ignore health and safety hazards when the price is right.

Shakedowns by state liquor inspectors who demand whatever is in a tavern's cash register for their silence about liquor violations.

Tax fraud by accountants who consort with taverns to cheat on state and federal taxes in a practice so widespread it may be costing Illinois $16 million in sales tax alone.

Misconduct and negligence by public employees who loaf on the job, use city equipment for private gain and routinely demand cash under the table for what should be public services.

Illegal kickbacks, tax skimming, and offers of political fixes from jukebox and pinball machine operators—including one from policemen who alone may be failing to report a half-million dollars a year in taxable income.

Pamela Zekman and Zay N. Smith, "Our 'Bar' Uncovers Payoffs, Tax Gyps," News Group Chicago Inc., 1985. Reprinted with permission of the *Chicago Sun-Times* © 1985.

Anthropologist Michael Moffatt profited from this entire range of opportunities during the two years that he lived in undergraduate dormitories at Rutgers University to learn what college is really like. His book, *Coming of Age in New Jersey*, portrays a campus that differs considerably from either academic or popular stereotypes. Neither party animals, drug/sex libertines, nor whiz kids were the central actors in this campus narrative. More than just a case study of life in

---

Box 13.2
Undercover Reporting

Do the special rights granted to the press under the First Amendment also impose upon the press special responsibilities that preclude deception and misrepresentation?

Or is the public benefit to be derived from the disclosure of certain conditions sometimes so great—and the obstacles to such disclosure sometimes so difficult—that reporters are justified in pretending to be what they are not?

In short, does the worthwhile end sometimes justify the deceptive means?

As recently as five years ago, says Thomas Winship, editor of the *Boston Globe*, "we got an excellent story by having a reporter pose as a guard at a youth detention center and report on the maltreatment he saw. We wouldn't do that now."

"We in the press are arguing for an open, honest society, demanding certain behavior from our public officials," says William Hornby, editor of the *Denver Post*. "We ought to be just as open and just as frank and straightforward in getting information as we claim other people ought to be in giving it to us."

But some editors see such proclamations as both unrealistic and self-righteous. Says Michael I. O'Neill, former editor of the *New York Daily News*, "there are some situations where it's the only way to get the story." That is the decision *Chicago Sun-Times* editors made when they assigned a team of reporters to operate the Mirage Bar incognito for four months in 1977 to expose graft and corruption in the city.

The results: City inspectors volunteered to overlook health and safety violations at the bar in exchange for money. Jukebox and pinball operators offered kickbacks. Accountants offered counsel on the fine art of tax fraud. Contractors served as bagmen for payoffs to public officials.

The *Sun-Times* ran stories on its discoveries for four weeks.

In earlier years enterprising efforts like that of the *Sun-Times* had often won Pulitzers—right in Chicago. The *Chicago Tribune* won in 1971, for example, when one of its reporters worked as an ambulance driver to expose collusion between the police and private ambulance companies.

But the *Sun-Times* did not win—largely because several editors of the Pulitzer advisory board objected to their journalistic methods.

"In a day in which we are spending thousands of man-hours uncovering deception, we simply cannot deceive," says Benjamin C. Bradlee, executive editor of the *Washington Post* and a member of the Pulitzer advisory board.

However, insists James Hoge, at the time editor of the *Sun-Times*, "We couldn't have gotten that information and presented it as effectively any other way. We had reported for a number of years on bribery in Chicago with . . . no effect."

Even Hoge agrees, though, that the kind of journalism practiced on the Mirage Bar story "should be used only with extreme caution and selectivity and only when certain standards are applied."

Most editors seem to agree, in principle, on those "standards":

The story involved should be of significant public benefit.

Past experience, common sense and hard work should first demonstrate that there is no other way to get the story, that conventional reportorial techniques just will not yield the necessary information. . . .

Executive Editor Gene Roberts of the *Philadelphia Inquirer* can remember using a variety of misleading tactics when he covered civil rights in the South for the *New York Times* in the late 1950s and 1960s.

"Reporters were systematically excluded from the first desegregated schools," he says. So Roberts, who has a Southern accent and could look quite young back then, always kept a sweater and a school notebook handy. On occasion he would throw his coat and tie under a nearby bush and stroll onto a high school campus, wearing a sweater, carrying a notebook and looking, for all anyone knew, like a typical white student.

Lois Timnick, human behavior writer for the *Los Angeles Times*, used a phony name and posed as a graduate student in psychology so she could work for two weeks at Metropolitan State Hospital and expose conditions for mental patients there.

Although Ms. Timnick signed her phony name to an "oath of confidentiality," promising "not to divulge any information or records concerning any client/patient without proper authorization," she did look at—and write about—patients' confidential medical records.

Did that violate her oath?

"No, I don' t think so," she says now. "When I wrote about the patients . . . I changed their names and some of the details about them so other people couldn't recognize them."

But Ms. Timnick took the job precisely because it would give her access to confidential medical records—something she felt was essential to her story, but something many editors see as an invasion of the patients' privacy, despite her subsequent precautions in writing the story. (Even Ms. Timnick admits she would not want a reporter looking at her own medical reports, whether he wrote about them or not.)

Although Ms. Timnick says she does not think she could have gotten as good a story by conventional interviews with patients, doctors and other hospital employees, Eugene Patterson, president and editor of the *St. Petersburg Times*, says "She'd have a hard time convincing me of that." Twenty years ago, Patterson says, a reporter who worked for him in Atlanta won a Pulitzer Prize for exposing conditions in a mental hospital, "and he did it with routine, above-board, reporting—without posing as anyone he wasn't."

A reporter for another paper says that when she assumed another identity to do an investigative story, all the questions of professional ethics did not bother her as much as those involving her own personal ethics.

"When I did my story," she says, "I had to make friends with the people I was working with. . . . I shopped with them and babysat for them . . . trying to get them to talk to me. I'd never made a friendship before that was blatantly [a] fraud.

"That bothered me personally a great deal."

But she did it anyway. And her editors supported her.

the dorms, this book is a detailed portrait of how college and such campus phenomena as bureaucracy, sex, intellectual work, and play are really experienced by undergraduates at a large state university. Mofatt wrote a book about one campus, a book whose title plays on anthropologist Margaret Mead's exotic classic, *Coming of Age in Samoa*. Her 1928 book created an enduring myth about growing up in the South Seas for generations of Americans. Moffatt presents a more mundane, but truer, portrait of contemporary college life. Every journalist has the same opportunity in his or her community.

Focusing Attention

Although participant observation allows a reporter to steep himself or herself in the richness of a situation, there are limits to the scope of this experience. To observe and understand *everything* is an unachievable goal. The participant observer must consider the 5 Ws of journalism—who, what, where, when, and why, albeit with less attention to the when than is typical for most news stories with their emphasis on timeliness. News stories based on participant observation usually concern continuing or evolving situations.

- The *who* is obvious, the group or organization of interest and its members. You want to know who the participants are, how they are organized in relation to each other, and their principal personal characteristics.
- The *what* consists of the activities of the group, the behavior of individual members, and personal relationships among members of the group and, possibly, with external persons or organziations.
- *Where* also is obvious, the physical setting for the who and what. Nevertheless, complete descriptions of the setting often are important context for the final news story.
- *Why* is the great advantage of participant observation over traditional news gathering techniques. In-depth knowledge of how a group thinks and behaves is far more likely to result from immersion in the life of that group than from short-term casual contact.

Some Guidelines for Participant Observation

Participant observation is not right for every situation. In particular, it poses major logistical problems for the television reporter. But if participant observation is the key to getting that major story about your community, here are some guidelines.

Be open and flexible. One of the great strengths of participation observation is its flexibility. Typically, you don't enter a situation seeking to prove or disprove a preconceived hypothesis. You discover the rules of the game as you observe and participate in it. Beware of the dangers of selective perception, seeing mostly those things that you expected to see at the outset. Because there is so much to see, participant observation involves complex problems of sampling—people to talk with, settings to observe, the relationships among the individuals of any group.

Strategies for coping with these problems include the use of informants, "snowball samples," and documents if they are available. But should an informant be a typical member of the group or a strategically located individual? And what about the ethics—and validity—of obtaining key information from an informant? With a snowball sample you systematically put together the connections among different persons. A conversation with a new convert to a religious sect may suggest a follow-up conversation with a friend who joined at the same time, and another follow-up with the sect member who recruited both. And then, another follow-up with . . . Of course, your snowball most likely will never be completed. You can't interview everyone in detail about every aspect of interest in the situation. But sometimes documents are available to fill in more of the details, such as minutes of meetings, memos, and even personal letters. Look for written materials.

Give yourself enough time to understand things. You will not gain instant acceptance in any group. When Elijah Anderson began studying Jelly's, he started by just hanging around the bar regularly, an outsider.

> It was a place where I would be relatively unobtrusive, yet somewhat sociable. It was here that the process of getting to know Jelly's began, where increasingly I gained some license to exist and talk openly with people.

Make complete notes on what you observe as soon as possible after observing it. Walking around with a note pad will not work most of the time, and simply cannot be done if you're working undercover. But don't rely on your memory. At the end of each day, make a record of what you saw, heard, and felt. Go overboard in note taking, especially at the beginning. When you begin a project, you can't know what will be significant or illustrative. An anecdote that seems trivial at first may prove to be central to what you eventually deduce about a situation. Your notes should include as much detail as possible on all five of the Ws.

It also is important to organize—and reorganize—your notes. Sort out what seems especially salient and give that priority attention. Also carefully distinguish between your *observations* and your *interpretations*. Objectvity is a familiar, albeit difficult, standard in journalism, but the involvement of the reporter in participant observation can create problems.

Don't take sides. In any participant observer setting, but particularly where you are watching a situation in conflict (union vs. management, inmates vs. guards in prison, or "regulars" vs. "wineheads" in a neighborhood bar), you cannot effectively observe the whole scene if you tie yourself to one camp. Position yourself socially so that you can communicate with all factions. Do this right from the start, or you may permanently forfeit any chance to obtain rapport with some sub-groups. This is one danger inherent in getting permission for a project from the higher-ups in an organization. If the rank-and-file see you being endorsed by the leaders, they may suspect that your allegiance is elsewhere. They will never act naturally in your presence, and your reporting will suffer.

Pay attention to how other people around you view the world. You are there to see how reality is perceived by others, not to impose your theories of reality upon them. Participant observation is a research technique in which data collection and the generation of hypotheses occur simultaneously. Like the open-ended question in survey research, participant observation emphasizes description and discovery. As Michael Moffatt remarked in the introduction to *Coming of Age in New Jersey*, there is "no single conclusion that can be stated in twenty-five words or less." When you are finished you do not have numbers to analyze and discuss. At least, not very many. Participant observation is essentially a qualitative technique. But there will be occasions on which you will need to count—the number of people at a meeting, the length of their comments to the group, and many other observations that can be quantified. Numbers can add precision and detail to qualitative observations. Unlike many of the techniques discussed in this book—surveys and document research, for instance—what you have for the most part are qualitative impressions. But the goal of these qualitative impressions is insightful, analytic description.

Planning Ahead

To succeed, you need considerable planning. The logistical problems of living with or at least living among your subjects are many. Michael Moffatt couldn't just stroll over to an undergraduate dorm and wing it. His plan included dressing and behaving like an undergraduate student—being someone he wasn't. It also took an investment of his time and energy.

It is important to be aware of the ethical reasons that could prevent you from gathering information through deception. Some news media have rules prohibiting or tightly circumscribing any use of deception by journalists. You have to decide in advance whether it is crucial to conceal your identity for the project to succeed. Was deception necessary to get the Mirage Bar story reported by the *Sun-Times*? Take a look at the arguments pro and con on this issue in David Shaw's article in box 13-2. In some cases, deception and concealment will be necessary. People in embarassing, illegal, or emotionally trying situations may not act naturally if they know a journalist is there working on a story that will turn up in the newspaper or on television.

For other studies, however, revealing your identity with some vague statement about the purpose of your presence may work. Some experts in the field believe that people find it impossible to be on guard constantly for long periods. After a while, people "let their hair down," forget what you're there for, and begin to act naturally. One advantage of not concealing your identity is that it gives you a plausible reason for asking people questions. A certain amount of structured interviewing, albeit in a more casual setting or manner than the usual survey research interview, is common in participant observation.

Planning also is important because of the investment in time and money required by a project. Social scientists can spend months or years on a project. That kind of commitment is not typical for news projects, but it usually will be necessary to spend a week or two, even a month or more, on one project. An investment of this type is not taken lightly by editors and news directors. Plan carefully!

Some Final Caveats

Participant observation is actually a kaleidoscopic combination of social science and journalism techniques: interviewing, direct observation, use of informants, use of archival records, and actual participation and introspection. A central theme of this book is that multiple techniques of observation yield a truer picture of reality. Participant observation is one avenue to that goal. However, caution must not be abandoned when undertaking this activity.

Beware of becoming such an active, wholehearted participant that you change the nature of what you want to report. Social psychologists Leon Festinger, H. W. Riecken, Jr., and Stanley Schachter had to walk an exceedingly fine line on this point when they joined a millennium religious group predicting the end of the world. This was not a situation where social scientists or reporters could sit around, notebooks in hand, asking questions about the beliefs and motivations of the faithful. They had to appear to be true believers, yet without such fervor that the very nature of the millennium movement would be changed by three college professors. Reactions caused by the very act of observation are, of course, a major problem for many modes of reporting. The presence of a TV camera, in particular, can change events. People act differently on camera.

Also maintain an awareness that even as a participant observer, you have a limited, sometimes highly selective, view of reality. Even a participant observer cannot be everywhere and with everyone constantly. Your role also limits what can be observed. If you are closely aligned with the leaders of a group, you have their perspectives on the members and not vice versa—you can't have it both ways. Although the traditional journalistic practice of interviewing all sides in a controversy is an attempt to have it both ways, it does not always succeed. But interviewing and participant observation can complement each other.

This question about the social distance between the observer and the observed has been discussed many times, including the explicit question of the distance between the reporter and news sources. It is not as easy in practice as it is in theory to maintain a distance that is sufficiently close to allow you to understand your subject but at the same time to avoid total identification and co-optation. Part of the task of the participant observer is to enter the world of the source's experience. But if we enter it too deeply and identify with his or her situation, then we have lost the neutral perspective of the professional journalist.

References

Anderson, Elijah. *A Place on the Corner*. Chicago: University of Chicago Press, 1978.

Brisbane, Arthur. The Death of Nellie Bly. *New York Evening Journal*. January 28, 1922: 1–2.

Fenno, Richard F., Jr. *Watching Politicians: Essays on Participant Observation*. Berkeley: Institute of Government Studies, University of California, Berkeley. 1990.

Festinger, Leon, Henry Riecken, and Stanley Schachter. *When Prophecy Fails*. Minneapolis: University of Minnesota Press, 1956.

Kroeger, Brooke. *Nellie Bly: Daredevil, Reporter, Feminist*. New York: New York Times Books, 1994.

Moffatt, Michael. *Coming of Age in New Jersey: College and American Culture*. Rutgers: Rutgers University Press, 1989.

Chapter Fourteen

FIELD EXPERIMENTS

. . . [L]ogiclally compelling results can be obtained only by using
an experimental design, one in which the investigator varies the
value of the suspected cause and notes whether that leads to corresponding variations in the suspected effect.

—Stanley Milgram and R. Lance Shotland
Television and Antisocial Behavior

Reporters soon learn that everyone thinks well of himself or herself, at least publicly, and that quotes are nearly always self-serving.
It is a rare politician who admits making a mistake, although it sometimes happens when he or she writes memoirs long after leaving
office. That is true of presidents, senators, mayors, company presidents, college presidents, police chiefs, fire chiefs, sports figures, and
cultural and entertainment leaders. It is true of everyone with whom
you will deal on a regular basis.

If quotes were true, then there would be:
- no racial discrimination, because everyone says he or she is
  without prejudice, and nearly everyone believes this is so;
- no gender discrimination, because everyone says he or she
  believes that jobs should go to the best qualified, regardless of
  gender (or race or other types of backgrounds) and nearly
  everyone believes in this type of fairness;

- no political unfairness, because political leaders say they act in the best interests of all their constituents, and they believe that they do so act; and
- no economic unfairness, because employers say they employ only with regard to the best potential employee and because most people believe and say that people who want to get ahead will do so.

People may say one thing and do another. They may say one thing and believe another, without realizing it. Reporters need to compare different sources and may even want to test reality with a field experiment, the subject of this chapter.

Simple Experiments

An experiment is a test of how things work. Scientists conduct experiments in laboratories. Journalists do not normally use the structured environment of a lab for their experiments. Instead, they go out into the field—the natural setting where the experiment is to take place. In 1959, reporter John Howard Griffin, a white man, used chemicals and ultraviolet rays treatments to temporarily blacken his skin and traveled through the South to live the experience of a black man. The experience was powerful. Griffin wrote:

> Walking ... through the ghetto, I realized that every informed man with whom I had spoken, in the intimate freedom of the colored bond, had acknowledged a double problem for the Negro. First, the discrimination against him. Second, and almost more grievous, his discrimination against himself; his contempt for the blackness that he associates with his suffering; his willingness to sabotage his fellow Negroes because they are part of the blackness he has found so painful.

This was an experiment in two ways: first to see what the experience of a traveling black man in the South might be, and second to see what kind of shock it would be to pass, temporarily, from white to black. However, strictly speaking, from a scientific point of view, this example is not a real experiment; there are no controls, no comparisons of one condition with another, and no careful plans for measurement. Yet it does test how the real world performs.

An experiment is an attempt to manipulate an event to find out how that manipulation affects reality. Physicists, chemists, and other scientists are able to control events; indeed that is part of their job. A scientist can set up an experiment to test how one chemical reacts with another in the following way:

Time 1: Measure the temperature, texture (or other measures) of chemical A,

Time 2: Introduce a controlled amount of chemical B, and

Time 3: Measure the changes in chemical A.

This provides a measure of chemical A before anything is done and then a measurement after the introduction of another chemical. If everything is controlled, any change in A should be a result of the introduction of the chemical B. If there is always a consistent change, then one could say that the introduction of chemical B is a *sufficient* reason for the observed changes in chemical A. If the scientist tries to get the same results from introducing every other known chemical to A and gets no results (or different results) as compared with the results obtained from chemical B, then the scientist could also claim that the introduction of chemical B is a *necessary* and *sufficient* condition for the changes in chemical A.

There are few instances in human affairs that are the definite cause of anything else—that is, a necessary (the one thing that is absolutely required to change something else) and sufficient (something that by itself will always change things, without any help from anything else) condition. Most human activities are best predicted from probabilities. For example, we know that drinking and driving is associated with traffic deaths, but we cannot say that drinking always leads to death, though the probabilities of death are increased. We know that cigarette smoking is associated with death from lung cancer, but it also is true that smokers do not always die from lung cancer. Smoking puts you in a category of greater risk of contracting lung cancer, but smoking is neither a necessary nor sufficient condition for lung cancer. People who never smoked get lung cancer. Still, who would advise one to drive drunk—indeed, it is illegal—or to begin a life of cigarette smoking? Probabilities are not certainties, but they certainly provide guidelines for daily living.

Many people use probabilities to plead causes, and that is why stories based solely on quotes are often misinforming. Those in the cigarette industry point out that the link between smoking and lung cancer is weak, meaning that if you smoke you may or may not contract lung cancer. Although the probabilities are greater, it is not certain you will develop cancer. If you drive drunk, it is not certain that you will kill yourself or someone else. Probabilities provide all kinds of room for interpretation, and reporters who match the quotes of one side against the quotes of the other side have simply opted for writing over reporting. Reporting requires additional kinds of data be introduced into the story. Merely matching quotes is often irresponsible, although, for most, it also is "objective."

The Journalistic Experiment

Contemporary journalists can set up loosely controlled experiments to test whether the perception of reality matches what is really happening. Technology allows small, unobtrusive cameras to peep into places where only print reporters formerly could go. In 1993, ABC's *PrimeTime Live*, a magazine-format news program, used a modified field experiment to see if an eye doctor was operating more often than necessary on older patients for cataract replacement, a relatively simple operation. The doctor or his associates developed a reputation for pushing patients through the operation process rapidly—as many as 40 per day—and on some days earned more than $100,000 from federal Medicare reimbursement.

ABC hired seven older people to show up for an examination to see if cataract surgery was in fact needed. In a crude way, ABC measured the volunteers in a "Time 1" condition by having two independent eye surgeons examine all seven of the voluntary "patients" before introducing the eye doctor's examination. The independent eye surgeons concluded that none of the seven needed cataract surgery.

When the volunteers visited the eye doctor in question, two of the seven—both under 65 and therefore not qualified for Medicare—were told they had no problem. The remaining five were encouraged to have the cataract surgery. In separate interviews, ABC also found evidence suggesting that, on occasion, the testing equipment was rigged to be sure the "right" outcome was indicated—that cataract surgery was needed.

The doctor who ran the operation declined an interview with ABC, although ABC did interview at least two satisfied patients in an effort to balance the story. This story went beyond quotes to add in evidence enabling viewers to evaluate the quotes. ABC actually intruded into the event to see how things worked—to see if the seven volunteer patients with healthy eyes would be seen as vulnerable older patients who could be induced into a quick operation in return for a Medicare payment.

This case also exemplifies the sensitive nature of many field experiments. The ophthalmologist whose clinics were the focus of this investigation filed a $50 million lawsuit against the ABC show, and portions of the case were pending at the time of this writing.

ABC's *PrimeTime* did another experiment, this time using cars to test the honesty of mechanics dealing with travelers who develop problems on the road. *PrimeTime* sent cars with known minor defects (for example, a disconnected spark-plug wire, which takes seconds to connect) to different garages to see what would be recommended and—if "fixed"— to see what would be the final cost to the distressed "travelers." Some mechanics spotted the minor problems immediately and reconnected the spark-plug wire without charge, but a few found major "problems." Hidden cameras revealed that some even created problems by punching holes in perfectly good parts. Repairs were expensive. Interviewed later, and shown the videotapes, the mechanics for the most part ran for cover—literally, in one case.

ABC's news program *20/20* sent two people shopping for shoes, cars, and other products. Both shoppers were middle class and in their thirties. Both were comparable in every reasonable way except one. One shopper was black; the other, white. Secret cameras recorded the differences in treatment—long waits or outright neglect for the black reporter but prompt attention for the white reporter. Despite their similarities in age, education, background, demeanor, and dress, their treatment by salespeople was distinctly different. The difference could be attributed to race. This was a reasonably controlled field experiment, and the result leads to the conclusion that, even today, race makes a difference in everyday shopping. If ABC had depended only upon personal interview quotes, no doubt every salesperson would say—and believe—that he or she is unbiased and treats everyone who comes through the door the same way. But the field experiment showed that was not true. Boxes 14-1 and 14-2 show how officials sometimes employ methods that borrow from field-experiment strategy.

Setting Up the Experiment

Journalists do not wait for news to happen. Instead, they develop hypotheses and test them. This has to be done carefully, otherwise it

---

Box 14-1
Testing Honesty

The couple who moved into the small brick colonial at 60 Alden Court in December seemed nice enough, but they sure had their share of household crises, neighbors recalled.

Almost daily, it seemed, repairmen were at the home to fix the furnace, clean the chimney or revive an appliance. Fourteen different repairmen, in fact, worked on the washing machine.

Today, Nassau County authorities revealed that the couple were actually investigators for the District Attorney's office and the Department of Consumer Affairs, that the home was equipped with hidden cameras and microphones and that of the 65 repairmen called to the house, 23 were being charged with breaking the law.

In one case, a chimney sweep climbed his ladder, looked down the chimney, and threw his brushes to the ground. He never touched the inside of the chimney but charged $56.91 for a cleaning. In another, a repairman found a towel that had been deliberately stuffed in a washing machine to block the water pump. He only removed the towel but submitted a bill for $146.67, saying he has installed a new pump. Before leaving, he pasted his name and telephone number on the machine, should anyone need to call him again for service.

"We found many honest merchants, but also some who crossed the line," District Attorney Denis Dillon said at a news conference. He said the six-month sting operation followed complaints from 30,000 people about their dealings with home-repair businesses last year.

---

would be little more than entrapment, a legal term that applies when an individual is encouraged to commit a crime and then is arrested for it. That is why journalists have to be sure beforehand—with independent assessments—that, as in our examples, the eyes of the volunteers do not need an operation or that independent mechanics have tested cars to make sure they are sound except for the minor problem created to justify taking the car to a mechanic.

In the laboratory the experimenter attempts to control everything except the outcome resulting from the introduced change. In our examples, the news media controlled everything possible. If they had

Box 14-2
Testing for Violations

After teen-age undercover agents documented a widespread problem, an alliance of state legislators and health authorities Wednesday proposed a bill to crack down on retailers who sell cigarettes or smokeless tobacco to minors.

The 17 Austin-area teenagers visited 165 stores and found that more than 60 percent were ready to violate the state law prohibiting the sale of tobacco products to people under 18.

"We asked for a tobacco product or a smokeless (tobacco), and they'd put it up (on the counter) and ring it up. They didn't care (about age)," said Jason Farrell, one of the teenagers enlisted by the Texas Department of Health to visit the stores.

Bolstered by the finding, State Representative John Hirschi (D-Wichita Falls) proposed a bill to punish with heavy fines and other action retailers who sell cigarettes to minors. He appeared at a press conference with Representative Mike Martin (D-Galveston), who filed a bill to restrict smoking in public by adults.

The Health Department and health groups are backing the legislation, which comes as the tobacco lobby is marking a victory in a recent products liability bill. Consumer groups and former Attorney General Jim Mattox have accused lawmakers of being in the lobby's pocket because they protected tobacco products from lawsuits. The bill was sent Wednesday to Governor Ann Richards for her signature.

Farrell, 15, a sophomore at Anderson High School, and Ivana Guzman, 15, a sophomore at Leander High School, appeared at a Capitol news conference to support a stronger law against selling tobacco products to minors.

At 61 percent of the supermarkets, convenience stores and other establishments visited, clerks were ready to sell the teenagers a pack of cigarettes when asked, the Health Department said.

However, to stop the transaction, the teenagers would announce they had forgotten their money and leave, said State Health Commissioner David Smith.

"Undercover Teens and Tobacco," *Austin American-Statesman*, Feb. 25, 1993. Reprinted by permission of *Austin American-Statesman*.

not independently tested the eyes of the volunteers, they could not assert that unnecessary operations were being recommended. If they had not independently tested the automobiles, they could not be attempts to control all the sources of variance that might influence the outcome except for the variable that you are examining. For sure repairs were not necessary. If the black reporter and white reporter had been very different in age, dress, and demeanor, the news medium could not be sure race was the reason for the difference in treatment. The experimenter attempts to rule out the possibility of changes resulting from anything other than what the experimenter is testing. Scientists call it "parsimony" when they try to find the single most influential cause of something. In our examples, the news media attempted to control everything possible to keep the focus on answering the questions that interested them.

If you want to do a field experiment, you need to think carefully, as a behavioral scientist might think, and lay out a strategy that attempts to control all the sources of variance that might influence the outcome except for the variable that you are examining. For example, suppose you are interested in knowing if there is a relationship between the number of well-equipped and available city parks and the frequency of crimes by teenagers in your city. This is more complex than it seems, but let's play with it a little.

You could look at crime statistics compiled by the local police over a ten-year period and compare those figures with the numbers of available parks open over the same period. If there was an increase in parks, but also an increase in teenage crimes, then you would be tempted to dismiss your hunch that kids would rather play basketball or engage in other legitimate activities than participate in crime. But you could not be sure that crimes would not have increased even more without the parks. Perhaps local teenagers just reflect a distressing national trend, a trend somewhat dampened by the availability of parks in your community. (Of course, you could compare your community with similar communities without parks to see if parks made a difference, but we are sticking to our own community in our example.)

You might consider examining the records of teenagers who are arrested in your community to see if they live within a certain number of blocks of a park. Arrest records list addresses, and you know the locations of city parks and when they were established. You can probably assemble the records as if they were part of an experiment. For example, consider figure 14.1.

If your hunch is correct, there should be proportionally more arrests of teenagers who live farther from parks. This is based on the assumption that it is harder to get to the parks and that teenagers

	Distance from City Parks		
	1–2 blocks	*3–4 blocks*	*5 blocks or more*
Number of teens arrested within . . .			
Total number of teens living within . . .			

Figure 14.1
A record sheet to keep track of how far teens live from city parks

Of course, you need to control for total teenage population. who live farther away may be more tempted to become involved in crime. Of course, you need to control for total teenage population. You probably can think of many other reasons why simple distance would not be enough to give a definitive answer to your hunch. For example, parks may be placed in "nicer" neighborhoods anyway.

So you could step up the power of your observation and combine the findings of your search of records with in-depth interviews of teenagers, as one possibility, if you or those helping you can obtain the trust of the teenagers. You could also have a teenager "move" into the neighborhood for a while to observe other teenagers, although this would require commitment and time to build trust and could be dangerous in some cities.

Pursuing the strategy of experimental design, you could study records of the past 10 years and see if there is or was a relationship between crime and city parks, with crime in a neighborhood rising or falling after the opening of a nearby park. To observe the changes that result in a neighborhood, you might even plan to do an in-depth series the next time that the city plans to open a park.

Of course, you can always make use of interviews, especially after you examine the records to test some of your hunches. Teenage leaders and followers and many public and private officials will have valuable and experienced views and observations on the relationship between parks and teenage crime. Quotes, with data, can be useful and valuable.

This example is not really a true experiment but uses an experimental *strategy* to gather and organize information as someone would who was trying to determine if one thing—here, parks—has a clear influence on something else—here, teenage crime.

Experiments can be done, if you have clear questions in mind. In Chapel Hill, several years ago, the members of one class at the University of North Carolina at Chapel Hill decided to see if manner of dress would influence how soon someone would pick them up as they thumbed for a ride on a major highway near the campus. There were enough members of the class that men could dress casual one day (jeans, shirt) and in more formal dress (suit, tie) on another (similar) day. The students used a stopwatch to measure how long it took before someone stopped to give each one a lift. (The drivers were then told this was only a class project!) The same experiment could be done with variations of dress with women, with black versus white students, and in many other ways. (For example, thumbing "aggressively" or "passively.") Incidentally, the class found few differences among the different conditions tried, suggesting perhaps that drivers expected and would tolerate a wide range of diversity in the students they picked up.

In our park example, you could step up the reporter power to the full field experiment. You might hire some youths—say a group of seven or eight—and have them follow a street map that keeps them in parks—part of the time in "good" neighborhoods and part of the time in "bad" neighborhoods. Their job would be to report feelings of danger in each sector. (Obviously, you need to be very careful.) What are some other ways you could test the role of parks with an experiment?

Students at an urban university were curious how close a person walking on a crowded sidewalk would let another person get to them. They set up an experiment on a street to measure the degree of closeness. A student would walk down the sidewalk and courteously yet firmly not move as he or she walked toward another person—who necessarily would have to move aside. The class varied the experiment in a number of ways. Male students walked toward other males and toward females. Female students walked toward other females and toward males. The students noted and measured the degree of closeness and found that men turned aside from men rather quickly and at a distance, while women allowed other women to come relatively close. Men and women sometimes nearly collided, so close did one sex allow the other to approach. Obviously, experiments present some ethical issues at the same time that they provide opportunities to gain interesting data.

Special Ethical Considerations

The essence of reporting is to cover community events as they happen, the world as it is, rather than to become entangled in events, as some of our examples show. While the field experiment can show how organizations actually operate, reporters should be careful that they do not commit illegal acts or operate with questionable ethics. Reporters have to be on the lookout for anticipated and unanticipated events. Several years ago, a television station in a Florida city wanted to see if bystanders would stop a crime in progress, so the station arranged for someone to break a jewelry-store window, seize some jewelry, and attempt to make off with it. The question was: Would bystanders intervene?

The station anticipated certain problems. For example, it informed the police, arranged with the jewelry-store owner to have fake jewelry on hand, and paid for the window replacement. The station did not anticipate that the confederate "criminal" would be cut. Also, it is possible that a bystander would be frightened and drop dead of a heart attack. That did not happen, but if it had, the station could have been in serious trouble. The experimenter is responsible not only for reactions that are anticipated but also for those that are not.

If the cataract-surgery patients hired by ABC News all arrived at the clinic at the same time for testing, lengthening the waiting line and delaying surgery for a patient who needed immediate attention, then the network could be in trouble. Obviously, ABC was careful to avoid such problems. If the students who were testing the effect of hitch-hikers' dress somehow caused an automobile accident, they also might be in serious trouble. If you tamper with mother nature, so to speak, then you must be prepared for the consequences.

Gloria Borger of *U.S. News & World Report* reported on how the notorious case of the exploding pickup truck illustrates a field experiment gone awry. A *Dateline NBC* segment charged that the fuel-tank position on one kind of General Motors truck might make the vehicle more likely to explode in a crash. To give the story visual impact, NBC staged a crash and fitted the truck with toy rocket engines to ignite flames. When GM threatened legal action, NBC denied the charges, then reversed itself. Ms. Borger wrote that "the effort to inform accurately had been overtaken by the need to dramatize."

Reporters can ask themselves these questions:

1. Is there any other way to test the organization? Perhaps some news medium has already published a study that addresses the same question. If someone else has done it, you probably do not need to do it. Remember, however, that nearly anyone you quote will always see organizational performance from his or her own perspective. News sources always feel that they are excellent leaders and that their organizations function fairly and efficiently. Therefore, you need to ask what are the ways, other than by asking people, in which the organization can be tested.

2. Is the experiment designed so that you can account for the influence of all factors except the one you want to test? The best way to do this is to sketch the experiment out on paper. There is Time 1—right now. You need to know how the system is operating. There is the change you want to introduce, and so you must think of anything else that might also cause change at the same time. There is Time 2—after your attempt to test the organization. Compare the organization at Time 1 with Time 2 and see if there is change. If so, can you account for the change as a result of what you did (and only that)? Sketching the experiment out forces you to think of other influences on the organization. It is best to ask others to consider your experiment because they are likely to spot possible sources of influence you should "control for," or attempt to neutralize. This is the ideal role of a "devil's advocate."

3. What other sources of information are available after the experiment? An experiment presents a unique and revealing perspective on organizations, but there are other perspectives. You also will want to plan to use documents, interviews, databases, and other appropriate sources of information. In the case of the eye doctor, for example, ABC gathered information about the number of operations conducted by the eye clinic and the average amount of money generated per working day. All public affairs stories are enriched by the addition of other perspectives generated from other appropriate sources.

4. What precautions must be taken to ensure professional attention to legal and ethical considerations? If you threaten or pressure citizens, you may jeopardize the legal standing of your news medium. It is best if you design a test that

does exactly what the average citizen does and nothing more. The volunteers for ABC were older patients who simply agreed to have their eyes tested and to report back to the network. They did only what many other patients did, nothing less, nothing more. (Of course, they did agree to a Time 1 test to make sure their eyes were healthy.) After that, ABC added interviews with patients and attempted without success to interview the doctor who owned the clinic.

Exposing the "Unseen"

Years ago journalist Walter Lippmann pointed out that journalists present the picture of the world upon which most of us rely, the world beyond our immediate environment. Lippmann called this world the "unseen environment" and pointed out that the press provides one of the few ways outside of personal contact that one can learn about distant places:

> The world that we have to deal with politically is out of reach, out of sight, out of mind. It has to be explored, reported, and imagined. Man is no Aristotelian god contemplating all existence at one glance. He is the creature of an evolution who can just about span a sufficient portion of reality to manage his survival, and snatch what on the scale of time are but a few moments of insight and happiness. Yet this same creature has invented ways of seeing what no naked eye could see, of hearing what no ear could hear, of weighing immense masses and infinitesimal ones, of counting and separating more items than he can individually remember. He is learning to see with his mind vast portions of the world that he could never see, touch, smell, hear, or remember. Gradually he makes for himself a trustworthy picture inside his head of the world beyond his reach.

With this power, journalists have a special responsibility to survey the events of the community and to make sure that important issues are presented on a regular basis. Journalists conduct field experiments to test reality and present the result to the public. In effect, the *experiment* makes news, putting issues on the public agenda whether or not news leaders want to discuss those issues. Hence there is a special need to consider the role of journalists as newsmakers.

Political scientist Bernard Cohen, in a study of the foreign news in the press, concluded that the press does not have power to determine what we think but does seem to have the power to determine what we think about, to set the agenda for community thought and discussion. Many studies suggest there is a limit to the number of issues about which citizens can think at any one time—about five to seven issues. One to three of those issues, such as the economy or concern about an ongoing war, tend to skim off the most attention, with the remaining issues receiving much less attention, perhaps the attention of only 3 percent to 5 percent of citizens.

Journalists can seize the opportunity to place important topics on the agenda, even if news sources do not want to discuss them. For example, it may be that city employees are paid so little that some are on public welfare to maintain their families. If so, city officials probably would not want to discuss this topic because it would mean they would have to raise taxes to increase salaries or that they had not been as sensitive as they should have been, regarding the lives of their employees. But the news media could look at the quality of lives of city employees from the point of view of housing, health, education, entertainment, and other areas.

In short, the news media could put the topic—not the solution—on the agenda. In San Antonio, one newspaper attempted to seize a small part of the agenda by deciding to focus each year on a topic of community importance. One year the newspaper decided to concentrate on children, so the paper presented many stories, editorials, and columns on various aspects of that topic. The newspaper did not promote a specific solution—that is the job of citizens and the political process—but did suggest the topic was worth discussion and perhaps action.

Professionalism

Experiments can put issues on the public's agenda. Are car thefts more likely on some streets than on others? Are people more likely to help strangers asking directions in neighborhood A versus neighborhood B? Many projects would generate solid news stories.

Some might find this approach too intrusive for a news medium. Yet dentists became involved in the political process when it became clear that the addition of small amounts of fluoride in city water would reduce tooth decay (and cause a decline in the business of dentists). Journalists, like other professionals, have a stake in the political, social, and economic condition of their communities. Steady mention of a topic over time is more influential than major, but passing, emphasis. Unlike other professionals, journalists also have an opportunity to test hunches in order to expose public issues and persistently put them on the agenda. The field experiment is one way to do that.

References

ABC. *PrimeTime Live*, June 11, 1993.

ABC. *PrimeTime Live*, September 24, 1992.

Borger, Gloria. "The Story the Pictures Didn't Tell," *U.S. News & World Report*, 114, no. 7(Feb. 22, 1993): 6.

Cohen, Bernard. *The Press, the Public and Foreign Policy*. Princeton: Princeton University Press, 1963.

Griffin, John Howard. *Black Like Me*. Boston: Houghton Mifflin, 1961.

Lippmann, Walter. *Public Opinion*. New York: Harcourt, Brace & Co., 1922.

Meyer, Philip. *Ethical Journalism: A Guide for Students, Practitioners, and Consumers*. New York: Longman, 1987.

Milgram, Stanley and R. Lance Shotland. *Television and Antisocial Behavior: Field Experiments*. New York: Academic Press, 1973.

Miller, George. "The Magical Number Seven, Plus or Minus Two," *Psychological Review*, 63: 81–87 (March, 1956).

Shaw, Donald L. and Shannon E. Martin. "The Function of Mass Media Agenda Setting," *Journalism Quarterly*, 69, no. 4(Winter, 1992): 902–919.

Chapter Fifteen

HOW VOTERS USE NEWS MEDIA TO LEARN ABOUT ISSUES

What the electorate needs from the press, in addition to a clear channel of communication that provides connection to its leadership, is a watchdog with the judgment to distinguish real abuse from normal political activity. Politics is the art of compromise.

—Thomas E. Patterson, *Out of Order*

Do Americans use the plethora of news materials available to them? Some recent communication scholars argue that there is an information "gap" between those of higher versus lower socioeconomic background and that those with a better education gain even more of an advantage when they confront new information—an example of the rich getting richer, in a sense. In addition, network television confronts a steady decline in audience, as do daily newspapers and commercial films shown in theaters. Newsmagazines also have struggled economically. It is possible that the information gap is growing larger, if those with more money are better able to take advantage of the newer forms of communication, such as home computers, faxes, and cable services.

In United States history, the emphasis has been on the opportunity for all citizens to participate in the political process, not just those of

This chapter was co-written with Edward Caudill.

283

Newsstands offer easy access to a variety of print media.

high social class or those with elite education. From the start, the United States was to be a country with opportunity for all, even if it took a Civil War to bring the beginnings of civil rights to black Americans and a century of struggle to bring the right to vote to all women. Many groups and organizations continue the struggle, but the promise for all has always been there.

The importance of political knowledge and participation is the basis for Seymour Martin Lipset's well-known analysis of political man, which argues that some occupational classes are better informed. The time that citizens spend reading, listening, and think-ing about politics is a sort of intellectual investment in the act of vot-ing and a first step to political awareness. Although Lipset cited the social problem of "chronic know-nothings," often from lower socio-economic classes, Lipset also argued that a key variable in any polit-ical and social system is the willingness of citizens to invest the time and commitment to learn about issues. For those who want to make such an investment, the information contained in modern mass media—newspapers, magazines, radio, television, and cable—can be gained relatively inexpensively. Thus socioeconomic backgrounds may be a less important determinant than the willingness of citizens to expend the effort to gain information, and the willingness of the general news media to supply a rich source of daily information about community life. That is the pattern we study here.

A Historical Test of Voters and Press Use

Using the strategy of a quasi-experiment, we conducted a test to compare how citizens during three national elections, picked to represent three time periods, learned about presidential elections and how much they knew about the candidates. Using recent history, we examined the notion that the press can, as French observer Alexis de Tocqueville promised, provide a way to equalize educational differences (among many other kinds of "differences").

Media Use

The elections studied were the 1956 contest between winning Republican President Dwight Eisenhower and Democratic challenger Adlai Stevenson; the 1968 election in which Republican Richard Nixon defeated Democrat Hubert Humphrey; and the 1980 election in which Republican challenger Ronald Reagan defeated incumbent Democrat Jimmy Carter. The 1980 election also included a major third-party candidate, John Anderson.

These studies allowed us to replicate findings across a wide period of time in which the mass media have played important political roles. From 1956 to 1980, television grew in importance as a major source of political information, with the 1960 televised debates between Democrat John F. Kennedy and Republican Richard Nixon establishing an important role for that medium. In the same period newspapers, magazines, and radio struggled to hold audiences or sought to find and maintain niches in the media marketplace. In 1980, network television had not yet begun the decline in audience that continues to this day (as it does for daily newspaper circulation). In these years network radio fragmented into many specialized stations, and there was a rapid growth of FM music stations while AM stations used talk shows to gain audiences. The 1950–1980 years, in retrospect, represent decades of great power for the mass media, providing citizens with many informational choices.

Democracy rests upon the idea of competing ideas and candidates, and citizens need the news media to learn about candidates and campaigns. Using national data from the Inter-University Consortium for Political and Social Research at the University of Michigan at Ann Arbor, we examined the political knowledge of citizens of voting age. Each of the Michigan presidential election surveys asked questions about both the candidates and media use, so we could compare the level of knowledge about candidates with the level of media use. As so often is true in survey research, the questions were not exactly the same across the 1956, 1968, and 1980 campaigns, so we cannot directly compare how audiences used the media, but we can come fairly close.

- In the 1956 survey, respondents were asked if they read or heard about the campaign in a particular medium—newspapers, magazines, radio, or television. Responses were "yes," "no," and "no answer" (to the question) or "don't know."

- In 1968, respondents were asked if they followed the election in newspapers, magazines, radio or television. Responses for newspapers were "regularly," "sometimes," "no," and "no answer." For the other three media, 1968 answers were "frequently," "sometimes," "no," and "no answer."

- The 1980 survey questions asked how much campaign news respondents received from each medium—"a lot," "a small amount," "none," "inappropriate [question]," and "no answer."

We can look at the extent of media use within an election year and compare it with how much information citizens knew about each candidate for that year, allowing us to examine the relationship between knowledge and media use for each of the three presidential elections in the study.

Voter Knowledge

The 1956, 1968, and 1980 surveys differed in terms of how much information about each candidate was elicited from citizens. In the 1956 survey, citizens were given the option to list up to five positive points about Eisenhower and also five positive points about Stevenson—a total of ten positive things in all. (Citizens could also list up to the same number of negative points, but we concentrated on the positive comments.) In the 1968 survey, voters were given the option to list two positive points about Nixon and/or Humphrey, making a maximum total of four. In the 1980 survey, voters were given the option to provide up to four positive comments about winning Republican candidate Ronald Reagan, Democratic candidate Jimmy Carter, or third-party candidate John Anderson, a theoretical total of up to 12 points for the really informed voter of that year.

Most citizens seem to make their choices about candidates based on relatively few pieces of information. For example, there is evidence that television advertising, which often does not even address issues, carries a lot of power during the course of a campaign. Citizens sometimes do not know a great deal about candidates, but what they do know can greatly influence their choices.

Some voters who were interviewed during these historical elections could provide only a single positive point about a candidate or could provide no information at all. Others could provide more positive things to say about candidates. Generally, but not always, people say favorable things about candidates they like and unfavorable things about candidates they oppose. Some people who have strong views may not express them during an interview.

Our test is based on the assumption that citizens with a lot of positive things to say about candidates were more likely to know more about candidates and issues than were citizens who could not (or did not) provide this information to interviewers. Assuming that those with the most to say were the most knowledgeable (we are aware that talkative people are not always well-informed, but we assume that talkative people who answer questions are more likely to be well informed than those who do not), we asked: do the most informed citizens make more use of the news media? We recognize there are many individual variations, but often in social science and journalism research one has to extrapolate from the data and make judgments and adjustments to find patterns. We argue for a collective pattern made up of roughly similar individual bits.

Patterns

We sought to find patterns in media use. After categorizing voters' level of knowledge into four different types, we compared the different "types" of voters according to the degree to which they (collectively) used the media to gather campaign information in 1956, the degree to which they regularly read newspapers or utilized other media to follow the 1968 campaign, and the amount of campaign news they received from the media in 1980.

Four "Types" of Political Citizens

Using positive comments made, we sorted citizens into four groups based on the quantity of information they could provide about presidential candidates. The categories are presented from least to most informed in figure 15.1.

ISOLATED———> ORDINARY————> TRANSITIONALS——> INFORMATIONALS
(Least Informed)   (Average informed)   (Very Informed)   (Most Informed)

Figure 15.1
Voters categorized by information types

These four categories allowed us to sort citizens based solely on their level of knowledge and did not take into account the citizens' level of formal education, interest in politics, sex, social class, or even the amount of time spent with the mass media. The advantage of this method of sorting is that it allows us to determine whether those who were more knowledgeable were the same people who made more use of the news media.

The "Isolated." This group of citizens could offer nothing at all, or they provided only minimal responses to questions about candidates. For example, 46.5 percent gave 0–2 reasons to support candidates in 1956 (scale of 0–10), 54.9 percent gave 0–1 reason in 1968 (scale of 0–4); and 70.4 percent provided 0–3 reasons in 1980 (scale of 0–12). Thus about half or more of the citizens interviewed knew little or nothing about candidates (or at least gave the interviewers little or no information). This finding was common to all three surveys.

The "Ordinary" and "Transitional." Citizens who provided a few positive comments about candidates but significantly less than "informational" citizens were labeled "ordinary." We labeled people "transitional" if they knew nearly but not quite as much as "informationals."

The "Informationals." About one of every 20 citizens surveyed provided numerous answers during these three elections. In 1956 we called voters informationals if they provided 7 to 10 positive points about the candidates. In 1968, informationals were those who provided four comments about candidates, and in 1980 those giving seven to 12 comments about candidates were judged to be informationals. Despite the range of the total number of possible answers (from 4 in 1968 to 12 in 1980), the percentage of the group who seemed to know the most was relatively consistent: about one of each 20 citizens. This number was consistent in each of the three elections studied in the three decades.

In 1956, there were 71 such highly informed citizens (4 percent of a sample of 1,762); 98 such highly informed citizens in 1968 (4.7 percent of a sample of 1,673); and 94 highly informed citizens in 1980 (5.8 percent of a sample of 1,614). These voters demonstrated the most knowledge, as measured by the quantity of answers provided to questions about the presidential candidates. Although we could not judge the quality of answers, we assumed that citizens with many positive comments about candidates were most likely to be well informed.

A Demographic Comparison of Political Citizens

Table 15.1 compares citizens who seemed least informed with those who seemed most informed. There were more similarities than differences across these four types of citizens—isolated through ordinary through transitional to informational—in terms of marital status, sex, age, and race. The table shows a small tendency for the "informationals" category to contain a higher percentage of whites than the other categories, although this reflects the far greater numbers of white people that fell into the Michigan Survey national sample. In general, informationals were as likely to be women as men.

There were also some differences. Informationals were somewhat more likely to vote, to have a college education (especially in 1980) and to have more money. In 1980, informationals were somewhat more likely to live in cities. These differences might be expected—more people were college graduates and lived in cities in 1980 versus 1956—yet they are not predictive of why some voters know more (at least in their ability to mention positive things about candidates).

In the case of formal education, a college degree in 1980 was associated with informationals 52 percent of the time, accounting for one of two of the informed citizens that year. This compares to the sometimes considerably lower levels of college degrees for the other groups. The clearest difference between informationals and transitionals was on the level of education and income. Also, those who were more politically informed were more likely to have higher levels of education and income. But education and income do not completely explain the different amounts of knowledge about presidential candidates.

Table 15.1 Percentages of Voter Types

	Isolated	Ordinary	Trasitional	Informational
Marrried				
1956	77	85	80	80
1968	70	69	54	67
1980	65	62	69	70
Male				
1956	42	47	48	45
1968	40	45	50	56
1980	40	42	46	55
Over 40				
1956	56	54	56	51
1968	60	65	62	61
1980	39	46	47	48
White				
1956	87	94	97	97
1968	86	79	79	81
1980	81	86	91	96
Previously Voted				
1956	64	78	83	89
1968	55	80	82	91
1980	47	59	73	87
College Degree				
1956	3	10	12	34
1968	9	15	22	25
1980	9	11	24	52
Above Median Income				
1956	32	50	58	80
1968	47	53	57	60
1980	35	37	48	61
In City of 50,000 or more				
1956	30	35	35	31
1968	19	22	25	22

Table 15.1 Percentages of Voter Types

	Isolated	Ordinary	Trasitional	Informational
1980	33	35	40	47

The Press as a "Leveling" Democratic Force

The news media played an important role in keeping citizens informed, if citizens made an effort to use the media. Regardless of levels of education and/or income, informationals seemed to learn a great deal about candidates by using the mass media, especially the print media. Informationals also used the mass media in consistent ways.

We compared citizens who had completed a college degree (or more) with those who had more than a high school education but less than a completed, four-year college degree. (We did not include voters with high school or less education because of the their very low representation in 1980; separate analysis of these voters demonstrated the same pattern as that resulting from our comparison of college-or-more with high-school-or-more voters.) We used education as a control because it is the variable most often used to explain why some citizens know more than others, on the assumption that education either enhances the knowledge of those who already have educational and social class advantages or at the least extends one's basic knowledge and awareness of life.

We used survey data as if it were a quasi-experiment by controlling for level of formal education. This allowed us to see how highly informed voters—regardless of level of education—came to know so much about presidential candidates.

Convergence: Print Media Use and Informed Citizens

Figure 15.2 shows that in the 1956 election, college-educated citizens generally used newspapers and magazines more than did citizens with less than a college degree. But for newspapers, there also was a convergence of newspaper use, at 92 percent for the most informed, regardless of level of formal education. Figures 15.3 and 15.4 show that the same converging patterns also occurred in the elections of

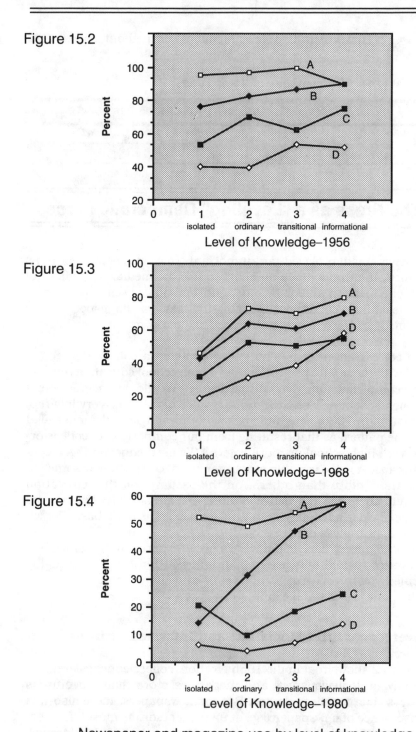

Figure 15.2

Level of Knowledge–1956

Figure 15.3

Level of Knowledge–1968

Figure 15.4

Level of Knowledge–1980

Newspaper and magazine use by level of knowledge
A=Newspaper use, college education   C=Magazine use, college education
B=Newspaper use, some college   D=Magazine use, some college

1968 and 1980. Political knowledge was associated with newspaper use, and this relationship could be detected despite some evidence of declining overall newspaper readership during the period.

All three elections tend to show more use of the news media by those who are informed—in the case of newspapers in 1956 and again in 1980, identical use. The most informed people also make use of magazines. We argue that print media used in these three elections demonstrate that the mass media provide routes that can be followed by citizens with less formal education to match citizens with more formal education. The print media apparently serve as an equalizer of informational opportunity—for those willing to use them.

Convergence: Electronic Media Use and Informed Citizens

The same trend is true in our three historical elections for television and radio. The most informed citizens made about the same use of television during the elections of 1956, 1968, and 1980 (figures 15.5, 15.6, and 15.7). Among college-educated citizens, the most informed citizens tended to use television only slightly more than the least informed. But among citizens with some college, there was a definite relationship between television use and high levels of information. With the exception of 1956, when the college-educated citizens seemed to use radio less and television more, there also was something of a convergence in use of radio during the three elections. Although the patterns are not quite as upward oriented, the trend is distinct: The most informed citizens use radio and television in similar ways.

Convergence and Democracy

Walter Lippmann said the press is like a searchlight beam, sweeping across the social landscape, highlighting first one episode and then another, and by implication leaving other events in darkness. A century ago, Alexis de Tocqueville declared the press to be an essential, if noisy, ingredient in American democracy. Tocqueville saw the press as a leveling force between the governed and governors, empowering people with community information that—even if distorted by partisan bias—would motivate interest and action in politics. The power of the press, Tocqueville wrote, was second only to the power of the people.

This chapter suggests several explanations for media influence. One is that some citizens are more active information seekers, espe-

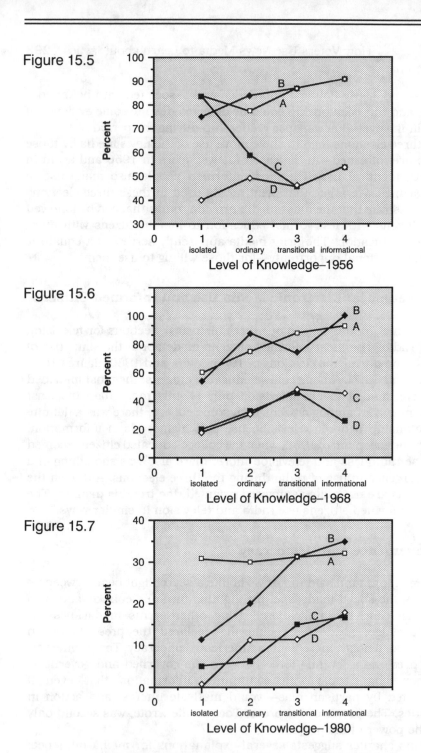

Figure 15.5

Level of Knowledge–1956

Figure 15.6

Level of Knowledge–1968

Figure 15.7

Level of Knowledge–1980

Television and radio use by level of knowledge
A=Television use, college education   C=Radio use, college education
B=Television use, some college   D=Radio use, some college

cially during campaigns or other times when particular information is needed. In these special times, citizens turn to the mass media—newspapers, magazines, network television (and cable), and radio—to satisfy their curiosity. These citizens may be driven by special interest, and this interest might be limited (as in this study) to campaigns and public life. Other citizens might use the media very actively to learn about entertainment, health, or business. However, one cannot be sure that subjects other than national politics would generate as much interest.

It also is possible that some citizens are inherently information seekers. If there is such a thing as a political person or a religious person, perhaps there is also an "informational person." If so, the informational person is as likely to be female as male, young as old. The informational person is likely to be non-Caucasian as well. If some are more tuned in to information, more interested in it, then the news media provide a way for those citizens to obtain vast quantities of pertinent community, family, and personal information.

Another explanation is that the news media provide the informational opportunities that our forefathers anticipated when they passed the First Amendment, guaranteeing that newspapers and magazines of the late eighteenth century would provide the richness of facts, views, and opinions needed by a young republic struggling to survive in the world's most recent experiment in democracy. The data we presented in this chapter, based on three historical elections, when all the contemporary mass media were strong, suggest that the news media provide informational opportunities to all citizens, if citizens will take advantage of them. Obviously millions do, and when they do so it makes little difference where they went to college, or even if they went to college. If a citizen wants to learn about public life, the news media provide ample and inexpensive opportunity. Tocqueville was right in the nineteenth century, and he remains so as we get ready to enter the twenty-first century. Still, we need to do some things right now.

Politics and the Press

The news media in general have fine-tuned the craft of covering and reporting stories, and technological advancements have enabled audiences to be better served than they were a half century ago. However, media still confront a special challenge in the area of political coverage and need to reorganize traditional approaches to covering campaigns. Political scientist Tom Patterson has described the evolution of national political coverage over the past few decades and suggests that there has been a serious erosion in public interest and participation in our collective political life. This breakdown is partially due to journalists themselves becoming tired of hearing candidates' major themes repeated as they try to get their messages across to the larger public. Consequently, journalists frame issues (often using terms common to battlefields), highlight candidate mistakes, and focus on new and unusual events or topics that are often extraneous to the issues or the candidates. In many cases the motivation behind this kind of coverage is the competitive drive to "beat" other reporters. Reporter Timothy Crouse in the 1972 campaign documented how reporters were more interested in what other reporters were saying and in the opinions of their editors back home rather than in what the candidates themselves were saying.

Over time, Patterson has documented how reporters have become less focused on issues and more on personalities, polls, and campaign strategies behind candidate activities—all legitimate news, of course. Theodore White's series of books about the "making" of the president in the national elections of 1960 through 1972 created wide public interest in the mechanics of campaigns and in personalities; investigations centered around the break-in of the Watergate housing complex in 1972 led to detailed behind-the-scenes stories about White House activities and eventually to the resignation of President Richard Nixon. Obviously, the public is interested in far more than issues.

At the same time that reporting moved the spotlight from the front-stage speaker to the back-stage staff members who handle the schedules, lighting, and sound system, the political parties were trading the smoke-filled rooms where party nominations were made after debate and tussle among professionals for the state and regional primaries where a party's most faithful (and most ideologically extreme) voters turn out to name their candidates. This process was in place by the 1970s, and the movement has continued to grow. Patterson points out that primaries often come very early in the campaign, in small unrepresentative states (such as New Hampshire), before most voters have any interest or knowledge of a campaign. The winners are therefore those picked by the most partisan within each party, or at least those most likely to vote. However the victory comes, winners become front-runners in the press, which continues to define candidates as winners or losers depending on shifting events and public opinion polls. Journalists are uncomfortable with ambiguity—about issues or candidates—and have framed recent election coverage within a horse-race, win-or-lose context. This current focus on the general public and what the general public is most likely to do (which is often measured by poll results) accounts for a fourth (or more) of national campaign stories.

In the early nineteenth century, so often dismissed as the era of a partisan press, the newspapers often carried an editorial paragraph or two to help readers "interpret" a speech, but then the newspaper carried the speech verbatim. Readers could make their own decisions. Press historian Dwight Teeter has argued that the newspaper political coverage of the early nineteenth century may be the best in the history of our country. It was a partisan era, but it was filled with views and facts obtained directly from the candidates.

This type of coverage is found less today, Patterson argues, because journalists now fill newscasts with their own interpretations, and editorial columnists spend far more time than ever presenting their own views. Today few papers other than the *New York Times* present the

The winner of a U.S. Senate primary election addresses questions from the press. Reprinted by permission of the Chicago Tribune.

entire speech (along with the shorter story on the front page) for the reader to peruse, as in the days of partisan journalism. Journalists sometimes have come between the events they are covering and the audience in the same way that a person at a cocktail party insists on telling everyone his or her interpretation of the events of the day, as though everyone was interested. In many settings, that person would be called a bore. In any event, political journalists seem to be talking to each other a great deal, but not necessarily to the citizens who are their audience. Perhaps this has contributed to the decline in daily newspaper circulation.

Patterson cites many studies to show that voters retain a strong interest in both issues and elections and that the increase in use of talk-show formats (without regular political journalists) is likely to continue despite journalistic grumbling that this is not real journalism. Perhaps it is not, but voters apparently are more interested in hard, unfiltered political information than they are in journalistic interpretations in lieu of that information.

A Reorganization of Political Beats

Major news media would be wise to reconstruct political beats into two teams. One team would have the responsibility for covering issues. Members of this team would concentrate on speeches, press conferences, and other campaign activities. If tired of hearing the same message, these reporters could use polls to find out the types of voters for whom an issue has the most appeal, but they would not link this to a speculation about the election outcome. Reporters on this team also could use polls to determine what issues interest voters in general in order to have some guidance in the types of questions to ask candidates. This is the essence of public journalism.

The other team would concentrate on the campaign as a horse race, consider strategies, evaluate advertisements for their honesty and intent, and present insider stories. This team would write stories about the challenges of campaign funding—legitimate news and a vital part of any campaign. Smart editors would aim for a balance of three issue stories to every one of the campaign stories. At present there is an imbalance between these two types of stories, forcing voters to reach through filters to learn about issues.

The teams should not mix, and members of one team should not write stories sometimes about issues and sometimes about the campaign strategies (during the course of a single campaign). The challenge for the issues team is this: Do voters know more about the issues (including the issue of personal style of the candidates) at the end of the campaign than they did at the beginning? It is a simple test. If voters do, journalists have succeeded in providing rich facts and opinions to the public. If voters do not, the failure must be attributed to journalism, not to the voters, for they have few other sources of public information. The challenge for the campaign strategy team is this: Do voters know more about the financing, polling, and mechanics of modern campaigns than they did at the beginning of the campaign? Do they understand the dynamics of democracy? These suggestions are related to national campaigns, but the same reasoning applies to campaigns and controversies at any level of government.

Journalists' Responsibility to Voters

No news is more important than news about government and politics. This chapter argued that the press is still an equalizing force, providing people who have less formal education an opportunity to obtain the facts needed to make informed judgments just as it does for those with high levels of education. The press allows citizens with perhaps fewer opportunities in life to participate fully in public decisions—even if citizens only pay attention to the stories that surround them daily in newspapers and magazines and on television and radio. However, we suggest that the current trends in political reporting need to be changed.

Journalists are educated to report, to comment, and to speculate, and this is part of journalism, if done responsibly. However, in the area of politics, much is done with little knowledge of the interests of voters and without an appreciation of the desire of citizens for plain, old-fashioned information. In the area of politics, journalists need to convey more information about social, political, and economic issues as well as the candidates' positions on these issues and less about the game of politics. It is a question of rebalancing the way news has evolved. A strong restructuring of political beats is needed if our government is to remain a popularly supported republic. There needs to be a convergence of the interests of journalists and citizens.

References

Campbell, Angus, Philip E. Converse, Warren Miller, and Donald E. Stokes. *The American Voter*. New York: Wiley, 1960.

Crouse, Timothy. *The Boys on the Bus*. New York: Ballantine Books, 1974.

Katz, Elihu and Paul F. Lazarsfeld. *Personal Influence: The Part Played by People in the Flow of Mass Communications*. New York: Free Press, 1955.

Lenski, Gerhard Emmanuel. *The Religious Factor: A Sociological Study of Religion's Impact on Politics, Economics, and Family Life*. Garden City, NY: Anchor Books, 1963.

Lippmann, Walter. *Public Opinion*. New York: Harcourt, Brace and Co., 1922.

Lipset, Seymour Martin. *Political Man: The Political Bases of Politics*. Garden City, NY: Anchor Books, 1963.

McCombs, Maxwell. "Mass Media in the Marketplace," *Journalism Monographs*, no. 24 (August 1972).

Patterson, Thomas E. *Out of Order*. New York: Alfred A. Knopf, 1993.

Patterson, Thomas E. and Robert D. McClure. *The Unseeing Eye: The Myth of Television Power in National Elections*. New York: Putnam, 1976.

Roper Organization. *Trends in Attitudes Toward Television and Other Media: A Twenty-Four Year Review*. New York: Television Information Office, 1983.

Teixeira, Ruy. "Will the Real Nonvoter Please Stand Up?" *Public Opinion Quarterly* 11, no. 2 (July/August 1988): 412–14, 59.

Tichenor, P. J., G. A. Donohue, and C. N. Olien. "Mass Media Flow and Differential Growth in Knowledge," *Public Opinion Quarterly* 34 (1970): 159–70.

Tocqueville, Alexis de. *Democracy in America*. New York: Vintage Books, 1945, reprint of 12th edition, 1848.

White, Theodore. *The Making of the President, 1960*. New York: Atheneum, 1961.

PART VI

PROFESSIONAL ISSUES

Chapter Sixteen

JOURNALISTS ARE OBJECTIVE

Journalism is probably the slowest-moving, most tradition-bound profession in America. It refuses to budge until it is shoved into the future by some irresistible external force.

—Timothy Crouse
The Boys on the Bus

When writing a story, journalists often balance the opposing sides of an issue as if their story is the only one that the public will see. Journalists do this because they want to be objective or, if that seems impossible, to be fair and balanced. This is true even though most journalists and editors have concluded that objectivity is impossible and, like magazine magnate Henry Luce, know they can only *aim* for fairness. Fairness and objectivity go together. Scholar Jay Rosen writes, "Objectivity is about informing the public; it tells us to worry about things like accuracy, balance and fairness."

In the late 1950s, there were two powerful national wire services, three commercial television networks, and a small number of major news magazines. There was much choice, yet not nearly as much as news consumers have now. Scholar Wilbur Schramm, who wrote an important ethics text during the period, devoted much time to the implications of choice, fairness, and balance in the news. The

This chapter was co-written with Jon Hill and Martha FitzSimon.

assumption was—and is—that audiences had a limited number of choices for obtaining news, and it was therefore important that each news source provide a balanced picture. Most journalists then, as now, attempted to do so.

However, the era of information scarcity is over. While we concentrate on making each message fair and balanced, audience members mix media messages routinely, for example by listening to radio at home or in the car in the morning and evening and reading newspapers at breakfast or lunch. Anyone relying today upon a single medium is likely to become informationally obsolete quickly. Audiences in the 1990s get perspectives from different media, not single messages from one source.

In the past, journalism educators spent much time emphasizing that journalists have the obligation to present a balanced set of messages. The power of choice was that of journalists and editors. Today the power of choice increasingly belongs to the audience. If people regard a message as unfair or unbalanced, they are empowered with the opportunity to find other messages, as indeed audiences seem to be doing. Today information is delivered by many kinds of media. Cable systems can deliver as many as 150 channels (some more than that), and as many as 500 channels may soon be available.

Where one person had, by chance, filmed what turned out to the assassination of John F. Kennedy in 1963, today many cameras record major events, and minor ones. Ordinary people videotape and photograph events and can even disperse pictures electronically. We are all on candid camera, from the time we make a deposit at the bank to the ride we take home on the subway. People can telephone, send faxes and e-mail to like-minded others; they can even organize people who live far away from each other, but who have common interests, into groups. Information professionals must remember that their customers can and do shop around.

An Examination of Current Trends

There are several important conclusions we might draw from the emerging era of information abundance:

1. The collective power of the established, major mass media to focus concerted national attention on important topics—to set the *collective agenda*—is declining. Twenty years

ago, a presidential convention would appear on all networks simultaneously, and there was little else to watch. Today only the most major events, such as assassinations and wars, receive that much attention, and even then, most Americans can turn to *Gilligan's Island* on cable. Indeed, in 1992, the national political conventions appeared most completely on the cable latecomers to political television— C-SPAN and CNN—as the networks cut back on their convention programming.

2. Leaders—including presidents, publishers, and broadcast owners—who depend on communication that primarily flows downward, with little coming back up, and who feel there is little need to justify orders and actions, are in trouble. Downward-only communication organizations assume there is a scarcity of information alternatives, which is almost never the case.

3. Ordinary people have become active information gatherers and disseminators. Inexpensive, easily operated, transportable audio and video equipment allow people to move from recording family reunions to filming chance real news events, such as the Rodney King beating—the incident in which white police offers were filmed striking a black suspect who was apparently already subdued—or the subsequent riots in Los Angeles. More "amateur" work is showing up on news and entertainment programs. "Real people" are on television and radio all the time. Just as Gutenberg's invention of movable type eliminated the church's control over information, new technologies are rapidly edging out traditional journalism. Facts and information are being democratized to millions of people.

4. Audiences make many more information choices than ever before. They select among hundreds of messages, both those that come down from above and those that come to them horizontally from others like themselves. In recent years, communication has allowed people to carry on a social dialogue that has nothing to do with the mainstream news media—witness "outsider" candidate Ross Perot's 1992 presidential campaign. There is no scarcity of news or alternative views of that news. Horizontal communication is almost as important as vertical communication; soon it will be equally important, with all that it implies for social,

political, and economic organization. Mass media should be exploring ways to use accumulated experience to help ordinary people speak with other ordinary people, as well as with leaders, and not always to tell the people what the leaders are thinking and doing.

5. Access to phones, faxes, electronic mail, and computer bulletin boards or computer-supported print publications allows people to organize and exchange information more than ever. Through this information exchange, people can communicate and band together to achieve common goals, pursue similar interests, or speak out in a united, collective voice. From the political point of view, the era of the silent masses is coming to an end, as witness activities and demonstrations in the former Soviet Union and in the United States (such as South Central Los Angeles), Cuba, China, and even, soon perhaps, North Korea. Autocratic leaders in nations, manufacturing plants, schools, governments, the arts, and universities should beware. A thousand points of light can illuminate your path, or consume you. Although those who are very poor may not have direct access to the information, now they are much more likely to be in touch with those who do than at any other time in history.

6. Information is like any other commodity, and information consumers are not especially loyal to a particular medium for the products they need, except (for awhile) to entertainment programs they enjoy. Media that rely mostly on loyal audience habit—newspapers are especially guilty of this— are doomed, individually if not collectively. The mass media are businesses that constantly have to assess their markets and adjust accordingly.

7. The abundance of information also provides journalists with new opportunities to show what they really can do. If a journalist carefully assesses all the appropriate sources (within reasonable deadline constraints), weighs facts and quotes, and balances the content without conscious effort to slant the conclusions, that journalist *is* being objective. Readers, listeners, and viewers may not agree or even like what they read, but their reactions cannot be the sole measure of objectivity.

Objectivity

Although most textbooks cite objectivity as a goal, many news editors avoid precisely defining the term. They feel that if readers from "both" sides of an issue complain equally (see box 16-1). The story by definition must be fair and balanced. Journalists usually leave the judgment up to readers.

The measure of professional objectivity can be found in the *process of reporting*. The focus, therefore, must change from the end product—the story—to the process of telling it, and journalists should tell readers more about how the facts were gathered, including all the appropriate sources used. Sidebars, used by some news media

---

Box 16-1
Teaching Balance and Fairness

Though most reporting textbooks today acknowledge the problems surrounding a standard of objectivity, some variation on that goal often can be inferred. These excerpts from recent textbooks highlight this issue:

Today, most journalists strive to be as impartial or "objective" as possible. Editors and other newspaper employees can express their opinions in editorial and columns, but not in news stories. Newspaper reporters are expected to be neutral observers, not advocates or participants. Reporters cannot discriminate against any ideas or tell their readers what to think about these ideas.

Fred Fedler, *Reporting for the Print Media*, 5th ed.

Journalistically, the challenge is to deliver to readers, listeners, and viewers a fair and balanced representation of viewpoints held by persons who differ markedly in their perceptions of what public policy should be.

A former editor quoted in Bruce D. Itule and Douglas A. Anderson, *News Writing and Reporting for Today's Media*, 2nd ed.

A more realistic goal is fairness and balance, combined with a continuing commitment to reflect the broad range of opinions and concerns held by diverse segments of the population.

Henry H. Schulte and Marcel P. Defresne, *Getting the Story: An Advanced Guide to Beats, Records and Sources*

---

already, should be used more to list and describe sources and procedures. If a story is objective, readers should be able to determine this from a sidebar, not from the lead of the main story with which audience members may not agree anyway. This re-education of journalists *and* audience members will not be easy.

Reporters find it easy to fall into the trap of rigid objectivity. They are even encouraged in this direction by their editors. After all, who can make a reasonable charge of biased reporting when a story contains roughly the same number and kinds of quotes from the main parties in a dispute? If the number of quotes is unbalanced, the editor instructs the reporter to pick up the phone and get one more quick quote from the other side, just to make sure both sides are equally represented. The pursuit of balance, then, may be as pragmatic as it is high-minded. But what about the substance that underlies the quotes?

Truth, as we all know, is relative, so rather than searching for the truth, journalists opt for reporting what the different players in a story say it is at any given moment. This is an especially dubious tack in an era of sophisticated spin control by governments, corporations, and special-interest groups. By no means can a reporter know or dig out the ultimate truth of every situation, and the media should make clear in these cases that much is still to be learned about the matter at hand or that reasonable people on opposing sides disagree.

However, when investigation can discern the fuller contours of the reality surrounding an issue, or as facts begin to flesh out the bare outlines, media must strive to communicate to the reader or viewer the full extent of the truth as it can be determined, not merely the shadow approximated by a collection of opposing comments marshaled in equal numbers and lengths. This is a more mature concept of fairness, one that treats news consumers "fairly" by pointing out when the facts do square with the arguments and when they do not.

Most journalism *is* objective, which is only to say that journalists fairly examine all appropriate and accessible sources within the structural constraints of time and space and draw professional judgments about how to present information. Most traditional journalists do not slant information or intentionally ignore some facts they know should be included or give undue weight to others.

The only journalists who are not objective are those who examine sources and—despite a thorough assessment of all the information available—still shape a story to fit a particular view as an *intentional* act. There are not many journalists like this, if only because the multitude of other accounts in an information-rich environment will spotlight any effort to distort. Journalists have the same respect for the body of facts with which they deal as do surgeons for the human bodies that are vulnerable to their skills (or lack thereof). Most journalists are objective. Increasingly, too, journalists realize that merely balancing all sides of a story may be unfair.

Let us examine two articles about smoking in an effort to assess fairness. Smoking is neither a necessary nor sufficient cause of lung cancer, but thousands of scientific studies have found a link. Yet when results are released of a new study making this connection, journalists balance these findings with quotes from tobacco industry representatives, who deny or downplay any relationship between smoking and lung cancer, usually with no specific hard evidence.

Journalists, however, are getting more sophisticated. Boxes 16-2 and 16-3 illustrate the kind of coverage the tobacco-cancer issue sometimes gets. The story in box 16-2 places the tobacco-industry arguments within the context of overall scientific findings, but the story also adopts the "balancing" approach. The story in box 16-3, on the other hand, goes much further toward the approach advocated in this chapter, clearly showing that the tobacco industry comment does not have the same weight as the scientific evidence.

Box 16-2
Tobacco Coverage—Balancing Views

Researchers sampled the air in workplaces that allow smoking and found that contrary to the tobacco industry's claims, workers are exposed to dangerous levels of secondhand smoke.

Nicotine levels in offices studied were more than triple the amount considered hazardous by U.S. regulatory standards, the researchers found in what is believed to be the largest study on secondhand smoke in the workplace.

"The tobacco industry says work exposures are trivial compared to home exposures," said lead researcher S. Katharine Hammond, an associate professor of public health at UC Berkeley. "And this paper says that's clearly not true."

A spokesman for the tobacco industry said the study's methods were faulty and that its conclusions contradict other research.

The findings appear in Wednesday's issue of the *Journal of the American Medical Association*. The study was conducted in Massachusetts, when Hammond worked at the University of Massachusetts Medical School in Worcester.

The researchers placed 25 fiber disks treated to react to nicotine at each of 25 work sites, including fire stations, newspaper publishing facilities, textile drying plants and various manufacturing plants. The disks were left for a week in offices, cafeterias, and production areas.

Nicotine levels ranged from 8.6 micrograms per cubic meter of air in open offices where smoking was allowed to 1.3 micrograms where smoking was restricted and 0.3 micrograms where smoking was banned. In nonoffice areas, the levels were 2.3 micrograms, 0.7 micrograms and 0.2 micrograms, respectively. Exposure to an average of 2.3 micrograms of nicotine per cubic meter of air for eight hours a day over 40 years creates a lung cancer risk of 3 in 10,000, the researchers said, citing previous research.

Secondhand smoke is believed to have an even greater effect on heart disease. Studies have estimated that secondhand smoke may cause 30,000 to 50,000 U.S. nonsmokers to die each year from heart disease, compared to 3,000 similar deaths from lung cancer, the researchers said. Hammond said she believes the Massachusetts work sites are typical of other U.S. workplaces.

Tom Lauria, a spokesman for the Tobacco Institute, a Washington-based trade group, said Hammond's method of monitoring at fixed locations failed to account for varying amounts of time employees actually spent at those locations.

"To measure workplace exposure properly, both concentration and length of exposure must be measured," he said.

Other research has found much lower workplace concentrations, Lauria added, citing a study by Oak Ridge National Laboratory in 16 cities. "Preliminary results from the Oak Ridge study show as much as 13 times less exposure in the workplace than at other locations," Lauria said.

He also said it has not been scientifically established that second-hand smoke contributes to lung cancer, as the government says.

Hammond said the Oak Ridge study has not yet been published in a scientific journal and subjected to review by experts.

The U.S. Environmental Protection Agency in 1993 classified secondhand smoke as a serious cancer threat and issued guidelines urging every company to have a policy protecting nonsmokers from involuntary exposure.

Michael Eriksen, director of the Office on Smoking and Health at the Centers for Disease Control and Prevention, said Hammond's study is not only the largest, but is one of the first to show the rela-tionship between secondhand smoke and work-site smoking policies.

Box 16-3
Tobacco Coverage—Using Professional Judgment

In the most comprehensive report of its kind to date, researchers have detailed the mechanisms by which secondhand smoke can damage the heart and circulatory system.

The report also concludes that nonsmokers are much more susceptible to heart damage from secondhand smoke than are smokers because nonsmokers' bodies haven't built up defenses against the onslaught of tobacco poisons. The conclusions are drawn from the most complete review to date of studies on how secondhand smoke affects the heart and blood vessels.

Stanton Glantz, a professor of medicine at the University of California, San Francisco, and Dr. William Parmley, chief of cardio-logy at UCSF, pulled together the data from more than 80 previous studies. Their review is published in today's issue of the *Journal of the American Medical Association.*

The evidence that secondhand smoke causes heart damage may accelerate the move toward smoking restrictions, said Scott Ballin of the Coalition on Smoking OR Health. The coalition comprises the American Heart Association, American Lung Association and American Cancer Society. Until now, most government regulations on secondhand smoke have been based on evidence that it can cause cancer.

But Walker Merryman, vice president of the Tobacco Institute, said the report "does not represent mainstream scientific opinion," including views from government research agencies and findings from large population studies.

The report includes recent clinical, laboratory, and epidemio-logical studies that demonstrate the underlying physiological and biochemical changes from ingestion of environmental tobacco smoke. The report concludes that secondhand smoke damages the heart by:

- Reducing the body's ability to deliver oxygen to the heart and inhibiting the heart's ability to effectively use oxygen.

- Increasing the amount of lactate, a salt derived from lactic acid, in blood, making it more difficult to exercise.

- Activating blood platelets, which increases the risk of blood clots and damages the lining of the coronary arteries.

- Aggravating tissue damage after a heart attack.

"About four years ago, what was happening in the heart could only be suggested. What's different today is that the studies have been done to show those things actually happen," Glantz said.

Using "A" to denote the scientific "side" and "B" to denote the tobacco-industry "side," figure 16.1 shows the more balanced effort represented by the first story—11 As, 6 Bs. Because the scientific evidence appears to be stronger, however, the second story has only 1 B to 10 As. Furthermore, in the "Air Quality . . ." story, 4 of the 11 As involve direct or indirect quotes (denoted by qs), but the remaining 7 are mainly facts. By contrast, the tobacco side (Bs), has direct or indirect quotes in all six of its paragraphs. In other words, in order to be fair, the reporter in "Air Quality . . ." had to balance hard scientific facts with tobacco-industry quotes. The second story, "Secondhand Smoke's . . .," used only one tobacco quote, then allowed the facts to overwhelm what was largely opinion. Which story is fairer? You decide.*

One can cite many similar examples in which journalists balance the comments of the informed with those of the self-interested or ignorant (even fools), all in keeping with goals of balance and fairness. In an earlier era of information scarcity, this ensured that even crazy points of view were given some public exposure. Even special interests charge bias if journalists do not give "their side," thereby making excellent use of this lingering notion of scarcity.

It is possible that the following hypothetical story is objective:

> Richmond—A new study released by scientists at the University of Richmond today made the link between cigarette smoking and lung cancer a very direct one, with smokers given a much higher chance of contracting the disease before they reach the age of 40.
>
> Tobacco industry representatives denounced the results, as they have in the past, although their denial lacked specifics to match either the newly released study, or any of the several thousand other studies that have established a link between cigarette smoking and lung cancer.

---

* For a study that takes the opposite and more traditional point of view, see Frederick Fico and Stan Soffin, "Fairness and Balance of Selected Newspaper Coverage of Controversial National, State, and Local Issues," *Journalism Quarterly*, 72, no. 3 (Autumn, 1995): 621–633

Figure 16.1
Examining Balance

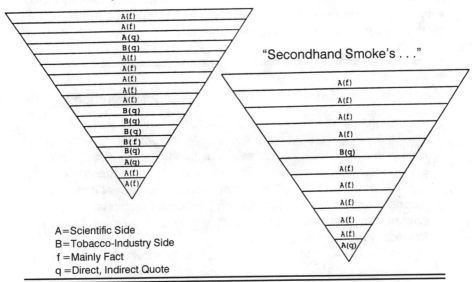

"Air Quality . . ."

"Secondhand Smoke's . . ."

A=Scientific Side
B=Tobacco-Industry Side
f =Mainly Fact
q =Direct, Indirect Quote

In the interest of fairness and objectivity, journalists often are denied the ability to exercise professional judgment, especially in politics. Journalists have brought this upon themselves. Journalists must review all the pertinent sources and weigh all the facts—that is being objective. When journalists write the story, they should ask themselves if all sides are equal or if one side is stronger than another. This process is not an example of bias; it is an example of professional skill and judgment.

Reeducating the Audience

Journalists operate in a marketplace of readers, viewers, listeners, and participants. Of course, it makes good economic sense to try to please the maximum number of audience members, but within the bounds of sound professional behavior.

Our philosophy of balance and fairness sometimes hamstrings the established media while many smaller, more individualized media fill all the informational needs of the very people who insist "their" point of view be represented in all stories. Audiences who charge bias are not necessarily loyal to established media, or indeed to any regular news media. Many people are loyal to their own causes, and usually they find or develop their own media. Yet it is in the hands of these very people that journalists leave the most important judgment of their work: Is it fair, balanced, and objective?

Box 16-4
"Good Reporting Is Fact-Finding without Prejudice . . ."

. . . [T]he job of journalism is to report, explain and clarify. We in the "serious" press—papers like the *New York Times* and the *Washington Post*—imagine ourselves as upholding the standards of a craft besieged by talk radio. The reality is that the "serious" press is often equally guilty of wild distortions, because editors and reporters are prisoners of prevailing intellectual fashions. A good example was last week's seven-part series on "The Downsizing of America" in the *Times*.

It has all the hallmarks of a project aimed for a Pulitzer. The *Times* anointed "downsizing" as a radical departure for the U.S. economy. In truth, "downsizing" is simply a new label for an old feature of a competitive economy: job loss. this is not dramatically greater than in the past, though it has affected some workers (generally older and with higher incomes) and companies (the IBMs and AT&Ts) that once seemed immune.

To convince us otherwise, the *Times* resorts to a pat formula: It introduces the new social trend with a compelling anecdote and a weighty statistic. The first personalizes the trend, the second proves that it's widespread. Thus, the series opens with Steven A. Holthausen, 51, who has gone from a $52,000-a-year job as a banker to a $12,000 tourist information officer. Then we're told that the "grimness" of his story is fairly common because "more than 43 million jobs have been erased in the United States since 1979." Gulp.

Actually, this impression is highly misleading. Averaged over 16 years, the 43 million lost jobs is 2.7 million jobs a year. The *Times* never points out that, in any one year, the loss is a tiny fraction of total jobs. The worse year was 1983 when 3 million workers lost their jobs out of employment of 101 million—about 3 percent. In 1995, displaced workers numbered 3.3 million out of 125 million—2.6 percent.

Not only do most well-paid, middle-aged workers not lose their jobs, but those who do typically don't suffer a 75 percent pay drop. Among rehired workers, only 31 percent suffered pay losses of more than 20 percent.

It's hard to see how a competitive economy could operate without job insecurity. New technologies and products create some jobs, eliminate others. Clearly, corporate managers are quicker to fire now than in the past; some "downsizing" is callous.

There is personal trauma and tragedy. Still, in some ways, the labor market is operating better now than 15 years ago. Between 1990 and 1995, unemployment averaged 6.4 percent, down from the 8.1 percent between 1980 and 1985.

Good reporting is fact-finding without prejudice. . . .

Excerpted from Robert Samuelson, "When Newspapers Turn Distortions into Compelling 'Stories,'" the *Chicago Tribune*, March 15, 1996, Sec. 1, p. 25. Reprinted by permission of the *Washington Post* Writers' Group © 1996.

One also wonders: Is this practice professional? If reporters present a balanced story when the facts do not conform to the findings of their own eyes and ears, they are not being fair and objective. Instead, they are acting like a surgeon who will not decide if an appendectomy was successful until the patient indicates whether he or she is satisfied with the inevitable postoperative scar. Patients wisely leave much to doctors, but mass media audiences do not allow much of journalists. Readers and viewers routinely blame journalists if they do not agree with a story, and editors understandably take these judgments seriously—too seriously in an age of information abundance. By conceding to readers and viewers the right to judge whether a story is fair, balanced, and objective, reporters allow their work to be evaluated—in a sense—on the basis of the scar, the most visible evidence of the operation rather than on the careful work done inside. One might call this the fairness fallacy—the assumption that there is always another side to which journalists must give equal weight (in the same story if possible), even if it cannot be supported, and even though such "objectivity" often presents a false picture.

Readers and viewers are accustomed to being asked whether they find messages objective. Most readers, unfamiliar with the journalistic process, are *not* objective in their collection and evaluation of facts—far from it. Readers and viewers who condemn news coverage always do so from the perspective of their own opinions. What these audience members are saying is, "I don't like or agree with the way the story is presented. It does not conform to my views, interests, goals, beliefs; therefore, the story is wrong, biased, insensitive."

A mass media audience member is no more likely than a politician to recognize that he or she might be "wrong" or that he or she only holds a different or incomplete view of the facts (because, after all, he or she did not interview the sources or cover the event). If audience members recognize that they might be mistaken, they do not admit it. They blame the press and have done so for centuries. Most members of the audience do not think they can do surgery, but they certainly feel they can do journalism—and, with new technology such as video cameras, increasingly they *are* (without worrying about professional fairness, balance, or objectivity).

Audiences will have to allow journalists to present pictures that are different from their own. So will leaders. When the late NBC correspondent Cassie Mackin reported that some statements made in the 1972 presidential campaign by incumbent Richard Nixon about Democratic challenger George McGovern were not true—said it on her own immediately on the air, without quoting anyone—she attracted immediate attention from the protesting White House. Who did Mackin think she was?! Today, John Milton's 1644 argument for diversity seems more pertinent than ever, if we have the courage, like Mackin, to pursue it by expanding our notions of professional independence. If audiences use technology to assess and compare different news sources, then journalists can use the same judgments to assess the information provided by news sources.

Reinventing Journalism

Some are concerned that the fabric of public life has been weakened—for example, there has been a long decline in voter turnout—and that the mass media have not remained in touch with the core needs of their audiences. Journalist Davis (Buzz) Merritt and scholar Jay Rosen have called for journalists to "imagine" *public journalism as an ongoing search for human connections that enrich public life*, in which journalism has historically been important. Merritt writes:

> "If journalists view their job as merely providing information—simply telling the news in a detached way—they will not be particularly helpful to public life or to their profession."

Rosen says:

> Journalism cannot remain valuable unless public life remains viable. Public life is in trouble in the United States. Therefore, journalism is in

---

Box 16-5
A New Movement in Journalism*

Public journalism is an unfolding philosophy about the role of the journalism in public life. The movement has emerged most clearly among print journalists who have tried to connect with their communities in a different way, often by encouraging civic participation or by grounding the coverage of politics in the imperative of public discussion and debate. In some of these experiments, newspapers have stepped out of a strict observer's role and occasionally become participants in the democratic process, helping to repair, support, and shape the civic culture that draws people into public life.

The Project [on Public Life and the Press] was established as a number of journalists came to see themselves as implicated in the troubles of America's civic culture and political system. These journalists began to question their roles as mere observers at a time when communities drift and unravel, when public discourse falters and politics earns the contempt of average citizens. The decay of civic culture and alienation from public life are increasingly associated with the long-term drop in newspaper readership.

While no journalist can afford to ignore the erosion of readership, public journalism emphasizes an equally troubling and related problem—the erosion of citizenship. By that we mean the weakening of a civic culture that draws people into public life, gives them a place in the political process, and encourages them to develop the skills of citizens in a democratic society. Rather than simply assume such a culture exists, the public journalist takes responsibility for helping to repair, support, and shape it.

*The Project on Public Life and the Press is a collaboration among The John S. and James L. Knight Foundation, Kettering Foundation, American Press Institute, and New York University.

From Merritt and Rosen, "Imagining Public Journalism," 1995.

---

trouble. Fortunately, there is something the press can do. It can help citizens participate and take them seriously when they do. It can nourish or even create the sort of public talk that might get us somewhere. The press can change its lens on the public world so that citizens aren't reduced to spectators in a drama dominated by professionals and technicians. Most important, perhaps, journalists can learn to see hope as an essential resource which they cannot deplete indefinitely without tremendous costs to us and them.

In the cacophony of messages in today's information market, thoughtful analysis, interpretation, and measured exercise of journalistic judgment is what is required, because for someone who disagrees with one voice, there are so many others available. Indeed, given the wealth of information possibilities presented by the latest technological advances, perhaps journalists may finally stop being scribes and stenographers, and apply to events the kind of judgment and critical thought for which they, as professionals, are well suited. Professional and independent journalists have never been more desperately needed.

News and Social Diversity

For the first time since the eighteenth and early nineteenth centuries, technology allows social diversity to flourish. The abundance of information choice has put communication technology at the center of human history, as suggested in a different context by Canadian economist Harold Innis and, later, in yet another way by Canadian communication scholar Marshall McLuhan. Both men saw communication as permeating all aspects of life and history. The 1992 presidential election campaign—in which some candidates used direct mail, telephone solicitation, faxes, videos, and cable channels to stretch their reach beyond the traditional mass media to reach voters—offers a telling illustration.

News media have new opportunities for creative experimentation with their faithful audiences because they no longer have to represent "all" points of view within every message, although they do have to remain professionally fair and objective as, indeed, most already are. Within the media market of the 1990s and beyond, the rules of scarcity that once required absolute (and sometimes mindless) adherence to rigid rules of fairness and balance because of the limited number of information sources available may no longer apply.

Journalists have exciting opportunities to present new ways of looking at old things—in objective ways—on the assumption that a variety of other facts and points of view will also surface. Journalists cannot please everyone in every message and should not try. Audiences can be fickle and whimsical. If an audience member does not like the final story, which is the journalist's best professional effort, let him or her look elsewhere. When it comes to surgery, it is advisable to get a second opinion; that also is true for journalism. That is what Milton had in mind when he spoke of diversity.

For their part, audience members must also be taught what journalists already know: Fairness does not always lead to objectivity; objectivity does not always lead to fairness. News consumers must learn some tolerance for news diversity, too, and develop their own critical thinking skills and judgment to be able to recognize the difference between fairness and truth. After all, communication technology is making journalists of us all. Our first challenge is to communicate with each other. The mass media have an important role in this challenge, and journalists have the greatest opportunity in the history of reporting to apply truly professional skills and perspectives to the hourly, daily, weekly, and monthly jobs we do.

References

Crouse, Timothy. *The Boys on the Bus.* New York: Ballantine Books, 1974.

Fedler, Fred. *Reporting for the Print Media*, 5th ed. New York: Harcourt Brace Jovanovich, 1993.

Innis, Harold A. *Empire and Communications.* Toronto: University of Toronto Press, 1972.

Itule, Bruce D. and Douglas A. Anderson. *News Writing and Reporting for Today's Media*, 2nd. ed. New York: McGraw-Hill, 1991.

McLuhan, Marshall. *Understanding Media: The Extensions of Man.* New York: McGraw-Hill, 1964.

McCombs, Maxwell E. *Mass Media in the Marketplace.* Lexington, KY: Association for Education in Journalism, 1972.

Merritt, Davis (Buzz) and Jay Rosen. "Imagining Public Journalism: An Editor and Scholar Reflect on the Birth of an Idea." Roy W. Howard Public Lecture in Journalism and Mass Communication Research, Indiana University School of Journalism, No. 5, April 13, 1995: 14.

Rivers, William L. and Wilbur Schramm. *Responsibility in Mass Communication.* New York: Harper & Row, 1969.

Chapter Seventeen

Encouraging and Influencing Community Change

This is to say, then that the press is significantly more than a purveyor of information and opinion. It may not be successful much of the time in telling people what to think, but it is stunningly successful in telling its readers what to think about.

—Bernard C. Cohen
The Press and Foreign Policy

There has been a decline in public attention to much of today's community media coverage resulting in the general decline in mass media circulation, and therefore power, during the past half century. Films, while important, do not attract the mass audiences they did in the 1940s and early 1950s, years which also saw the effective end of network radio. Mass magazines like *Life* and *Look* died in the early 1970s, and a decade later the major television networks saw a steady decline in their audiences that continues today. The question is: Can mass media reestablish a relevancy for the communities they cover? Can *mass* media matter?

One way that mass media can reestablish useful contact with communities is by focusing on community issues rather than on community events alone. Things that happen in a specific time and place are events. A civil disturbance is an event. But the causes of the disturbance may have been building for years and may be based on discrimination, the lack of economic opportunity, police-public relations, or other factors. Because these factors are not immediate and dramatic, the mass media spend less time searching for patterns, although they are as important in their own way as the disturbance itself.

Yet recent winners of the prestigious Pulitzer Prize for reporting have been journalists who used databases to dig behind events, exploring the shadows thrown by things that happened. About one-ninth of an iceberg lies above the ocean, with the remaining eight-ninths of the iceberg immersed below the waterline, out of sight. It was the unseen part of the iceberg that sank the *Titanic*. Today stories about the part of the iceberg that is not visible win prizes. In other words, by going beyond obvious conditions journalists *are* creating news, or at least creating new perspectives on events.

In-depth reporting is nothing new. Northwestern journalism professor Curtis MacDougall wrote an important textbook in the 1930s in which he argued that journalists need to dig deeper and to seek the whys of events. Journalists are accustomed to putting into every story the who, what, when, and where of events. Often journalists add the how. Journalists do not often address the most difficult of questions—the why—because the answers to that question are hard to determine or are controversial.

We do not argue that journalists keep the spotlight on events with the intent of always answering every one of the five Ws and one H. Instead we argue that journalists need to identify selected social challenges and keep the spotlight on a few selected issues long enough for the community to come to terms with them. That might require more in-depth coverage or it might only require simple stories about events and issues in a consistent way. While editorial function of the mass media allows them to contribute thoughts on particular solutions, the real power of the media is in the consistency and quality of the coverage of the spotlighted issue.

Mass Media and Agenda-Setting Power

The media have power to gain public attention. We know from hundreds of agenda-setting studies that the media do have the power to tell people what to think *about*. That is true of people who attend to the media; it also is true of people who do not pay attention to the media but who learn about issues from others. The press does not tell people *what* to think. Press attention does not lead to a specific action, or if it does, that action is not necessarily logical or reasonable. Once an issue is on the public agenda, one can never be sure of the outcome.

Recent research shows that the press is able to pull together different segments of the community in terms of agreement on important issues. Those of different gender, race, and age may agree on important issues—for example, crime or the quality of health care—but they may not agree on solutions or approaches to these issues. You cannot know how people will think about the issues emphasized in the mass media, but you can safely guess that substantial numbers of people will at least think about the topics published, and many will talk to each other about these public issues. The ability to stimulate interest is, in itself, great power. However, this ability alone may not result in a public effort to confront public issues.

Although the ability to set the agenda is great power, the press normally does not emphasize the same story every day. Variety, within reason, is the spice of life in journalism as it is elsewhere. The spotlight moves on. But if a news medium used its agenda-setting power to keep the light focused on an issue, then gradually turned the spotlight down so it was not so bright, public attention would stay on the issue, perhaps uncomfortably.

Research shows that the public seldom keeps more than five to seven issues in mind at any one time, with only one to three issues gaining the most attention. For a reasonable period of time, a news medium could select a limited number of key community issues to put on the agenda for public attention, even if news leaders do not emphasize these issues or ignore them altogether. For example, several years ago, a newspaper in San Antonio concentrated on a community issue—children's quality of life—and kept attention on this issue for a year. Because stories about children deal with a wide range of topics such as health, education, play, and safety, and nearly all beats touch on the lives of children (as they do adults), reporters from different beats were able to keep an eye open for stories that involved children. So did columnists and editorial writers. It was a collective effort.

Any news medium could—and should—perform the same public responsibility. Figure 17.1 shows one way that the press can give major attention to a topic, then gradually step down the attention to a lower level. For any topic, there should be some, if sometimes slight, continuing attention by the news media. Research demonstrates that longer, lower-grade media attention rather than passing, intense media attention has greater impact on public awareness. If the spot

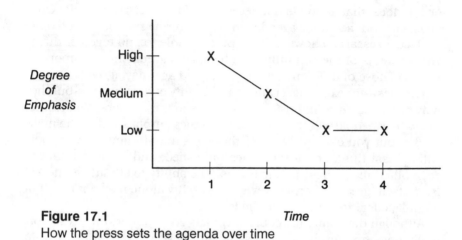

Figure 17.1   *Time*
How the press sets the agenda over time

light moves on, the dark corners of the stage still receive some illumination, the mass media equivalent of stage lights.

Some journalists will protest that the news media cannot possibly become entangled in events like this. But this is exactly what news media do by establishing regular news beats. The selection of news beats—courts, mayor's office, police, and so forth—has a powerful and predictable influence on the news agendas and therefore presumably on what people think about.

The news beats that have been developed by news media over the past half century have not maintained the audiences that newspapers, news magazines, network radio, and network television used to attract. Old news patterns apparently do not always fit audience interests. The traditional beats do not fit life especially well. Some mass media have experimented with new beats such as the environment, health care, minority affairs, and other areas.

It seems unlikely that news media will remain vital to communities if they merely convey information from (mostly) official news sources, especially when audiences can obtain all kinds of information from many sources, often immediately. Yet the mass media remain among the few institutions that attempt to serve the entire community and still can focus substantial and continuing attention on social issues that affect the quality of community life. Simply by holding the spotlight on key events and/or issues the news media can be advocates, and, within reason, the news media should be. This will require courage and a break from generations of doing things pretty much the same way.

The Role of People in Social Change

Although central to community change, the press is one of many institutions involved in social change. The press provides an agenda of social issues for public consideration rather than a series of final solutions. Solving community problems is the role of citizens and leaders, with the involvement of many other institutions (such as the press) and special-interest groups. However, editorialists and columnists have opinions on solutions just like any informed citizen.

Communication scholar Everett Rogers in 1962 highlighted an important line of research when he examined the process of innovation—how the press helped spread new ideas or new products. Rogers summarized many studies that showed the key role that people play in social change, *after* the mass media arouse interest by means of advertisements, news, or editorial emphasis. For example, nurses are more likely than an advertisement alone to persuade a married woman that a birth-control method is safe and effective. The advertisement may cause interest—may put birth control on the agenda of things to think about. But that often is as far as it goes.

Rogers points out that many people, not just political leaders, are interested in spreading ideas. For example, a nation's department of agriculture may want farmers to use a new high-yield wheat seed to increase the nation's food supply. Adopting a new seed is a risk for a farmer who may have used the same type of seed all his life, as did his father and grandfather. Change is risky, even if the payoff is potentially great for the individual farmer (and for the nation as a whole). Rogers assembled many studies to find patterns in the way that ideas about doing things a different way or in using new products spread. These studies are called *diffusion studies* because they trace how information, products, or ideas spread—or diffuse—throughout a social system.

Diffusion studies reveal that mass media news stories and advertisements are usually not sufficient by themselves to get people to change their ideas or behavior. The more important the decision, the more people seek advice from someone else who they like or respect. In the case of farmers, a visit from a respected agricultural agent is likely to be more effective than a mass media message or advertisement alone. But the combination of mass media agenda-setting (news and/or advertising) and individual support from others can be powerful.

For convenience, Rogers has given labels to five "types" of people:

1. *Innovators*—venturesome individuals who quickly seize new ideas. For a few in this group, the mass media messages alone may tempt them to experiment, but this is a very small, if bold, group.

2. *Early Adopters*—individuals who are highly informed from both mass media and interpersonal sources, and so they too are fairly quick to accept new ideas.

3. *Early Majority*—those who watch and learn from the first two groups—innovators and early adopters—before taking action.

4. *Late Majority*

5. *Laggards*—like the first group, also is small.

Even with the power to set the agenda, the mass media alone have limited power to change things. Most people are cautious and will talk with others before taking action.

Rogers also describes a pattern in the way that individuals consider new ideas. He cites five key steps. The first step, gaining *knowledge* of the new idea or product, involves having exposure to the new idea—along with curiosity, and understanding.

The next step is *persuasion* and involves forming an attitude about the new idea or product—for example, whether or not it is good. Then there is the big third step—people must decide whether to *adopt* (or reject) the idea or product.

The fourth step, *implementation*, is when an adopter puts the innovation to use—tries it out. The fifth step is *confirmation*, and that happens when a new idea/product proves to be a good one and reinforces its adoption, *or* it proves to be a bad idea/product, and we suddenly are back at step one, ready to consider another new idea or product, although perhaps a little wiser. Community change does not come easily because individual change does not come easily.

In sum, diffusion research suggests that there is a logical expectation that media attention to an idea or product may be a sensible investment of attention at first, with less attention given to the role of other people. Before long, the role of other people becomes more important and even crucial if the idea is a hard one to accept or the product is an expensive or risky one to buy. Hypothetically, we can sketch the role of interpersonal communication and change as in figure 17.2.

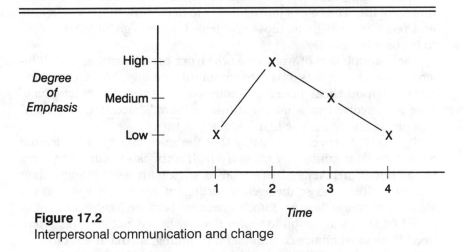

Figure 17.2
Interpersonal communication and change

In this hypothetical model, one can see that there is little need for interpersonal contact at Time 1 because the media only spark curiosity or impart initial knowledge of the innovation.

When curiosity is aroused, there is a need for immediate information and reinforcement from other people (Time 2).

The need for reinforcement declines as people actually try the product or idea and find it useful (if not, it will be dropped), and this is represented by a decline in need for interpersonal contacts at Times 3 and 4.

The amount of time between Times 1 and 4 varies with each situation of course, as do the numbers that constitute "light," "medium," or "heavy" contacts. These are all judgments that have to be made in light of every product or idea in the context of the local community. This model suggests a starting place.

Combining Traditions

We do not argue that the mass media should press for specific solutions to the various economic, social, political, and cultural problems that are challenging our communities. We do argue that mass media should focus steadily on these challenges, seek patterns, and keep the spotlight of attention on key issues that must be addressed if communities are to achieve a fair-minded and equitable quality of life. The role of journalists is to determine major challenges and keep the spotlight on those problems long enough for other people to become involved.

The combination of what we know from agenda-setting and diffusion research suggests a path to community change. We can combine our two hypothetical models, without worrying about what lengths of time are involved or what constitutes a "low," "medium," or "high" amount of attention. The figure looks like this:

Figure 17.3 reflects the reality that the mass media influence the agenda for community audiences if a high emphasis is put on an issue for a short time. Newspapers tend to stick with issues longer than television does, and so the agenda-setting influence of newspapers is slower but longer lasting. Public attention is more likely to be influenced by steady attention to topics than by heavy, but passing, attention. The model shows continuing, if declining, media attention.

As mentioned previously, agenda-setting research often has shown that the public keeps only about five to seven issues in the collective mind at any one time. So if a "new" issue comes along, it "pushes off" an older issue. Therefore if a mass medium decides to keep a steady spotlight on a particular topic—say, local crime or local educational opportunities (perhaps creating a temporary issue beat around the topic)—that topic is more likely to become part of the collective mind. That is why the news media that give massive but brief attention to social problems—for example, drugs in the street—are far more likely to influence cocktail conversation than social policy. Consistency is the key.

Leaders are well aware that mass media attention soon slips away. It is the steady, if lighter, attention that drops the kind of rain that forces leaders and citizens reluctantly to pull out the umbrella, not the sudden squall that soon passes, that can be waited out by pausing beneath a store awning, and is quickly forgotten. Figure 17.3 shows that the ideal way to gain public attention is to combine the major mass media emphasis with a gradual dropping away of the topic to a lower but continuing level of attention. At the same time, the interpersonal community resources become more involved—or should, if community leaders want to address the policy implications of the issue.

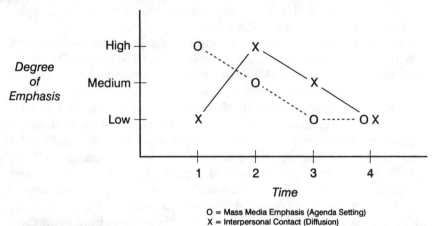

Figure 17.3
Combination of agenda setting and diffusion

Allocating Time and Resources

Our model is a rough guide to community change, based on communication research. The model obviously goes beyond the role of the mass media. Those who apply this model need to decide how long Time 1 should be for a particular campaign, as well as how long Times 2, 3, and 4 should be. These will vary, with more time required for some campaigns than for others. Decisions also have to be made in terms of what constitutes "high," "medium," or "low" mass media and interpersonal emphasis. Some people buy public attention to get on the public agenda through advertisements. At other times, consistent news and/or editorial attention results in a spot on the public agenda.

One can use the model to make guesses about campaign starting points and the allocation of any resources. To demonstrate this, we push our hypothetical case further, using a community challenge broader than journalism. Suppose that we have $14,000 with which to do something that experience has shown is really challenging: To convince married men and women in Village X in Country Y to use a new, safe birth-control method. We select this assignment without drawing inferences about the use of birth-control methods and whether we "should" try to do such a thing. In any event, this is a difficult sell in many places in the world.

Our model provides a starting point. If you imagine that "high" is set equal to an imaginary score or scale value of 3 (up from 0), while "medium" is set to a score/value of 2 and "low" is set at the score/value of 1, then you can actually make some initial judgments about how to allocate your money. One can also imagine values set for the time periods, but there is no need to do so in our hypothetical example.

Look again at figure 17.3 and imagine a score for both mass media and interpersonal emphasis. Obviously, the major attention at Time 1 is given to mass media (score = 3) to gain attention, such as the use of an advertising blitz. Less attention (score = 1) is given to interpersonal sources (such as visits by family-health nurses in our example) at Time 1 because it would be premature to use them until people are exposed to the issue.

Time 2, however, would bring a big increase in use of interpersonal sources (score = 3), once interest presumably is aroused by the mass media attention, while the attention by the mass media gradually declines (score = 2). You strike while the iron is hot. Time 3 shows that both media and interpersonal attention are stepped down in emphasis.

By Time 4, both mass media and interpersonal attention have fallen to maintenance levels (both scores = 1), but—perhaps—the change in behavior has begun to take root. If not, it is not likely to do so. If a change is completely accepted in a community, you eventually can drop the emphasis even more.

Look again at figure 17.3, and you can even construct a kind of mathematical formula to describe this process of encouraging change *if* you will pretend that one "unit" of mass media attention (from 0 to 3) is exactly equal to one "unit" of interpersonal attention (from 0 to 3). That is "low" would equal 1, "medium" would equal 2, and "high" would equal "3." The formula would look like the following (T represents time; M represents media emphasis; I represents interpersonal emphasis):

T1 (3M+1I) + T2 (2M+3I) + T3 (1M+2I) + T4 (1M+1I) = Total Resources = Change?

Here T1 through T4 equals all phases of the entire campaign, M equals mass media emphasis, and I equals interpersonal emphasis. Also, "low" is equal to one unit, "medium" is equal to two units, and "high" is equal to three units.

Do not worry whether one unit of media attention is really equal to one unit of interpersonal attention or whether the costs for mass media and interpersonal resources are the same. Costs are not the same because people are more expensive than media attention, even television advertising. In our example, we decided to set each unit of media or interpersonal attention at a value of $1,000. If we hold that they are equivalent for the moment, we can see that our $14,000 would be allocated in the following way:

Time 1
    Media Emphasis (3M)   = $3,000
    Interpersonal Emphasis (1I)   = $1,000
    Total   **= $4,000**

Time 2
    Media Emphasis (2M)   = $2,000
    Interpersonal Emphasis (3I)   = $3,000
    Total   **= $5,000**

Time 3
    Media Emphasis (1M)   = $1,000
    Interpersonal Emphasis (2I)   = $2,000
    Total   **= $3,000**

Time 4
    Media Emphasis (1M)   = $1,000
    Interpersonal Emphasis (1I)   = $1,000
    Total   **= $2,000**

    Grand Total   **= $14,000**

In general, most of our expenditures are in Times 1 and 2, with mass media given the most initial emphasis and interpersonal follow-up coming second. About two-thirds of the money should be spent in Times 1 and 2, with the remaining third spread out over Times 3 and 4. In other words, the best strategy for the expenditure of our money for both the mass media and interpersonal contacts would be something like that shown in figure 17.4.

This approach helps with planning because the shape of the line, as a starting point, should fit whatever amount of money is used (of course, you will have to do some adjustment because people are more expensive than media). As a model, this can also be a guide to the allocation of resources other than money, such as the use of volunteers.

Some will be outraged by our suggested approach because of the assumptions made about the equivalents of units or the phasing of the time periods. They may feel that there is too much journalistic

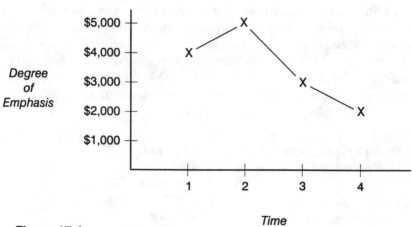

Figure 17.4
Allocation of resources—a theoretical perspective

involvement. Certainly journalists might take exception to the suggestion that the mass media in any way should be involved with trying to engineer social change, although the mass media do this all the time through advertisements, editorials, and columns and through the types of beats selected and covered. But this is not the purpose of this illustration.

We simply suggest that communication research shows informed strategies for beneficial community change, which has been a traditional mass media goal; editorials constantly call for change. If you take our example and strip it of money, you still have an indication of how effort, however defined, could be expended sensibly. Generally, one expects that the mass media will highlight issues in news coverage and that community leaders or community action groups will provide the interpersonal contributions to solving problems, which is a step beyond where most mass media leaders want to go. The mass media may not have an interest in any particular solution to community challenges, only that the community address those issues to improve the quality of life.

Community Patterns and Change

Today, journalists dig beneath news events as never before. With databases, journalists gather and analyze data in ways that do not even occur to the agencies that gather it, or perhaps that may not be in their best interest. With faxes and expanded telephone service, journalists can contact people all over the world. Private citizens also do much of this, but journalists have a professional interest in finding patterns.

The search for patterns in any important area will result in many stories far beyond those that journalists might obtain from interviewing leaders. Journalists are in a position to put issues on the public agenda on a steady basis, and journalists are as prepared as anyone else to know the important issues—they deal with them every day.

If journalists discover and turn selected patterns into continuing issues, then it is up to leaders and citizens to address these issues in a fair and equitable way. Journalists will still be publishing all the news that is fit to print, but also will be doing what any responsible citizen should do: Alert responsible citizens about the dry woods of social conditions before lightning strikes to ignite the forest into the flames of social disruption. If citizens are surprised at the turn of events, it is always partly due to the failure of the press to inform them. Alert journalistic sentries find many patterns from the watchtowers of communities and have more tools than ever to keep citizens informed. Journalists have far more knowledge of how communication actually works than they did 30 years ago. Journalists no longer have to wait for events to happen. In fact, journalists *should not wait*. But change is dependent on people, and people have many informational choices.

Individual and Group Empowerment

Modern media give people access to global communications through satellites and the ability to interact with the world through faxes, telephone, or computer link-ups. French traveler Alexis de Tocqueville noted the tendency of Americans to read newspapers and to join various community associations. Now Americans, like others, can read, view, and listen to many messages and join associations far beyond their local communities. People can physically reside in one community but intellectually live in another one (or several). Place is not always a good description of where people live anymore.

Once, average individuals were at the bottom of a community's social pyramid; political leaders comprised the top stone, and others involved in political, economic, and cultural duties comprised the broadening layers on the way down. This is an image of a world best served by the old mass media, which mostly focused on news about the powerful people at the top and published millions of copies of this news for those on the layers toward the bottom.

This orderly world has been disrupted by communication technologies that give individuals at any level some ability to gather information on their own and, very importantly, to communicate with other people on their same level. This is especially true for the millions of people linked together with the instantaneous communication of electronic mail. It is as if the stones of the social pyramid were pushed apart somewhat. There is still a social pyramid, but air now passes between the stones at all levels. There is potential improvement of life for all levels, except perhaps for those at the very top who now can feel a certain wobble in the pyramid. Some national pyramids already have collapsed. Even the older mass media feel threatened—and little wonder, because these media historically have covered those at the top for those at the bottom. Mass media information traditionally has flowed down the pyramid, as air over the surface of an airplane wing. Now the wings have holes.

The Challenge for Mass Media

Walter Lippmann compared press attention with the beam of a spotlight that fixes powerfully on a spot momentarily and then moves on. That metaphor, from his 1922 *Public Opinion*, fits modern mass media. Television usually gives brief attention to important stories. Newspapers devote large amounts of space to only the most important stories. For all topics, the spotlight eventually moves on.

What is natural for mass media—passing attention—does not fit the challenges of modern society. Problems of education, work, faith, family, poverty, transportation, discrimination, crime, and drug or alcohol abuse continue, whether in the public spotlight or not, seemingly without solution. We also know from decades of communication research that, for many citizens, out of sight is out of mind. When press attention shifts, public attention fades. Journalists have a responsibility to keep the spotlight on certain issues so that community leaders cannot evade them but instead address them to improve public life.

There has never been a more pressing time for the mass media to focus on commonly shared community issues. "Niche" media such as many special-interest cable channels or magazines, for example, aim at a narrowly defined segment of the market and do not address the issues of the larger society. That leaves the spotlight power of the traditional mass media with a more important mission than ever—the power to focus on common community issues in a consistent way.

The challenge for the general mass media is to focus light on important community issues long enough so that leaders from all levels of society cannot escape the glare and therefore will attempt to address community social challenges. We suggest, like Lippmann, that the spotlight of media attention should focus on community problems and issues. Unlike Lippmann, we suggest the spotlight should follow some issues for a substantial amount of time until the dynamics of community change begin to work. If members of a society become isolated, responsible collective social life ends. That should be the concern of all citizens and institutions, not just the press.

There is no shortage of subjects for the spotlight, if journalists will force the light on key subjects long enough for leaders and citizens to take note of the important issues that we share. Although members of the audience live in a variety of communities, they still share much.

References

Cohen, Bernard C. *The Press and Foreign Policy*. Princeton, NJ: Princeton University Press, 1963.

MacDougall, Curtis D. *Interpretive Reporting*, 5th ed. New York: Macmillan Company, 1968.

Miller, George. "The Magic Number Seven, Plus or Minus Two," *Psychological Review* 63 (March 1956): 81–97 .

Rogers, Everett M. *Diffusion of Innovations*, 4th ed. New York: Free Press, 1995.

Shaw, Donald L. "The Rise and Fall of American Mass Media: Roles of Technology and Leadership," Roy W. Howard Lecture presented April 4, 1991, at Indiana University, Bloomington.

Shaw, Donald L. and Shannon E. Martin. "The Function of Mass Media Agenda Setting," *Journalism Quarterly* 69 (Winter 1992): 902–920.

Chapter Eighteen

GETTING READY FOR THE TWENTY-FIRST CENTURY

. . . Oliver Wendell Holmes told . . . about the circus parade coming to town. The elephants always went first. And the little boys in the town would dance in front of the elephants, pretending to be leading them. But, of course, the elephants were going to march on, regardless of the little boys. And Holmes said those little boys were the politicians of any era. And the elephants were the great social movements of the time. They would march on, regardless.

. . . [I]n the press . . . it seems to me, we can either throw obstacles in the paths of those elephants and slow down the great social movements, or we can try to make smooth the path; get things out of the way.

—Cokie Roberts
ABC News correspondent

Journalism students are often driven by idealism, regardless of their communication career goals. If aiming for a news career in magazines, newspapers, television, or radio, students hope to produce the kind of stories that will clean up government, correct social or economic wrongs, and make life better for all citizens. If aiming for a career in advertising, students aspire to sell products that will improve

This chapter was co-written with Jon Hill.

337

Television network newscasts are traditional sources of information. Photograph by Larry Busacca, Courtesy CBS.

life; if aiming for a career in public relations, students plan to represent industries that stand for the best in American organizations. Sometimes the ideal is attained, sometimes not. It is a credit to the field of journalism that so many idealistic young (and older) students are attracted to it.

Journalism always has covered change, but journalism is also part of change. Today journalists confront an audience that often is just as confused by the multiplicity of voices as are journalists who have to select a few stories from a large number of possibilities. For the first time in the history of mass media, journalists cannot be assured that an important story will be widely shared, unless it is about a very major event.

Audiences have many ways to gather information of personal interest, but journalists also have a wide array of methods to gather, organize, and present information. Other than national leaders, journalists remain in the best position to monitor the whole society of their neighborhoods, cities, states, regions, and the nation. If journalists search for patterns reflected in our daily lives, they will help build the kinds of public agendas and awareness that may lead to a better life for all of us. That has always been the challenge of those who practice the profession of journalism.

Journalists have tried to counter the loss of audience. Many newspaper publishers watched *USA Today*, founded in 1982, successfully reach a national audience with well-written and well-illustrated stories. The *USA Today* emphasis on colorful and simple graphics has inspired imitation. Beauty, however, often has proved skin deep, and the problem seems to be more substantive. A loss of contact with the core audience and the issues that affect them has caused metropolitan daily newspaper circulation to stagnate or even drop year after year.

One of the most intriguing developments is the effort of some publications to promote *public journalism* (see also chapter 16). Definitions of public journalism differ, but Jay Rosen and Buzz Merritt in a 1995 lecture concluded that:

> The viability of public life and the value of journalism are inextricably bound together. . . . The objective of our journalism must be to re-engage citizens in public life.

Pursuing this theme, the *Charlotte (N.C.) Observer* used public opinion surveys in the 1994 election to determine the issues that concerned voters in the Charlotte area, then put fire to the heels of any candidate who would not address the same issues. Journalists in a sense became an extension of the public.

The success of the public journalism movement has yet to be evaluated completely in terms of circulation (although there are hopeful signs), but certainly journalism that tries to meet the needs of its audience cannot be wrong. That is what the most successful journalists have done throughout our history, from Benjamin Franklin to Horace Greeley to Frederick Douglass to Ida Tarbell to Walter Lippmann to Neil Sheehan and David Halberstam and to David Broder and Barbara Walters.

Yet the long-term trends for mass media metropolitan newspapers, mass distribution magazines, and network television are not promising. A study by one of the authors suggests that all mass media live through three stages of development—youth, adulthood, and old age in terms of the ability to attract audiences. Figure 18.1 illustrates these trends.

Journalists therefore are writing for smaller audiences than before. This is both a challenge and an opportunity. The challenge is putting public events and issues before enough people that the society will take notice. The opportunity is to provide news for the remaining, important audiences that is consistent and well contextualized so audience members can and will be able to participate in the impor-

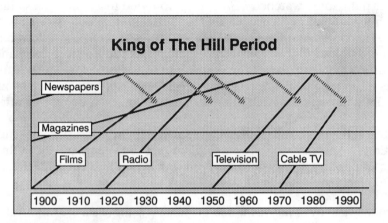

Figure 18.1
The rise and fall of American mass media

tant decisions of society. In this, newspapers confront the same challenge as schools, government, churches, and other institutions that serve wide audiences rather than just selected niches carved from the larger audience.

Changed Roles

The role of journalists has evolved, along with the skills needed to pursue the profession. Adolph Ochs purchased the *New York Times* in 1896 and promised to publish all the news that was fit to print. By the 1930s, it was evident that facts alone often did not provide the context needed to understand complex events, such as why World War I got started or why, in a world so apparently prosperous, a Great Depression brought the industrial giants to their knees.

In the 1930s, journalism scholar Curtis MacDougall called for interpretative journalism. Within about a decade the Commission on Freedom of the Press suggested that the time had come to put the facts of the news into some kind of context and that facts alone were not sufficient to help readers and radio listeners understand the complexities of the modern world. At the turn of the century, muckraking journalists such as Ida Tarbell and Lincoln Steffens had used facts to force public issues on the agenda, with some success, and proved that facts were more powerful than opinion. Yet facts have not always been sufficient to illuminate public issues, even when journalists have gone far beyond a single event to explain important developments in a community or in the nation or world.

Of course journalists come from many educational and practical backgrounds, and journalism has always been enriched by a variety of perspectives. Regardless of educational background, today's journalists confront a challenge in reaching broad masses of the public. Nearly everyone has contact with the ubiquitous and expanding media. However, the number of citizens reached at roughly the same time with roughly the same message—no matter how important—by network television or radio, metropolitan daily newspapers, or news magazines has been in steady decline, at least in terms of the percentage of the total mass media audience. At one time, for example, the three major commercial television networks, NBC, CBS, and ABC, covered the nominating conventions of the Democratic and Republican parties nearly from the opening to the closing gavel. Today these networks cover only the most important aspects of these events, while only C-Span, CNN, or some other cable outlet is likely to focus full-time on the conventions. On the other hand, in 1994, when football celebrity O.J. Simpson was pursued by the Los Angeles Police, soon to be charged with the murder of his ex-wife and one of her friends, all the networks switched to the event, as did CNN and other channels. One could not escape coverage of Simpson's arrest and later trial.

This power of the mass media to focus collective attention on one spot at one time—journalist Walter Lippmann called it "the spotlight power of the press"—seems to be apparent only with unusual, out-of-the-ordinary incidents such as assassinations or with other major—and usually "bad"—events.

Most of the time the mass media are engaged in a massive struggle for public attention. In such a struggle, the journalist of the twenty-first century needs to have superb command of traditional journalistic tools, the ability to write quickly and clearly and to obtain facts from documents and interviews without error. Earlier we suggested that journalists may need to dig up documents from the files of reluctant officials and to use databases, public surveys, and other resources to improve and deepen public affairs knowledge.

Changes in the Field

If journalists hope to translate the idealism that attracted them to the field into meaningful social stories, they need to use all their skills to present stories that interest and inform people who have many choices about how to spend their time. The journalist (and editor) needs to be a strategist about informing their communities. Some trends of importance already are evident as the new century approaches. Some trends have to do with audiences, some with technology, and some with newsroom organization. Here we discuss some of the changes.

Mobility. Audiences are increasingly mobile, and the media will have to move to where the audiences are. Already an issue for many media, the reality of an audience that is constantly on the move and able to choose from a host of options forces the journalist to compete against a multitude of distractions. Audience mobility will only increase with the spread of small computers, personal phone systems, and satellite transmissions. To get through, messages will have to be striking enough to catch the audience members' attention and redundant enough to sink in without being boring. Graphics will remain one way to sharpen messages so a wide range of audience members can be reached. This trend represents new opportunities for news media.

Globalization. Local stories increasingly take on global implications. Rural communities become home to international manufacturers. Large immigrant populations retain interest in their home regions. Narrowcasting, far-flung computer news groups, and other forms of specialty media make it possible for a consumer to have as much or more in common with people in another state or country than with the consumer's own neighbors. Such a consumer may consider distinctions between local and international news to be unwarranted and even irksome. With e-mail, direct-dial phones, and, perhaps someday, communication by way of virtual reality, local reporters can follow up on stories wherever they lead. This trend already is evident at many local television stations, which often send their own crews to cover remote events that were once left to the networks.

Audience Involvement. Improved communication channels—especially the Internet—make it possible for news organizations to get immediate and continuing feedback from their audiences. Newspapers already are seeking reader input through informal telephone (voice mail) surveys and e-mail. Stories are written based on some of this feedback. Television shows regularly use phoned-in comments. Audience participation can go even further when the members begin to assist in newsgathering by, for example, recording events with video cameras. The Rodney King case, which involved the beating of a black motorist by white Los Angeles police officers, became one of the biggest stories in years because of this kind of eyewitness journalism. Home talk, videotape, or other such materials may be part of the attraction of many talk shows. Perhaps this development opens the door to a more active audience, one that not only selects what it will read and watch but also plays a role in what will be covered and how. Some members live so much in their own media worlds, such as on the Internet, that they have departed the reality of the mass media world for the "virtual reality" conveyed through the media to which they attend.

The Merger of Entertainment and News. The televising of major events such as the Simpson trial and the 1991 Persian Gulf War joins with tabloid-style and reality-based shows to blur the line between entertainment and news. Audiences seem to watch them at least as much for vicarious thrills as for information or enlightenment. Like many of the trends cited above, this factor places the reporter's work into a fiercely competitive arena. A news story must "sell" itself as something more than important information that should be taken like medicine. How do journalists make the unimportant important, the ordinary extraordinary? This trend also raises serious ethical questions: When does it go too far and result in media manipulation? At what point have the media created the news? At what point does giving the audience what it wants become pandering?

The Redefinition of Objectivity. With the dizzying growth of communication outlets leading to highly specialized broadcast channels, cable services, and publications, mass media such as the television networks and major daily newspapers appear to be losing audience members. Specialty communication will allow—even require—most reporters to address particular niches. Reporters will report from an obvious perspective, without making any secret of it, and will strive for explanation, entertainment, and even advocacy at times, rather than for bland objectivity. This may represent a welcome opportunity for journalists to apply long-suppressed analytical skills in their jobs, but it also may be a step toward the further fragmentation of society as individuals retreat into their own ideological ghettos.

A Convergence of People and Technology. If newspapers, television, radio, computers, and magazines converge in various online formats, journalists assembling stories will have to think in broader terms. To a certain extent, this already is the case with television reporters, who must work closely with camera and sound teams to complete a story. This trend is evident at newspapers such as the *Norfolk Virginian-Pilot* and the *Minneapolis Star Tribune*, where reporters regularly work within teams that include photographers, editors and page designers. This trend carries newspapers further down the path toward magazines such as *National Geographic*, where extensive collaboration between writer, graphic artist, page designer, photographer, and editor have been routine for decades. Reporters and editors will have to pull together visual material (still and moving) and written material and provide ways for audience members to tap into more in-depth information on the subject. Perhaps the increase in multimedia heralds the growth of a shared community that communication philosopher Marshall McLuhan projected a few decades ago.

Revamped News Beats. Beats should be adjusted to the way people live their lives. Are traditional beats out of sync with modern lives? Perhaps. One example of this is a beat that might be labeled "jobs." Information under this heading may be covered on multiple beats—business, government, features, consumer affairs—but audience members probably see it as relating to their lives in some crucial way: "Can I find a job?" or "Will I keep my job?" Economic restructuring and increasing mobility mean that workers are likely to find attractive opportunities in other cities, regions, or countries. A reporter's on-the-job beat, then, could represent a valuable link between workers, business and government as he or she presents comprehensive information about this topic.

Walled-off Societies

Our current era could not be more challenging for those interested in improving society. It is beyond dispute that social improvement is needed. Within recent years, there has been an explosion in illegitimacy and a widened gap between rich and poor. Many public schools have lost support as they have become more racially and ethnically diverse, and in some cities the neighborhoods around them have become battle zones in the drug war.

The ideal of the post-World War II years that the United States could create an equitable and just society at home while expanding freedom abroad—that the country had unlimited possibilities—has been frayed by tears in the social fabric at home and by a succession of small wars and conflicts abroad that replaced the cold war and the threat of the former Soviet Union.

Few would have guessed that in 1989 the wall that divided Berlin into communist and capitalist sectors for nearly half a century would come down, or that the process of national fragmentation would shatter Yugoslavia like glass. National systems have been knitted together by history or ethnic or religious identity, by the force of outside power, or by the attraction of an idea, as with the very early Marxist Soviet Union, now disintegrated into 15 different national parts.

Many people exhibit a tendency to withdraw from the general concerns of society. We have seen some housing areas featuring expensive homes that only can be reached by passing a gate-house. Some are built on islands, surrounded by moats as in the days of castles. People who live in these places do not worry about crime in the streets. Problems are walled out.

There are many kinds of walls, real or imaginary. Many middle-class whites and blacks have left the central city to live in suburbs. Nearly 40 million Americans do not have health insurance because they cannot afford it, although those who can afford it easily slip behind hospital walls—passing the gate house of the business office— to receive perhaps the finest medical care in the world. As a result of economically influenced housing patterns, American public schools are often segregated by race. There is no end of economic, social, and cultural walls. Nothing is inherently wrong with walls, but if enough are built there no longer is a central community, just a collection of private interests fighting for dominance.

The mass media address the concerns and issues of communities where people actually live. The term "mass" media suggests that a medium addresses the concerns of large, unspecialized groups of people who are only asked to pay a small price for newspapers or magazines or for the electricity that powers radios and TV sets. The mass media historically have served those who have a specific home or mailing address.

But that historical mission confronts the contemporary reality that audiences are reconfiguring their communities according to their own agendas and are actively sampling media from a large number of choices, for example from cable channels or tiny specialty magazines. As never before, people are what they choose to read, hear, and watch, just as they are what they choose to eat. In the past, a person's home address fixed him or her in place and interests, but today an electronic address applies to a world community. Even American

Southerners can no longer agree on what that region means, if in fact the region means anything special anymore. A sense of community is as vital as ever to humans, but the traditional role of geography is in decline. There are many communities, and individual audience members belong to several of them.

Fitting the Newspaper to the Audience

One could speculate about the best fit of a metropolitan newspaper to the collective audience. There are some realities. For example, advertisers concentrate on Thursdays through Sundays, leaving Monday-through-Wednesday issues relatively bare of advertisements. There is some evidence that readers differ for different days also, as many readers pick up the newspaper at news stands when they want and need it rather than subscribe to the newspaper at home.

Mondays through Wednesdays in most communities are days for public meetings. Many, if not most, councils meet on one of those days. Those are the days for civic lectures, book clubs, and other civic and cultural engagements.

Thursdays through Saturdays, however, is when the work week winds down and most people turn their attention to shopping, household activities, and recreation. These are the days in which most food stores concentrate their advertising to attract shoppers, and the days for most activities that deal with nightclubs, concerts, and other types of entertainment. On Thursdays through Saturdays, most communities are involved with marketing or entertainment engagements.

Sundays are different, and Sundays typically are the days with the largest circulation. Many people read the Sunday newspaper who may not read other days. On Sundays, people are likely to have time for leisure or community activities. Sundays, therefore, are days of family and community engagement.

If you look at a typical community calendar that lists community events, you will see that most communities roughly follow this division. It is not unreasonable to argue then that newspapers—in our example—have at least three different groups of readers. Those deeply involved with community issues and improvement are likely to be Monday-through-Wednesday readers, the issues that advertisers avoid. Those interested in marketing and/or entertainment read Thursday through Saturday. The final group reads the Sunday paper. Of course, some read all days; others mix up the days they read.

Still, there is an opportunity for newspaper editors to distribute "serious" in-depth news about community issues on Monday through Wednesday, where the readers are open to such news, and the lack of advertisers allows more space for such issues. Major news on entertainers or recreation activities would be published on Thursdays through Saturdays. In-depth pieces on the community or family issues would fit into Sunday's format. Breaking news on any beat would be displayed daily, of course, but otherwise editors would try to fit news to the audience. An in-depth study of a local symphony—with its problems of building an audience, obtaining funding, and finding qualified musicians—would run Monday through Wednesday because it is more "serious" in a sense than a profile of the hottest pop star or the newest blockbuster movie. The latter would appear Thursday through Saturday. According to this line of reasoning, a trend story about religion would not appear on Saturday, as it often does, but on Monday through Wednesday because that audience is most receptive to serious, in-depth news.

To a certain degree, editors are aware of these realities and sometimes try to juggle their news budgets accordingly. But what if a newspaper decided to quit tinkering around the edges and openly acknowledge these audience subdivisions? It could experiment with treating the different segments of the week almost as different publications. Not only would the copy in each segment reveal a different emphasis, but the look and feel of the paper also could metamorphose throughout the week. The Monday-through-Wednesday editions could be heavier on type and lighter on color photos and graphic displays. It might even be printed on pages half the size of the average broadsheet, along the lines of the *Christian Science Monitor*. Thursday-through-Saturday could be modeled after the trend-setting design of *Rolling Stone* magazine or perhaps *USA Today*. Sunday could contain a blend of the styles, perhaps opting for a colorful but less-hip look that in places might even encourage use by children. The *Minneapolis Star Tribune* and the *Atlanta Constitution* can be cited as examples of the Sunday format. In addition, each segment could promote material appearing in other weekday segments in hopes of spurring crossover readership.

Such a major restructuring would have a significant impact on reporting, the main concern of this book. Reporters could "take ownership" of their assigned segments, striving to define them and make them successful. Breaking news on every beat would compete for good play each day, but reporters would be assured of a special place in which to display their best work. This could benefit lifestyle writers,

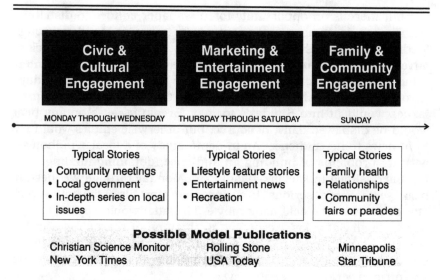

Figure 18.2
Fitting the newspaper to the audience

who would not always have to compete with hard news for top play, as well as hard-news writers, who would be able to more fully explore serious topics with fewer space and design constraints.

We have used newspapers in our example, but the same reasoning would roughly fit local television as well, although that medium always has to take advantage of visual opportunities. Regardless of medium, journalists and editors need to fit the medium to the community.

Beats

Media need to accommodate audiences in two ways: to reflect their lifestyles and to reflect the way people still seem to relate to communities. One might consider organizing beats according to the way people live. For example, everyone is born, lives within some kind of family, gets educated, works, plays, has health problems, and is curious about new and strange events; beats could be organized accordingly around "health," "relationships," "work," "play," and "frontiers." There are many other possibilities in matching beats to the way people actually live.

Media need to be less predictable. One example of predictability is the abundance of stories about anniversaries of past events. These stories are important because they tie us together in history, and for many, the mass media convey history far more adequately than do formal courses in history (to which people are exposed for only a tiny part of their early lives, anyway). But is it possible that one day a newspaper will be entirely filled with anniversaries—in the year 2000, say, stories marking five years since the trial of O.J. Simpson, 225 years since the opening battles of the American Revolution, 135 years since the end of the Civil War, 40 years since the first televised presidential debates (between Richard Nixon and John F. Kennedy), 50 years since the beginning of the Korean War, 55 years since the end of World War II. Carried to its extreme—and many news media do—this type of coverage will leave little room for current news. The mass media should provide context, but if a mass medium becomes a history text, then the medium will be too predictable to attract interest to the lively events of today.

Every day a news medium should have one story that could not have been predicted, either a new topic altogether or an old topic presented in a new way. The story should provide a new perspective on the event or issue covered.

Skills of the Twenty-First Century Journalist

The journalist in the twenty-first century will need to have some special perspectives and skills.

- The ability to use computers to gather, organize, and—in time—present information
- The knowledge of basic statistics, enough to be able to work with numbers from databases and surveys
- The flexibility to adapt messages to a variety of distribution means
- The knowledge of what audiences want and need and the ways in which audience members actually use media to gain information
- A sense of fairness and balance to seek stories from those at the margins of society—the poor, for example—who may not even be customers of traditional news media

Effectively coordinating visual and written material enhances a newspaper's appeal to its audience. Courtesy Chicago Tribune.

- A faith in communities, including the belief that involved citizens and local government can solve problems
- The flexibility to work in teams, as mass media focus more on depth in trend stories, while remaining able to relay routine events very briefly
- The ability to see stories graphically and not just with words
- A willingness to stop, listen, and learn from the agendas of audiences along with the ability and willingness to blend special inside knowledge of issues with those of the audience

Journalists have to remember that they are citizens, with a stake in representative democracy, as the First Amendment assumes. One prominent writer for a major newspaper called the White House after a presidential address to ask whether a particular passage was quoted from the Bible, as it seemed to have been. An aide checked, then called back and confirmed President Clinton's use of the biblical passage. This exchange was cited in the story apparently to make a point about the president but also about the power of a major journalist to get others at high levels to run down information readily available from other sources. To the extent that journalists use position and power that average citizens cannot use to gather information, journalists will be seen as a breed apart as much as are politicians, who, like journalists, have fallen in public esteem since the days of the Watergate investigations in the early 1970s. Journalists need to remind themselves frequently that they also are a type of public servant in the marketplace.

Journalism has attracted men and women from many backgrounds since the beginning. In the twentieth century, journalism, like medicine and law, was formalized into regular curricula in university settings. The first school of journalism was established by Walter Williams, a sports writer, in the first decade of the twentieth century at the University of Missouri; Sigma Delta Chi, a society that promotes high-quality journalism, was started shortly after. Although men and women trained in formal journalism programs account for about six of every ten new hires today, people from many personal and educational backgrounds still enter journalism, a profession enriched by a diversity of perspectives.

Regardless of background, journalists enter a career in which they need to have high skill in gathering, organizing, writing, presenting (and storing), and evaluating the effects of information. This requirement is strong for lawyers, physicians, and other professionals, and is a summary of what universities themselves do: gather, organize, present, store (in data libraries), and evaluate information. Journalists are in the information business in the information age.

Digital Thinking in a Disappearing Analog Age

Analog thinking can be defined as thinking that things in the future will be pretty much as they have been in the past, as one looks back from the rear platform of the caboose of a train and has a good idea of the upcoming forward direction of the train by seeing if the rails lie straight over flat ground or are curving in a mountain terrain. Digital thinking is better defined as looking up at the wisps of vapor that trail a passenger jet and knowing those wisps are not going to remain to mark the future direction of the plane. The analog world is secure and steady, if sometimes dull. The digital world is less predictable and sometimes scary but also exciting.

In the twenty-first century, journalists will need to be flexible digital thinkers ready to use their skills and perspectives in new ways. Journalists, as always, will need to demonstrate sound professional values, knowledge, and skills. Changes in established mass media, evolving communication technologies, and shifting loyalties to different types of communities mean that journalists may work for media that we cannot imagine right now, just as eighteenth-century journalists did not imagine the large city daily newspaper, and nineteenth-century journalists did not imagine radio and television. Journalists are not defined by their medium so much as by professional knowledge and a commitment to enrich community knowledge. That has always been true. Regardless of where and how we work in the twenty-first century, we will always be journalists.

Reference

Roberts, Cokie. Fifth Annual Theodore H. White Lecture, The Joan Shorenstein Center for Press and Politics, Harvard University, 1994.

INDEX